EDP Systems For Credit Management

EDP Systems For Credit Management

CONON D. WHITESIDE
President
Whiteside Associates, Inc.

WILEY-INTERSCIENCE, a Division of
John Wiley & Sons, Inc.
New York · London · Sydney · Toronto

Library of Congress Catalogue Card Number: 74-156330

ISBN 0-471-94080-1

Printed in the United States of America.

10 9 8 7 6 5 4 3 2 1

Introduction

There has been an amazing growth in the volume of business done on the basis of trade credit during the past fifteen years. The corollary growth of receivables as an asset escaped the attention of top management or was largely ignored until about 1966. Charles C. Manger, writing in the June 1967 issue of *Credit and Financial Management* provides some interesting figures and comments:

"The credit executive in contemporary U. S. business is all too aware of the rapid growth in accounts receivable during recent years. Since 1951 they have been increasing at a compound rate of 8.5%, *faster than any other asset item*. This uptrend has exceeded by a wide margin the relative growth in, for example, cash or inventories.

"During the last decade the investment in accounts receivable has grown, in fact, from 14.7% to 17.7% of total assets. The 'National Summary of Domestic Trade Receivables, Manufacturers' Monthly Supplement' for November 1966, published by the Credit Research Foundation, illustrated through use of a trend chart how receivables during the period of April 1, 1959 through September 30, 1966 grew much more rapidly than sales volume. While the latter rose during that interval by 47%, the trade receivables investment increased by 73%."

In recent years the cost of borrowed funds has reached the highest level in business history. As a result, many business firms (1) cannot obtain bank financing at rates they can afford, or (2) management decides to use every resource available to avoid borrowing. An inevitable consequence in either situation is that the trade creditors of these business firms wind up providing the needed financing albeit unofficially and probably most unwillingly.

The current situation, overall, has caused a recent change of emphasis in the view of top management executives responsible for financial planning and control. Financial matters are now in the forefront of management; therefore, the planning of programs and the stature of credit management have been enhanced at long last.

The one factor that focused top management's attention on receivables in recent years was the fact that—for the first time in business history—the total investment in funds in receivables began to exceed those tied up in inventories. As mentioned above, the high interest costs and the profit squeeze have also contributed to the belated realization that trade receivables require close control at all times. Factors requiring control are variable sales terms, extended dating and the resulting financial costs—and the direct profit losses represented by unadjusted deductions and customer claims of all types.

Impetus Toward Mechanized Receivables

Since early 1966, there has been a constantly growing trend in industry toward computerizing trade receivables. There is little doubt that the business conditions cited in preceding paragraphs have had a great influence on this trend because of the recognized need to gain better control, to obtain more accurate and timely management information, and to reduce the investment in receivables as much as possible.

Since the credit manager is the one financial executive closest to sales financing and receivables administration, he must control the granting of extended sales terms, changes of terms, handling of unadjusted deductions—and he must also tighten up on collection policies and procedures. As the Credit Research Foundation admonished its members in a letter dated December 19, 1968: "Unless credit managers control receivables vigorously they may have no alternative but to carry many customers far beyond the normal time for payment of their bills. This will represent an added cost to their companies, either in loss of opportunity for other investments, or the need to borrow funds to replace uncollected payments, or actual bad-debt losses. Not only will these extra costs decrease profits but they could very well impede future growth."

Unique Challenge

There is little doubt that the computer age provides both a unique challenge and an opportunity for the forward-thinking credit executive. Today's most remarkable business tool, the electronic computer, has come of age at a time when the duties and responsibilities of the credit executive were never greater. By harnessing the power of this new management tool, the progressive credit executive can continue to move ahead and can take his rightful and possibly long overdue place in the executive hierarchy of his company.

Considerable evidence at hand points to the fact that the computer, if intelligently applied to the receivables, credit, and collection functions, can free the credit executive from the confines and the burden of routine work. Through thorough planning and imaginative systems and procedures aggressively developed and installed, the credit manager and his staff can handle greater sales volume, cut operating costs, improve collections, and still have time to assist with various customer development and marketing plans.

Customer Data Base Required

It has long been recognized that executives in many areas of industrial management require a continuing stream of current, accurate information for making vital decisions on a sound basis. Now is the time for top management to recognize that the credit manager also requires accurate, timely information and analyses provided through special reports of many types. Failure to recognize this fact has, in many firms, caused the credit manager to be the ''forgotten man'' among the users of data processing services in the firm.

Objectives of this Book

This book is intended to provide guidance and assistance to three different groups of individuals involved in applying the computer to financial applications:

- Credit executives
- Systems analysts assigned to computerizing receivables
- Members of top management

To assist credit executives, this book outlines in detail what the credit department usually requires from a computerized receivables system and explains how to develop the required information. It specifies the credit manager's key role in the systems design and development work, and it explains the very successful committee concept as applied to systems design. The latest credit operating tools are fully explored, such as automatic order approval, automated dunning procedures, and various methods of cash application and control over differences. The concept of developing a complete customer data bank is outlined in depth.

This book also includes a complete chapter on ''information retrieval'' as it pertains to credit management. It explains the concepts behind ''on-line'' credit inquiry utilizing a computer—and presents a modern, alternative method of obtaining equivalent results without the high cost of the on-line approach. This unique chapter also explains the benefits of micromation (Conversion of computer-printed reports at tremendous speed to film for visual display on microfilm readers) and describes how ''microsystems'' techniques are rapidly reshaping modern credit departments.

The second section of this book is specifically directed to systems analysts and project managers who have been given the tremendous responsibility for the development and installation of a comprehensive and successful receivables-credit-collection system. The systems group should not underestimate the magnitude of the assignment, nor the difficulties involved in a typical mechanization project. The group will benefit greatly from the documented, combined experience of many firms that have already gone through a computerization program; the different chapters present various methods and approaches accompanied by evaluations and specific suggestions.

For financial executives concerned with money management, this book contains many special ideas and suggestions based on concentrated experience and research in the trade receivables and credit field. Special management reports are discussed and illustrated. One chapter of special interest covers the 11 different types of losses accruing through receivables administration—and offers solutions for controlling them.

Preface

An Important Message for Credit and Financial Managers

SECTION I. FOR FINANCIAL AND CREDIT MANAGEMENT

The eight chapters that comprise Section I of this book are written primarily for the General Credit Manager and the credit executives concerned with obtaining the necessary working tools and other credit-oriented information from a computerized receivables system under discussion or in the planning stages. These chapters also provide a useful blueprint and suggestions for major additions or improvements to existing computerized trade receivables installations, where credit management desires to implement and gain benefits from some of the more modern concepts, for instance, credit checking by computer and automatic dunning.

Speaking directly to the General Credit Manager, if your firm is currently considering a computerization of receivables project, be sure to study Chapter 1 carefully to determine your appropriate role in this very important undertaking. You will find the computer reports shown in Chapter 3 to be of special interest, since they have proved to be, in many installations, the primary working tools for credit department operations.

The attention of financial managers is directed to Chapter 8, which explains how a properly structured computer system for handling trade receivables can provide valuable financial data and special analysis reports for the financial management of an asset consisting possibly of many millions of dollars, that is, accounts receivable.

SECTION II. FOR SYSTEMS ANALYSTS AND CREDIT MANAGERS

The eleven chapters that comprise this section include considerable technical information and cover topics of special significance to systems analysts, who are entrusted with the responsibility for developing a successful and profitable trade receivables computer application. However, the General Credit Manager—in the interests of better understanding and more effective communication with the systems team responsible for designing and specifying the new system—should also read this entire section for these reasons:

- The credit executive should assist with the compilation of a master list of invoice terms, which must be mechanized.
- He will be called on to help decide the data contents of the Customer Data Bank.
- Knowing that cash application methods and control of remittance differences are the most vital elements of a trade receivables system, he will be very interested in working with the systems analysts on this segment of the overall system, and in assisting with making many key decisions as to approach and procedures.
- He will want to know how unadjusted deductions should be handled—and will review the methods for input and processing of all types of journal entries.

Conon Doyle Whiteside

Contents

EDP Systems For Credit Management

Section I.

For Financial and Credit Management

CHAPTER 1

The Credit Manager's Role in Systems Design and Development

When top management of a firm approves a project to computerize the receivables and related credit and collection functions, the credit manager should begin at once to plan for his role in the project. He should regard the situation as both a challenge and an opportunity and should prepare to assume his rightful participation in—and responsibility for—the many key decisions that must be made. If he remains silent and passive he may pay a rather high price subsequently for his inaction. Without full and continuing participation in the project the credit manager's position and control over his department will be in danger simply because many systems analysts do not understand the credit/collection function. Usually they view a receivables project as an assignment to develop an *accounting system* for receivables. Invariably the system developed under such a concept will properly handle the mundane aspects of posting sales, applying cash, and reporting totals posted or applied. However, quite often vital requirements of the credit and collection departments are either ignored or recognized only to the extent of a customer statement and an aged trial balance being provided for.

The fact that top management itself may very well consider receivables as a simple accounting operation makes the potential problem even more acute. Proof that this concept exists is found in a great many firms where management has placed the receivables administration under the accounting department reporting to the controller—and completely separate from the credit department.

For all these reasons, experience has shown that it is imperative for the credit manager, or a designated representative, to take part in the systems project from its inception to the final installation stage. Not only should the credit manager participate in the systems design and development work, he should be one of the key executives directing the entire project. This thought will be pursued at greater length in subsequent sections of this chapter.

SYSTEMS PLANNING FOR COMPUTERIZED RECEIVABLES

A decision made by top management of any firm to computerize the receivables accounting, credit, and collection functions starts a chain of events that involves a great many different work phases and other activities. Here is a list of what may be involved in a project of this kind:

1. A basic review of the existing system, procedures, and policies.
2. The determination of management objectives and results wanted from a new system.

3. Systems design, development, and documentation.
4. Programming, testing, and debugging.
5. *Planning and setting up new departments:*
   Account coding
   Input
   Proof and control section
   Terms coding, batching, proving sales
6. The selection of a numbering system—and preliminary numbering of customer accounts.
7. Site Planning for the computer . . . if a new installation.
8. Floor planning for the new sections or departments.
9. Conversion planning—preliminary and final conversion.
10. Preparing a master schedule of all events and work phases and assigning target dates for beginning and completing each work phase. (This is usually done as one of the first steps in order to plan and control progress on the project.)

TWO MAJOR WORK PHASES

The two major work phases, other than the basic review, included in the above list of events are:

- Systems design, development, and documentation
- Programming, testing, and debugging

The other work phases listed are performed intermittently and concurrently with the work being done to complete the two major jobs mentioned above.

THE SYSTEMS TEAM

A systems group or team does the work described above as "systems design, development and documentation." The work done by this group provides the foundation for all the subsequent programming, testing, and other work required by the project. In the computer field the individuals who are assigned to systems design projects are called *systems analysts.* Some systems analysts have a broad background that has been developed through public accounting practice or experience in depth with many different business applications over a period of years. Others typically begin their business career in the data processing field—possibly beginning as programmers—and gain their business experience by working with supervisors and department heads in various departments or sections of the business. Thus we see that the background and experience of individuals qualified to do creative systems design and development work vary widely in this computer age.

Programmers are specially-trained individuals who analyze the systems requirements as provided by the systems analysts, then prepare work flow diagrams as the basis for coding all instructions necessary for the computer to produce the desired results from each computer run.

DIVIDED FUNCTIONS

In those firms that separate the functions of the systems analysts and programmers, the systems analysts design, develop, and document the proposed system in great detail. On completion of a segment or an entire unit of the new application, the documentation is turned over to programmers to begin their work. In some firms these two functions are combined. That is, the systems analyst and the programmer are the same person. However, the systems design work necessarily is done first, then the programming work is performed.

THE PROJECT MANAGER

Any computer project requires that top management assign a project manager who assumes full responsibility for the completion and success of the project. Contrary to popular belief this man should not be an outsider brought in because of his data processing skill and experience. Preferably he should be a capable employee with many years of actual experience with his current employer. Selecting the right individual for project manager is a most important step and one that should be considered with care. Too often the data processing manager controls this assignment and routinely delegates the responsibility for the new project to the senior systems analyst assigned to the job.

Many experienced authorities in the computer field believe that this is the wrong approach. There are many excellent reasons for this belief, based on the analysis of scores of unsuccessful and successful computer installations. Successful, practical computer systems are invariably the ones designed and developed by people who *know the job to be done thoroughly* from first-hand experience, and who also know and understand the firm's current operations and policies.

Therefore, the project manager should have the following qualifications.

- He should be very familiar with the operations and procedures of the various departments of his firm.
- He should be fully qualified to discharge management responsibilities.
- He should be intelligent and capable of understanding the function of computers and how to apply them to business problems.
- He should be the type of individual who welcomes change and is willing to take on new, challenging assignments.
- He should have the knack of working smoothly and harmoniously with people at all levels and of enlisting their full support and cooperation. This is a most important characteristic.

In summary, the project manager primarily directs the efforts of the systems analysts. He sets up the interviews with department heads and operating supervisors; he plans, guides, and directs all of the work necessary to design and lay out, in detail, a complete, well-documented system ready for programming.

THE PLANNING AND ADVISORY COMMITTEE

Before discussing the purpose and functions of the planning and advisory committee, let us pinpoint a fundamental principle that should be observed in all systems design work. That is, any new system should *reflect the combined experience and views of all key USERS of the proposed new system.* For this reason it is a mistake for systems analysts to withdraw into the seclusion of their offices or work areas, and to proceed to develop a system based almost solely on their own ideas as to what the users require and how the job should be done. Such an empirical approach is all too common in the data processing environment. A system developed without the users' full participation will be subject to critical inspection and even to rejection when it is finally ready and is presented to the users as a *fait accompli.*

The valuable lesson learned from the combined experience of many firms over the years is this: set up an *advisory or planning committee* to assist the project manager and the systems analysts. The properly oriented systems group actively solicits the assistance, counsel, and suggestions of the committee at frequent intervals throughout the entire systems development work.

COMMITTEE MEMBERS

Members of the committee should be selected primarily from a list of the key users of the new system. Therefore, the job titles will vary considerably from one computer application to another. For example, a committee set up to guide the design of a production and inventory control system would be composed of individuals active in the related manufacturing operations and support functions. Members of a committee to guide an accounts receivable computerization project should be selected primarily from the credit, collection, and accounts receivable departments.

COMMITTEE CHAIRMAN

Since the credit department is the one department most vitally concerned with receivables administration, the key member of the committee should be the General Credit Manager. He should, in fact, act as chairman at all committee meetings.

In addition to committee members representing credit, accounts receivable, and collection functions, one member should represent the financial management in order to be sure that the necessary accounting controls are built into the system. Another function of this member should be to suggest various reports developed especially for money management.

THE COMMUNICATIONS PROBLEM

It is essential for the credit manager to realize that the basic problem he will be faced with to obtain all the necessary reports and working tools from a computer system—essential for operating his department efficiently—is the difficulty of *communicating* with the systems group.

Most systems men have only an academic knowledge based on hearsay as to the function and operation of a credit and collection department. On the other hand, the credit manager should recognize that he does not understand data processing nor the problems faced by systems analysts and programmers charged with developing and programming a successful system. The solution is for both parties to break the communications barrier and enter into the systems design sessions with open minds, with complete goodwill, and with the common objective of producing, as a team, the best possible receivables system for the benefit of everyone concerned.

DETERMINE SYSTEM REQUIREMENTS

If the credit manager is to be an effective chairman of the systems team he must show leadership. He should actively seek out information and develop a list of reports that he thinks his department will need from the new computer system for effective functioning. One way to do this is for the credit manager to visit installations wherever possible and to talk to his counterpart who has had experience with mechanized receivables. If he can obtain copies of various forms and credit department reports in actual use, they will be invaluable in the planning sessions.

Another source of information is credit association seminars or luncheons. Most people in the credit field are extremely cooperative and eager to assist their fellow credit men with problems. Therefore, it follows that the credit manager can pick up valuable ideas from attending these lunches and seminars.

Another resource that should be considered is the use of consultants who specialize in data processing as it relates to trade receivables, credit and collection functions. Specialists in the field usually have access to a large library of forms and reports that have been obtained from many successful installations. They can bring concentrated experience and knowledge accumulated from a number of installations to bear on a receivables project for the benefit of top management and the systems development team.

Consultants who have had experience with many different installations can offer very valuable guidance and counsel for the entire project, since they know what NOT to do, as well as what to do. For example, one of the most appealing concepts that always enters the picture when mechanization of trade receivables is being considered is that of applying cash "automatically."

This approach obviously has considerable basic appeal. And, it has been successfully implemented in a few firms with uniquely favorable conditions. However, it should be noted that scores of firms in trade receivables have experienced great difficulties when they installed this method of cash application. In some instances, the problems and outright dollar losses resulting from installation of "automatic cash" have caused the eventual discontinuance of the technique.

The primary point here is that top management should give consideration to the fact that it may be advisable to secure experienced counsel and advice on all aspects of the proposed project *before* a large investment has been made in systems work and programming.

SPECIAL MESSAGE FOR THE CREDIT MANAGER

Many credit managers involved in computerizing receivables have said that they were reluctant to request everything that they thought they needed for the efficient operation of their department—because of the lack of understanding about what a computer can or cannot produce. The fact is that you should not permit this consideration to influence your thinking and planning in the early stages. The best approach is to develop a list of forms and reports the computer should produce, without your being unduly concerned about possible computer limitations. Let the systems men inform you about problems if there are any. Then you can discuss the situation with them on a cooperative basis to develop alternative approaches that may be equally satisfactory as the idea you originally broached.

Another point is that the computer is merely a highly versatile and efficient piece of office equipment. It is a tool to be used to implement the requirements of the credit department as well as others. Therefore, why not plan and develop the new system to serve your needs and requirements fully without undue worry about computer operational problems? Too often a system is warped toward accommodating the computer; the reverse approach is strongly suggested.

A CASE HISTORY

Unfortunately there are many case histories in the industrial business world that point up the possible consequences of a communications failure between the systems design group and the credit management group during the critical period of systems design and development. Consider the situation that developed within a large, well-known industrial manufacturing firm as typifying what can happen unless some of the fundamental recommendations discussed in this chapter are carefully followed.

This firm manufactures a line of plumbing and hard goods that is marketed nationwide. The organizational structure features a decentralized credit and collection function, with a group of credit men located in each of six geographic divisions. Top management decided to centralize accounts receivable, using a computer adjacent to company headquarters in the Midwest.

The project was assigned to a group of systems analysts working out of the home office, and under the control of the data processing manager representing a corporate service function. The systems group had little, if any, communication with the credit and collection department at any time. They developed a mechanized system in accordance with their own concept of what was required. The computer system which they designed, programmed, and installed was one that brought the account balance forward at the end of the month to a new month's statement. All details of what made up the account balance were dropped when the balance was brought forward. Probably without realizing the inevitable consequences, the group had developed and installed a *retail* receivables system in a company that had *trade receivables* with the usual wide variety of invoice terms and many unadjusted deductions.

In a few short months the collection effort came to a complete standstill, since the collectors found it literally impossible to follow and to collect individual past due items. It was impossible to analyze a customer's account and to answer customer inquiries and complaints. The adjustment function also began to deteriorate, since the customer's account no longer showed the details of open items, including credit memos processed and posted to cover prior deductions. Since all cash received was posted to the account, instead of being used to remove specific paid items from the account, the grand total of open, unapplied cash rose to an enormous figure in a few months' time. This, in turn, meant that the past due statements and the aged trial balance were meaningless.

Obviously, if there had been close, continuing discussion and cooperation between the systems design group and credit management, this catastrophe would have been averted. The systems group would have avoided the frustration and stigma of a complete, costly failure; credit management would have obtained the necessary reports and information designed to best serve all legitimate needs and requirements.

The situation described above is not at all unique in the computer age. The problem begins with the fact that nearly everyone from top management on down to the systems analyst underestimates what is really involved and the many difficulties of properly mechanizing trade receivables. There is a tendency for many business people to consider receivables as a "simple debit and credit posting operation." Computerizing trade receivables is not that simple. If the new system is to properly handle the seven major functions listed and explained in Chapter 2, it requires scores of different computer runs and a great many difficult management decisions, which range from selecting the best account numbering system to determining the most practical and efficient method of applying cash and controlling remittance differences.

Summary

In summary the credit manager's role in the systems design and development project is, indeed, a vital one. He should assume the responsibility of securing for his department the necessary working tools from the new system. To accomplish this, he cannot remain passive and on the sidelines. He must actively participate in the planning and implementation of the new system, beginning with the very first planning sessions. As recommended in the first section of this chapter, he, in fact, should be the key individual on the Advisory and Planning Committee, which assists, guides, and directs the systems group in their work.

Guidelines for Top Management

Careful and thorough planning is absolutely essential to the success of a computerized receivables project. Top management should provide guidance for the project in the form of a list of objectives and management goals that has evolved from a series of meetings between the General Credit Manager, the Treasurer, and the Financial Vice-President—or some other officer of the firm representing top management.

Management at all levels must be careful not to adopt the attitude that is frequently found: "Don't bother me with the details of this project; I don't understand computers." Management must get involved and *stay involved*—or the ingredients for a "successful failure" are present. A successful failure in the computer age is the mechanization of work formerly done manually—which results in a high-cost operation with meager peripheral results or minor benefits accruing from the expensive process of mechanization. Furthermore, quite often the general confusion and general dissatisfaction with the new system may actually represent a liability in many ways.

It is essential for top management to support a receivables project fully because the systems analysts must cross many departmental boundary lines while doing their work. This is essential in order to integrate the functions of many different departments and to assure that the new system will serve many different departments and divisions of the company. This requires that they have the appropriate backing and authority stemming from top management to work on any aspect of the system in any area that has a bearing on the new, automated receivables system.

LIAISON OFFICER

Top management should select a key member of the management team to assume the responsibility for controlling the planned project. The systems group and the advisory committee will report directly to him from time to time—to report progress and to obtain guidance when needed. He should be the final authority concerning the major decisions that must be made as the work progresses. His function is to represent the management viewpoint and objectives in all discussions with the systems team and others.

CHAPTER 2

The Seven Major Functions Served by a Comprehensive Computerized Receivables System

The purpose of this chapter is to provide an outline and certain guidelines with respect to the overall structure, data contents, and reporting structure of a truly comprehensive trade receivables system, designed to serve the many diverse functions found in credit department operations and receivables administration. The system should provide appropriate working tools for the following functions.

I. Credit checking.
II. Answering credit interchange requests.
III. Collection activities.
IV. Cash application and accounting.
V. General reference and account reconstruction.
VI. Controlling customer deductions and adjustments.
VII. Monitoring the receivables investment and reporting to financial management.

This chapter provides details concerning the data and report requirements for each of the above-named functions; this makes it possible for both the credit manager and the systems analyst to use this chapter as a reference source when designing the new computer system for receivables.

SOURCES OF INFORMATION

Information required for various credit department reports and for support of credit functions can be divided into two categories:

1. The information about a customer that is descriptive, historical, or statistical. *Examples.* Customer name and address, Dun & Bradstreet rating, the assigned credit limit, order limit, industry classification code, pay habits history, etc.
2. The information extracted from the receivables accounting records that reveals the current status of the account from an investment standpoint, such as the account balance, the past due situation, future due items, etc.

CUSTOMER DATA BANK

Information that is descriptive, historical, or statistical is usually stored in special records which together constitute a "customer data bank." The records that represent the accounting situation, for instance, invoices, credit memos, deductions charged back, on-account cash, etc., are referred to as the "open item file." It is very feasible to keep both types of records for a common customer together on a computer file. However, some systems analysts prefer to structure the computer system so that two separate files are kept:

- Customer Data Bank
- Open Item File

The credit manager and the systems analysts should bear in mind, during the systems design phase of the project, that a great many reports call for data and information from both files. For instance, data required for credit checking is taken from information stored in the open item file—such as the account balance and past due status—and also from statistical information stored in the customer data bank.

From a systems design standpoint and from a practical operating viewpoint, it is logical to combine these two files into one complete, integrated customer file. It is no coincidence that this arrangement parallels the old customer ledger sheet that was so popular over the years before computers became available. The customer's name and address appeared on the top part of the ledger; all posted debit and credit entries were found in the body of the ledger sheet. The balance usually appeared on the right side of the form and was printed with each additional posting. It was possible to record pencil notations as to pay habits and high credit on the bottom section of the ledger card. Overall, the old ledger sheet provided considerable information of both types about an account. It was supplemented by certain documentary information that was filed in the customer's credit folder.

When a customer data bank is mentioned in connection with computerized receivables, most laymen envision the information as being stored physically inside the computer. This is an erroneous impression. Computers typically store information in coded form on reels of magnetic tape or on random access devices—outside the computer memory. The most popular type of random access device features data recorded on the surface of disks that resemble phonograph records. When information about an account is required for any reason, the computer brings the data stored on the random access device inside the central computer memory for processing or for answering inquiries.

Additional information about customer data banks is given in Chapter 11, which covers the concept and contents of a data bank in considerable detail. The subject was introduced here to provide an initial understanding about the source of various types of data listed on subsequent pages as being required for specific functions or reports.

I. Credit Approval (Credit Checking)

When a credit man is checking credit on an order, he usually seeks the following information to use as a basis for his decision:

- Latest account balance and status of the account.
- How much is currently past due?
- What is the total of open orders approved but not yet shipped?
- What is the credit limit? The order limit?
- How has the account paid his bills in the past?
- How long has the account been in business?
- What is the financial position of the firm?
- What is the current sales volume; is the account a major source of sales revenue?

Now, it is understood that the credit man does not require this extensive data for every order received in the department. Credit checking should be done on an *exception basis*. This is a fundamental principle behind the modern concept of automatic order approval by computer. The computer first screens all orders and then calls the credit man's attention only to the ones that require his personal inspection and approval.

You can see from the nature of the information listed above that all of it would be stored in an integrated file that consisted of open items representing dollar amounts, plus a customer data bank. However, you may wonder about the type of report to which the credit man would refer to obtain the desired answers. There are several ways in which a well-designed computer system can provide this information.

One method is to print a monthly Customer Credit Guide for credit checking. This brings all the desired information into one specially designed report which is used primarily for credit

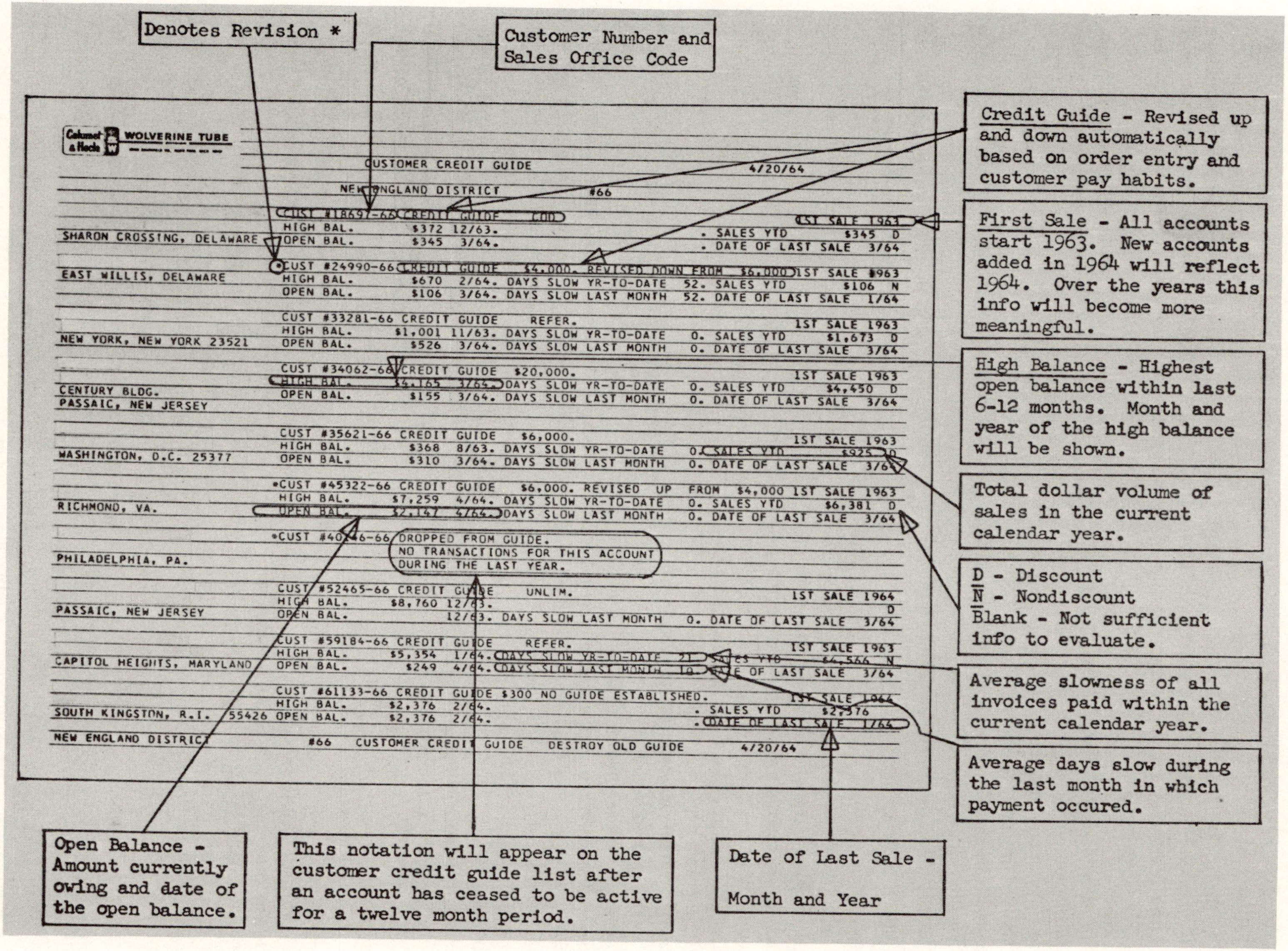

Figure 2.1 Customer Credit Guide (courtesy of Wolverine Tube Division of Calumet & Hecla).

approval work. The Wolverine Tube Division of Calumet & Hecla prints such a report on a monthly basis. Mr. William Bruder, General Credit Manager, states that this report has served the purpose very well over a period of years (see Figure 2.1).

Many computer installations do not provide a special report that is specifically for the credit-checking function. Instead, all of the data bank information appears as part of basic working reports such as the Monthly Aged Trial Balance and Weekly Status Report. Both of these reports are explained and illustrated in Chapter 3.

OVER CREDIT LIMIT REPORT

Firms that operate over large geographic areas may face the problem of scattered warehouses or distribution centers in locations that are far removed from the centralized receivables and credit administration center. This situation requires that credit reports be supplied to order-handling points on a scheduled basis or order referral through direct data-communications lines to the central administration center. Order approval on a decentralized basis is usually based on the principle of "negative credit approval." That is, if a customer's name does *not* appear on the latest list, the order can be approved and shipped without referral to the credit department.

Typical criteria that may cause a customer's name to appear on the list are the presence of past due items on the customer's account—or the account is over limit. Credit men should have the privilege of adding and removing names from time to time as the collection situation requires. An Over Credit Limit Report should be updated at least once each week; some firms update the customer lists on a daily basis and distribute them at once to order-shipping points. This type of report is illustrated in Chapter 5.

II. Handling Credit Interchange Requests

If a credit man expects to receive credit information from other creditors doing business with the same customers carried by the credit man, he must be prepared to reciprocate when other firms send in requests for credit data on designated accounts. During the years when many large firms were using punched cards (before computers were available) as a basic receivables records, credit interchange information was usually lacking. However, in the current computer age there is no good reason why this type of valuable data cannot be carried in the computer file routinely—available for in-house reports and for answering credit interchange requests, such as:

- Sold since.
- High credit for one or more time periods.
- Terms.
- Pay habits; pays on discount basis, prompt or slow.
- Total now owing.
- Account status; status of past due items.

This data may be found on the customer Credit Guide or extracted from the Weekly Status Report—or Monthly Aged Trial Balance.

III. Cash Application and Accounting

Cash application is the heart of any trade receivables system, since cash cannot be merely posted to the account; it must be carefully and accurately applied to specific open items. Furthermore, the gross credit is not posted to the account when data processing methods are applied to receivables; the cash is merely the authority for flagging all paid items or for physically removing them from the customer's open item file.

Cash application and control over differences require very stringent accounting methods and control procedures. The functions of cash application and control over differences cover all of these work phrases:

- Identification of paid items
- Setting up unadjusted deductions
- Auditing the remittances and pinpointing major differences
- Disposing of the major difference amounts
- Reporting differences to management
- Posting all debit and credit amounts (chargebacks) to the receivables file
- Preparing all necessary paper work

This book includes two complete chapters covering five different ways to apply cash. It also describes the audit function and how it works. Bear in mind, as you develop your system, that an overriding objective of a computerized trade receivables system is to develop a system that will utilize a simple approach to identifying paid items, with the computer required to perform the remittance audit—and to report major differences. Finally, the system should positively control the resulting disposition of differences and should report the details of the disposition decisions to management.

OTHER ACCOUNTING TRANSACTIONS

The system obviously must provide for posting sales transactions to the customer file. Also, a provision must be made for handling journal entries of all types. Chapter 18 covers the journal entry requirements in detail.

The easiest type of transaction to process to the customer file is sales. "Posting" sales in a data processing system refers to the process of adding new invoice or credit records to the existing customer file of open items. If the open item file is kept on reels of magnetic tape, it is necessary to completely rewrite the tape file when adding one or more sales records to one or more accounts. The reason for this is that no blank areas are left on the reel of tape for the subsequent insertion of new sales or other types of records. Accepted procedure, then, is for the computer to copy existing records from the old tape file to a new tape, then to add today's new records in the appropriate position. Today's tape handling units are so fast that this requirement of reading and rewriting the entire file is not a serious problem from an operational viewpoint.

This apparent disadvantage is actually a benefit. By retaining the old tape file, you obtain "backup" files for protection against the loss of the latest customer file, which may well represent scores of millions of dollars. And, since all of the information is copied from the old file to the new one, the computer can provide a new trial balance total on receivables each and every time the tape file is updated for any reason.

IV. Automatic Dunning

The very nature of the work done in the collection department provides great opportunities for saving time and operating costs when trade receivables are computerized. Consider the fact that collection procedures are usually well defined and routinized. A Past Due Statement may represent the first collection effort, which is then followed by two or three standard letters. A further point is that the review cycle is usually a fixed time period. All of these factors lend credence to the feasibility of utilizing automatic dunning.

Under manual methods the collection function is apt to represent a very expensive but necessary operation. In many firms there are three groups of people involved in this function: credit men, collectors, and typists. The work is apt to be behind schedule quite often, and the overlooking of large amounts that are past due is easily possible.

By contrast, automatic dunning with a properly structured computer system is not only feasible, it is very practical. Chapter 6 provides the guidelines as to how this can easily be built into a mechanized system. Experience has conclusively shown in recent years that computerized dunning effectively reduces operating costs and improves cash flow.

DOCUMENT COLLECTION POLICIES, FORMS AND PROCEDURES

In preparation for subsequent system design and writing procedures, the systems analyst should spend considerable time working with the collectors to determine how they follow past dues and to document the rules that determine the type of collection document to be sent out; that is, a statement, a second statement, collection letter No. 1, Collection letter No. 2, etc.

The analyst should accumulate a file of actual forms in use and should inscribe notes on the face of each form as to how and when it is used. He should also inquire about suspense accounts—those that have been placed in the hands of attorneys or collection agencies for outside collection.

An important consideration to bear in mind is that there are documents or reports involved in collection work other than statements and collection letters. When an account has been dunned repeatedly, the dunning paper work halts—and the credit man or collector takes personal charge of all subsequent collection efforts. In some firms the Monthly Aged Trial Balance becomes the basic report that will display the details of the accounts which are seriously past due. More often, the Weekly Status Report becomes the basic working tool for use by the collection personnel to follow the accounts that require close personal attention.

V. General Reference and Account Reconstruction

Many computerized receivables systems in existence today fail to provide adequate reference or the capabilities for reconstructing a customer's account when it is necessary to do so. Another important ingredient that should be built into any system is the "audit trail": the basic reference keys for tracing backward from any entry on the computer file to the *original source* document. Public auditors will insist that any computer system provide this capability. Review the proposed new system with your firm's outside accountants to obtain their cooperation and approval.

THE REFERENCE PROBLEM

Collectors often are faced with the reference and backtracking problem. When a customer is dunned for a past due invoice, the customer may claim that he never received such an invoice and may request a copy. Formerly, this required that someone find the original document in the files and prepare a photographic copy for transmittal to the customer.

As mentioned above, any good, well-planned system will include basic data as part of each open item that will make it possible to find easily the original source document. For example, the use of batch dates and batch numbers has solved the problem for many years. Now, with Micro-Systems becoming more and more accepted, there are additional techniques available for finding the desired document in seconds rather than in hours. (Chapter 7 explains the fascinating new field of Micromation and Micro-Systems in general).

Another reference problem which can be anticipated is that a customer, when remitting, may provide invoice numbers and amounts on his remittance voucher that *cannot be found on his account.* This indicates that the invoices have been miscoded (wrong invoice number applied) and have been posted to the wrong account. Locating misposted items in a large customer file can be an extremely difficult problem unless the system provides periodic printouts of cross-reference reports.

CROSS-REFERENCE REPORTS

The way to obtain cross-reference reports is to store the invoices and credits on a work file for one week or one month, then use the computer to sort the records on invoice number, and then print the entire list in *invoice number sequence.* This enables any one to find any invoice in question on the printed list. Since the customer number to which the invoice actually has been posted is part of the printed information, the search for the missing invoice is ended immediately.

The same type of report can be provided after the source records are sorted into *amount sequence* and printed. This makes it possible to search for a missing invoice based on the amount only (see Figure 2.2).

MISPOSTED CASH

Bookkeepers may miscode cash taken on account; this will cause the computer to post the remittance to the wrong account. This, in turn, will lead eventually to dunning a customer for open items that he has actually paid. When the dunned customer proves that he sent in a check, then the search begins to determine which account got credit for the cash.

If a work file is created weekly and monthly for all received-on-account cash records, the file can be sorted on *amount*—and a cross-reference report printed in this sequence. This effectively solves the problem of tracing misposted cash.

DUPLICATE DEDUCTIONS

Quite often a customer's accounts payable section will take the same deduction twice. This may easily occur because of the following series of events.

- The customer writes his own debit memo and deducts an amount from a remittance which represents a claim, such as an alleged wrong price, the goods having been damaged, seller having made a short shipment, merchandise being returned, etc.
- The seller, on processing the remittance, researches the customer's claim and prepares a credit memo eventually—if the deduction is allowed. Now, since the credit memo is an offset to a deduction already

Figure 2.2
Cross Reference Sales Register

Date: 05-31				
Customer Number	Invoice Date	Invoice Number	Amount	
		Invoices by INVOICE NO.		
017-3125	05-01	12345	212.44	Note that the invoice number is the basis for this register.
332-6771	05-01	12346	24.78-	
444-3332	05-02	12347	35.66	
054-0175	05-02	12348	345.88	
123-0247	05-02	12349	515.32	
Date: 05-31		*Invoices by AMOUNT*		
555-2331	05-29	14599	1.49-	Note that all items are in AMOUNT sequence.
018-1222	05-01	12111	1.85	
123-4567	05-15	13000	2.50	
332-1263	05-19	12350	10.00	
144-5023	05-24	14444	15.50	
444-3332	05-02	12347	35.66	

taken, a copy of the document should not be sent to the customer. However, for various reasons, a copy of the internal credit memo may find its way into the mails and, subsequently, into the hands of the customer's accounts payable department.

- The customer's accounts payable clerks will subsequently deduct the credit memo amount from a remittance. The original claim amount has now been deducted from two different checks. On the receiving end the cash application bookkeepers or the adjusters must be able to prove, by reference to appropriate history records, that the deduction really has been taken twice. If the system does not provide this capability, the deduction amount will inevitably be lost by default.

CUSTOMER CLOSEOUT REPORT

A customer history file printed periodically has been shown to be an excellent source file for general reference, and for proving duplicate deductions. It is also very useful for assisting customers in reconciling their payables records with the seller's receivables records.

This special report is usually printed in check date sequence within customer account number. The cash application procedures should make it possible for the computer to *pull together all items paid by one check* (see Figure 2.3).

Notice that this report shows all records deleted by journal entry, as well as the ones deleted by cash application.

VALUE OF A CREDIT MEMO FILE OR LIST

When a customer deducts what appears to be a credit memo from his remittance, this causes the cash application clerk to review the open credit items on the ledger sheet first. If such a credit does not appear on the latest ledger record, the cash application bookkeeper may feel it necessary to do some research on the amount deducted because of certain questions that may arise:

- Is this customer using a credit memo that has been previously used as part of a prior check?
- Has the credit memo been posted to the wrong account?
- Is this really an unadjusted deduction and, therefore, no open credit memo exists at this time?

To aid and assist cash appliers with this type of decision making, it is very helpful to accumulate all credit memos received and processed to receivables and to print a complete list of them weekly and monthly—available for quick reference.

VI. Handling Adjustments and Customer Claims

A difficult problem shared by all manufacturers selling to business firms is the unadjusted deduction situation. The customer may attach

MONTHLY 05266

CLOSE OUT REPORT

5-26-6

CO	CUSTOMER NUMBER	STORE NO.	CLIENT		RISK	ENTRY	INVOICE		DATES			RECEIVABLE	PAYMENT	DEDUCTION	JR CODE
			NUMBER	NAME			NO.	DATE	DISCOUNT	DUE	PAID				
												21.38	21.38	.00	
	0018939	A	& M KNITWEAR CORP					BROOKLYN		N Y					
1	0018939		2-676-01	NYNOTION		1	08589	3-23	4-10	4-10-6	5-06-6	72.36	423.12		
1	0018939		2-676-01	NYNOTION		1	08510	3-21	4-10	4-10-6	5-06-6	66.33			
1	0018939		2-676-01	NYNOTION		1	08413	3-17	4-10	4-10-6	5-06-6	174.87			
1	0018939		2-676-01	NYNOTION		2	04938	3-31	1-30	1-30-6	5-06-6	26.53-			
1	0018939		2-676-02	PRESTIL		1	13310	2-10	3-10	3-10-6	5-06-6	84.42			
1	0018939		2-676-02	PRESTIL		1	13265	2-08	3-10	3-10-6	5-06-6	60.30			
												431.75	423.12	.00	
1	0019670		5-517-01	LAZARUSM		1	08915	4-08		6-08-6	5-16-6	67.00	67.00		
												67.00	67.00	.00	
	0021074	A	& P NOVELTY					N Y C		N Y					
1	0021074		2-676-04	ADVNOTIO		1	15389	4-29	6-10	6-10-6	5-26-6	5.50	5.50		
												5.50	5.50	.00	
	0021595	A	R KNITWEAR CO					N Y C		N Y					
1	0021595		5-790-01	SPARKLE		1	06346	3-08		5-08-6	5-10-6	792.00	1,971.00		
1	0021595		5-790-01	SPARKLE		1	06372	3-14		5-14-6	5-10-6	891.00			
1	0021595		5-790-01	SPARKLE		1	06333	3-03		5-03-6	5-10-6	288.00			
												1,971.00	1,971.00	.00	
1	0022150		6-753-01	P&M DIST	C	1	BK173	12-17	1-10	1-10-6	5-04-6	168.00	382.57		
1	0022150		6-753-01	P&M DIST	C	1	BK640	2-25	3-10	3-10-6	5-04-6	174.24			
1	0022150		6-753-01	P&M DIST		1	39751	3-11	4-10	4-10-6	5-04-6	40.33			
												382.57	382.57	.00	

	0022785	A	R S INC					N Y C							
1	0022785		6-445-01	HARBRCLO		1	03424	3-23		5-23-6	5-25-6	93.29	738.04	3.25	
1	0022785		6-445-01	HARBRCLO		1	03425	3-23		5-23-6	5-25-6	63.00			
1	0022785		6-445-01	HARBRCLO		1	03426	3-23		5-23-6	5-25-6	286.00			
1	0022785		6-445-01	HARBPCLO		1	03427	3-23		5-23-6	5-25-6	299.00			
1	0022785		6-445-01	HARBRCLO		4	03161	2-18		4-27-6	5-26-6	2.86			41
1	0022785		6-445-01	HARBRCLO		4	03247	3-04		5-05-6	5-26-6	4.18			41
1	0022785		6-445-01	HARBRCLO		1	03247	3-04		5-04-6	5-05-6	388.93	384.75	4.18	
1	0022785		6-445-01	HARBRCLO		1	03327	3-14		5-14-6	5-11-6	175.50	175.50		
1	0022785	1792	6-445-01	HARBRCLO		2	00373	3-28		1-28-6	5-12-6	571.36-			
1	0022785		6-445-01	HARBRCLO		1	01793	9-24		11-01-5	5-12-6	571.34			
1	0022785		6-445-01	HARBRCLO		1	02709	1-03		3-03-6	5-16-6	5,065.48	6,015.19	839.03	
1	0022785		6-445-01	HARBRCLO		1	02788	1-24		3-24-6	5-16-6	368.46			
1	0022785		6-445-01	HARBRCLO		1	02779	1-20		3-20-6	5-16-6	503.28			
1	0022785		6-445-01	HARBRCLO		1	02710	1-03		3-03-6	5-16-6	384.34			
1	0022785		6-445-01	HARBRCLO		1	02521	12-07		5-01-6	5-16-6	573.16			
1	0022785		6-445-01	HARBRCLO		2	00376	4-12		2-12-6	5-16-6	40.50-			
1	0022785		6-445-01	HARBRCLO		1	03370	3-17		5-17-6	5-18-6	2,010.66	955.74	22.62	
1	0022785		6-445-01	HARBRCLO		2	00377	4-12		2-12-6	5-18-6	1,040.44-		8.14-	
												9,137.18	8,269.22	860.94	
	0023800	A&S MFG CO						CLEBURNE		TEX					
1	0023800		1-030-01	ABBT MLS		1	31555	3-08		5-08-6	5-03-6	32.45	73.53		
1	0023800		1-030-01	ABBT MLS		1	31395	3-03		5-03-6	5-03-6	5.71			
1	0023800		1-030-01	ABBT MLS		1	31082	2-21		4-21-6	5-03-6	6.46			
1	0023800		1-030-01	ABBT MLS		1	31049	2-18		4-18-6	5-03-6	6.03			
1	0023800		1-030-01	ABBT MLS		1	40172	2-21		4-21-6	5-03-6	22.88			
1	0023800		2-510-01	MAG KNIT		1	11175	12-23		3-03-6	5-03-6	175.30	175.30		
1	0023800		1-780-01	EXEC FAB		1	11308	2-17		4-27-6	5-02-6	8.41	22.68		
1	0023800		1-780-01	EXEC FAB		1	11257	2-10		4-20-6	5-02-6	10.09			
1	0023800		1-780-01	EXEC FAB		1	11338	2-21		5-01-6	5-02-6	4.18			
1	0023800		2-190-01	INWOOD T		1	04599	12-21		2-21-6	5-02-6	33.00	68.83		
1	0023800		2-190-01	INWOOD T		1	05028	1-17		3-17-6	5-02-6	35.83			
1	0023800		1-670-01	DIAL FAB		1	64632	2-15		4-25-6	5-10-6	19.40	19.40		
												359.74	359.74	.00	
	0023825	A	& S OUTLET					BROOKLYN		N Y					
1	0023825		5-420-01	IMPERLTX		1	95513	1-28	4-08	4-08-6	5-13-6	717.79	717.79		

ENTRY LEGEND

1—INVOICE 4—DEDUCTION 7—EXCESS ANTICIPATION
2—CREDIT 5—INTEREST 8—CASH ON ACCOUNT
3—NOTE 6—EXCESS DISCOUNT 9—N.G. CHECK

EXHIBIT ______

Figure 2.3 Computer-printed paid item report (courtesy of James Talcott Factors, Inc.).

his remittance explaining the reasons or justification for the deduction—or he may casually make a pencil notation and deduct a large amount of money.

Depending on the amount involved, the usual procedure is to set up the deduction amount as a charge-back to the customer's account—and to prepare paper work for internal use in researching the claim to determine its validity.

An increasingly common approach is to charge certain types of deductions, such as documented freight claims or advertising allowances, directly to the department responsible for researching claims of this kind. As an example, suppose a customer attaches a signed Bill of Lading document to his remittance which indicates agreement by the driver of the common carrier's vehicle that freight damage occurred during transit. The cash application bookkeeper, under these circumstances, may be instructed to charge the amount deducted directly to the traffic department. The department, in turn, will file a claim against the carrier.

If a customer deducts a large amount for an advertising or display allowance, the cash applier may charge the amount directly to the sales or advertising department. In either instance, the department receiving the notice of deduction takes over the problem and sets up the deduction amount as a receivable. If the department, after appropriate research, subsequently notifies the credit department that the claim has been disallowed, then papers should be prepared to set up the amount in dispute on the customer's account as a receivables item. The customer would be notified, and collection efforts would be made to collect the cash.

EVALUATION OF THE CLAIMS PROBLEM

Computer analysis of open items found on trade receivables files reveal that up to 4% of all receivables at any moment consists of unadjusted deductions pending research and disposition. To say that these items are questionable assets is to understate the case. This figure of 4% appears in various types of firms, including manufacturers of soft goods as well as those that manufacture metal goods.

Analysis of open items shows further that any manufacturer selling to retail outlets can expect to handle a larger number of deductions than the manufacturer who sells to other manufacturers or distributors.

Since the deduction and adjustment functions are a very important aspect of receivables management, this book includes a special chapter on this subject (see Chapter 17).

VII. Monitoring the Receivables Investment—and Reporting to Financial Management

As stressed in the introduction to this book, recent years have shown the investment in trade receivables to be constantly increasing. One interesting result of this constant increase has been that, for the first time in the history of most firms, the total funds invested in receivables have exceeded the funds invested in inventories. Inevitably, as the cost of financing increased to the highest point in business history in late 1968—then climbed again in early 1969—financial managers became increasingly aware of the positive need for better control over all aspects of receivables.

It certainly is true that computerizing receivables provides a fine opportunity to provide top management with special reports of great value, for money management and evaluation and control of this vital asset. Credit management, working closely with the systems design team, should make every effort to help design special reports that will be effective working tools for credit control and also will point the way to better money management and increased profits. See Chapter 8 for examples of special management reports, along with explanations of how they are used.

CHAPTER 3

What the Credit Department Requires from a Computerized Receivables System

The purpose of this chapter is to name and to describe the various reports that a comprehensive, well-designed computerized trade receivables system should produce for the credit department. The reports and forms illustrated in this chapter, in actual use in several very successful computer installations, may be considered to be the WORKING TOOLS FOR THE CREDIT MAN.

Before computers became available for keeping large-volume customer receivables records, the primary source of credit reference was the conventional customer ledger record. Even now, ledger sheets are found in the majority of trade receivables installations. However, during the 1950 decade many large firms converted to tab equipment for their accounting work—and replaced the ledgers with punched cards. Many of these early installations have, in recent years, moved ahead to keeping customer accounting records on magnetic tape or disk files.

In a receivables installation using hand-posted or machine-posted ledger sheets, the ledger records are generally used by several different groups for different purposes, for example:

- Credit men—for order approval.
- Collection department for dunning.
- Bookkeepers for cash application.
- Machine operators—posting sales and gross cash credits.
- Adjusters—for applying credits to open deductions.

RELIANCE ON LEDGERS

It is easy to understand why early designers of computer systems met with immediate resistance from credit men and others who were reluctant to give up the conventional ledger card. And, in fact, those of us engaged in recent years in developing workable and practical computer reports—intended to replace the old type of customer ledger records—did, indeed, find it a very difficult task. However, we gradually developed the concept of a customer data bank and designed reports of various types which presented—on a scheduled basis—all the data a credit man needed to perform the credit granting function, plus meeting the requirements of dunning and answering credit interchange queries.

Eventually we reached the point where the new working tools produced by the computer were superior in many respects to the old ledger sheets. In theory, the ledger sheet was a central source for all types of information. In actual practice the desired information was not readily available, or it took considerable study to extract the desired data from all the many ledger pages that may constitute one account for a period of time. Let us examine the difficulties of extracting certain specific types of information from a conventional ledger card.

Pay Habits Data. This information is not easily determined when postings representing sales and cash credits cover several pages, front and back. Pay habits are never summarized and presented in summary format.

High Balance Owed. Only by scanning the ledger balances over a long period of time can the high balance for a specific period be determined. And, the practice of filing filled ledger sheets in storage cabinets always complicates the task of trying to ascertain high balances.

Credit Limit. This is usually not available at a glance, even though the original intent was to type the credit limit at the top of each ledger sheet.

Past Due Status of an Account. This is not easily determined unless the debit postings on the ledger include the invoice terms and the final due date. Very few bookkeeping machine installations provide the final due date for each invoice posted. This means that the reviewer must mentally calculate the due date for each open invoice when reviewing a ledger sheet to determine the past due status.

In all fairness, the conventional customer ledger card is not as satisfactory a source of information as sometimes represented; the most valuable functions it accomplished was to provide the latest balance at a glance plus a chronological history of all charges and credits.

Special Reports Available from a Computerized System

The various special reports that can be produced from a computerized receivables system may be considered to be the working tools for the credit department. Most of them are produced on a weekly and a monthly basis; only one is required daily.

The reports illustrated in this chapter are taken from actual, successful installations in several large factoring and industrial firms. Even though these exhibits will be helpful in designing a computerized receivables system, the credit manager, as a key user of such reports, should assist in designing the reports for his department so that the information included in the report will represent *his* views as to what he wants for the efficient operation of his department.

Here is a typical list of computer-produced reports for the credit department:

- Monthly Aged Trial Balance
- Weekly Status Report
- Customer Account Statement—Monthly
- Past Due Statements (printed on a cycle basis)
- Special Collection Report (daily)
- Customer Open-Item Ledger—prepared periodically for cash application

Monthly Aged Trial Balance

The monthly aged trial balance report has gradually evolved as one of the prime working tools for a credit department under a computerized system. Some of the early computer installations provided separate, special reports for each major function, such as order approval. It quickly became apparent that a credit man should not be required to refer to two or three different reports to get all the needed information about an account. An awareness of this fact brought about the concept of designing the aged trial balance as a basic source for *all information* required for order approval, credit interchange, collection review, and for general reference or account reconstruction.

TWO TYPES OF TRIAL BALANCE REPORTS

One basic decision that a credit manager must make early in the systems design phase is whether he wants a detailed trial balance or a summary-type report. Each has its merits and disadvantages as outlined below.

A detailed trial balance report lists every open item on each account, in addition to the name and address. Usually, the report provides several horizontal columns for distributing each open item amount by aging category: current, future due, and past due—which is recorded in aging columns, such as 1 to 30 days, 61 to 90 days, etc.

The last print line for an account shows the account balance, and summary figures for each distribution column. To provide one basic source for all types of reference, the report may also include data extracted from the customer's data bank, for instance:

- Date account was opened
- D & B Rating and date
- Credit limit and order limit
- Pay habits history for two or more time periods
- High credit for two or more time periods, etc.

The Aged Trial Balance shown in Figure 3.1 is a "unit-type" report; one page is printed (minimum) for each customer on the trial balance list.

SUMMARY-TYPE OF TRIAL BALANCE

The summary trial balance features only one line of dollar totals for each account. Typically it shows the latest account balance—and the totals for each distribution column. In addition, the report should show a variety of historical and statistical data on each customer for credit checking, collection followup purposes—and for answering requests for credit information.

REPORT EVALUATION

Many credit managers prefer the detail-type of trial balance report for several reasons:

- It provides a permanent record of the *open items* which constitute the account balance as of the monthend.
- It provides a complete working report for adjusters, collectors, credit men, et al—since all open items are shown in detail.
- It may replace use of other reports for the first week of each month (or longer), since it is a complete account record as of the end of the month.
- It provides a source for answering the requests of outside auditors for the verification of account balances, or open items as of a specified monthend date. For example, a request may be received in January requesting the status of a particular account as of December 31.
- It provides complete reference and an audit trial for tracing specific items, or for account reconstruction. By working from this detailed report plus the Paid History File, an accounts receivable clerk can trace items from the open file to the paid file—and easily can assist a customer in bringing his records into agreement with the computer records.

DISADVANTAGES OF DETAILED TRIAL BALANCE

By contrast with an aged trial balance which includes all open items, the summary-type of report requires far less computer time, less paper, and is easier to use because of its reduced bulk. After discussing these two types of trial balance reports with various credit managers over the years, it gradually became clear to me that the decision to utilize a summary report should be based on a review of other reports that complement or support the trial balance. For example, if a firm has a great many retail customers, or its invoice terms are Prox or EOM, the computer system will be required to print a complete account statement at monthend for every customer in the retail category. Now, if the credit department retains a copy of each statement, the credit men have available a complete open-item list for every retail account. Under these conditions, the summary-type of aged trial balance may be preferred over the detail-type of trial balance.

On the other hand, if it is decided not to print full customer statements at monthend, there is considerable merit in opting for the detail aged trial balance.

CREDIT MAN SUMMARY

Either type of aged trial balance should include summary totals developed for each credit man. If each customer is assigned to a specific credit man, then the open items should be sorted by credit man number before the print run is made. This makes it easy for the computer to print the report so that each credit man's accounts are grouped together—and the summary totals of credit man responsibility are printed on the last page for his group of accounts.

Typical summary totals are:

- Total number of assigned accounts on report
- Number in each credit risk category: A, B, or C
- Number of past due accounts and dollar totals for each past due aging column

TRIAL BALANCE BY EXCEPTION

Edward Frank, formerly Credit Manager with the Schering Corporation, is now in the

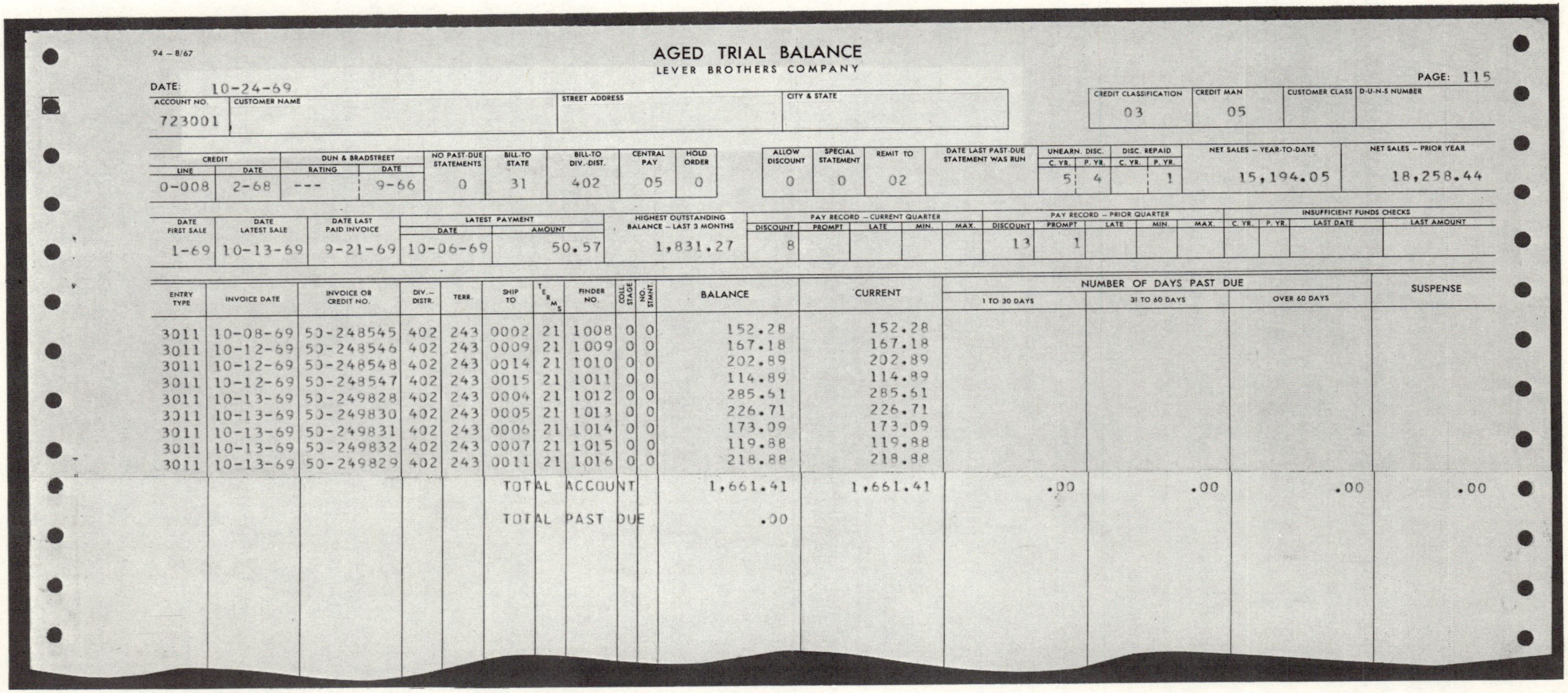

94 – 8/67

AGED TRIAL BALANCE
LEVER BROTHERS COMPANY

DATE: 10-24-69 PAGE: 115

ACCOUNT NO.	CUSTOMER NAME	STREET ADDRESS	CITY & STATE	CREDIT CLASSIFICATION	CREDIT MAN	CUSTOMER CLASS	D-U-N-S NUMBER
723001				03	05		

CREDIT LINE	CREDIT DATE	DUN & BRADSTREET RATING	DUN & BRADSTREET DATE	NO PAST-DUE STATEMENTS	BILL-TO STATE	BILL-TO DIV.-DIST.	CENTRAL PAY	HOLD ORDER	ALLOW DISCOUNT	SPECIAL STATEMENT	REMIT TO	DATE LAST PAST-DUE STATEMENT WAS RUN	UNEARN. DISC. C. YR.	UNEARN. DISC. P. YR.	DISC. REPAID C. YR.	DISC. REPAID P. YR.	NET SALES – YEAR-TO-DATE	NET SALES – PRIOR YEAR
0-008	2-68	---	9-66	0	31	402	05	0	0	0	02		5	4		1	15,194.05	18,258.44

DATE FIRST SALE	DATE LATEST SALE	DATE LAST PAID INVOICE	LATEST PAYMENT DATE	LATEST PAYMENT AMOUNT	HIGHEST OUTSTANDING BALANCE – LAST 3 MONTHS	PAY RECORD – CURRENT QUARTER DISCOUNT	PROMPT	LATE	MIN.	MAX.	PAY RECORD – PRIOR QUARTER DISCOUNT	PROMPT	LATE	MIN.	MAX.	INSUFFICIENT FUNDS CHECKS C. YR.	P. YR.	LAST DATE	LAST AMOUNT
1-69	10-13-69	9-21-69	10-06-69	50.57	1,831.27	8					13	1							

ENTRY TYPE	INVOICE DATE	INVOICE OR CREDIT NO.	DIV.–DISTR.	TERR.	SHIP TO	TERMS	FINDER NO.	COLL. STAGE	NO. STMNT.	BALANCE	CURRENT	NUMBER OF DAYS PAST DUE: 1 TO 30 DAYS	31 TO 60 DAYS	OVER 60 DAYS	SUSPENSE
3011	10-08-69	50-248545	402	243	0002	21	1008	0	0	152.28	152.28				
3011	10-12-69	50-248546	402	243	0009	21	1009	0	0	167.18	167.18				
3011	10-12-69	50-248548	402	243	0014	21	1010	0	0	202.89	202.89				
3011	10-12-69	50-248547	402	243	0015	21	1011	0	0	114.89	114.89				
3011	10-13-69	50-249828	402	243	0004	21	1012	0	0	285.51	285.51				
3011	10-13-69	50-249830	402	243	0005	21	1013	0	0	226.71	226.71				
3011	10-13-69	50-249831	402	243	0006	21	1014	0	0	173.09	173.09				
3011	10-13-69	50-249832	402	243	0007	21	1015	0	0	119.88	119.88				
3011	10-13-69	50-249829	402	243	0011	21	1016	0	0	218.88	218.88				
					TOTAL ACCOUNT					1,661.41	1,661.41	.00	.00	.00	.00
					TOTAL PAST DUE					.00					

Figure 3.1 Detail Aged Trial balance report (courtesy of Lever Brothers Company).

factoring business in New York City. From considerable experience in past years with computerized credit department reports, he believes that a trial balance should include *only* those accounts that represent problems, or meet specified tests. The tests would normally include accounts over credit limit, those with past due items, and those that have been classified as marginal—or new accounts less than six months old.

Mr. Frank found that, on the average, only about 20% of the total accounts appeared on the trial balance report in detail; he states that credit men used the report to much better advantage than one that included all accounts.

The Weekly Status Report

The weekly status report has proved its value in the daily functions of a typical credit department. Even if a random access, on-line credit inquiry system were installed as part of a computer complex, this report would still have considerable value. The reason is that it is an exception report—it includes only accounts that meet certain designated tests:

- Accounts with one or more invoices past due
- Accounts that are over credit limit
- Those flagged as marginal or restricted for any reason

This report is actually a part of the automatic dunning system because it is the prime means of following delinquent accounts after the computer has produced the series of dunning statements or letters as is prescribed by collection procedures. When the customer still fails to pay the past due item or items, and the production of dunning documents ceases, the credit man works from the weekly status report to follow the account (see Figure 3.2).

Daily Collection Report

As a by-product of the credit checking process, credit men will mark certain orders as "hold" pending receipt of cash from a marginal or delinquent account. Once these orders are filed in the "hold" file, procedures must be set up for releasing them on a consistent, routine basis. The daily collection report, prepared by the computer as part of cash processing and cash application, informs the credit men of all past due items now paid by today's cash. This daily report is prepared on an exception basis; in addition to reporting cash from past due accounts it reports checks received from over-limit accounts—and possibly all cash received from restricted accounts.

Not only does this report provide the means for clearing orders from the "hold" file, it informs collectors of payments that may serve to halt unnecessary collection efforts from taking place on past due accounts (see Figure 3.3).

Special Collection Report

This report may be designed as a unit form, or it can be printed as a continuous register. Some firms prefer the unit form or ticket, since this makes it easy to sort the forms by credit man or by credit group. The use of the continuous register format may make it necessary to pass the collections report from desk to desk for review and notation.

Morton Reitman, Senior Vice-President of A. J. Armstrong Company, Inc. (New York, New York), utilizes this type of report as a credit control device. After studying the report and noting past due items paid, he calls in the credit man to explain why the items were past due in the first place. Typical responses to his questions are:

- A duplicate invoice had been requested by customer and sent.
- The past due invoice represented a dispute.
- The customer claimed that merchandise arrived late.
- The customer paid late for no known reason.

Mr. Reitman stresses that the psychology behind reviewing all past due items on this exception report with the individual responsible for collections is excellent. It offers a continuing, positive indication that the General Credit Manager is constantly watching the overall past due situation.

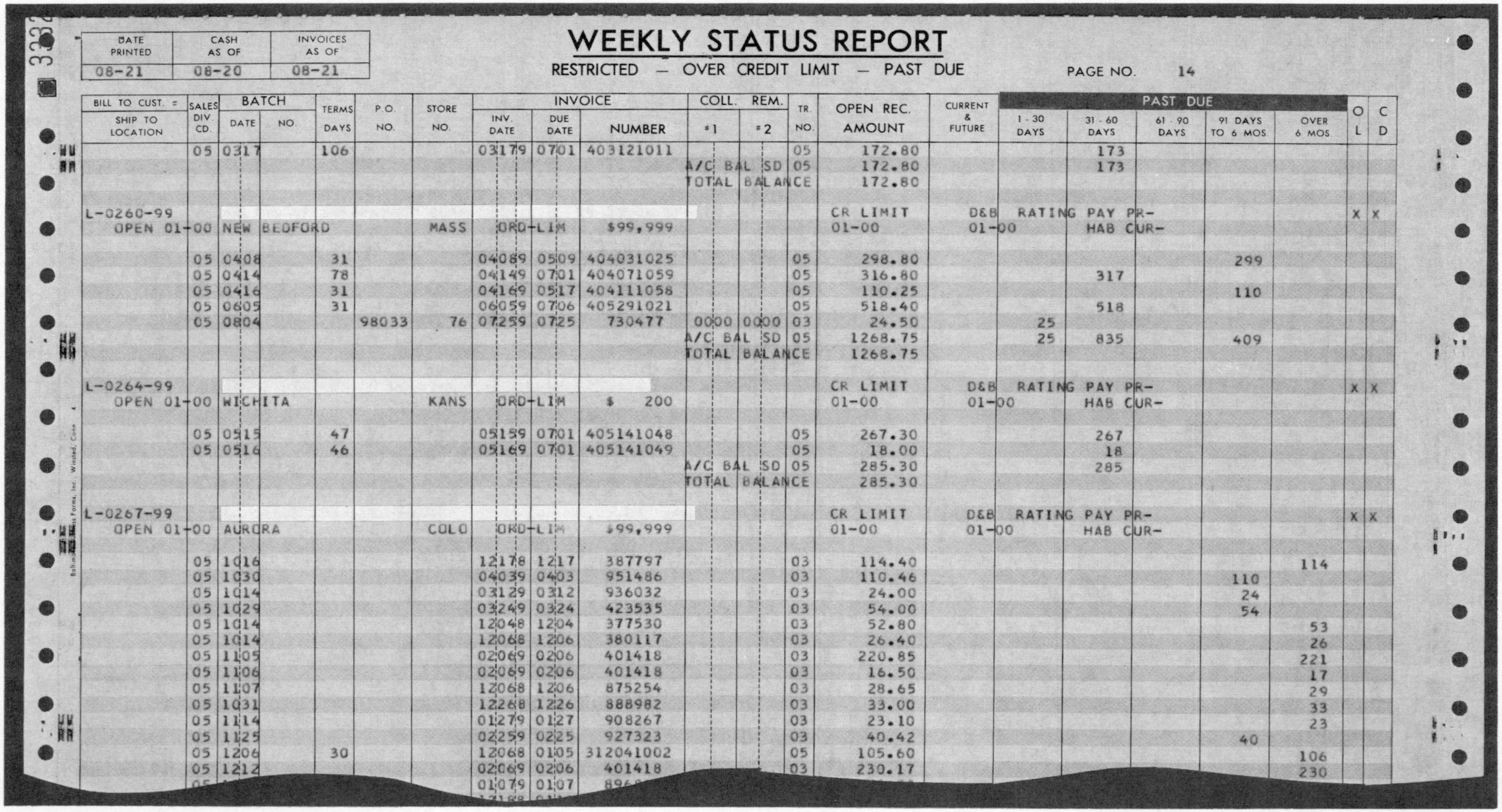

DATE PRINTED	CASH AS OF	INVOICES AS OF
08-21	08-20	08-21

WEEKLY STATUS REPORT

RESTRICTED — OVER CREDIT LIMIT — PAST DUE

PAGE NO. 14

BILL TO CUST. # SHIP TO LOCATION	SALES DIV. CD.	BATCH DATE	BATCH NO.	TERMS DAYS	P.O. NO.	STORE NO.	INVOICE INV. DATE	INVOICE DUE DATE	INVOICE NUMBER	COLL. #1	REM. #2	TR. NO.	OPEN REC. AMOUNT	CURRENT & FUTURE	PAST DUE 1-30 DAYS	PAST DUE 31-60 DAYS	PAST DUE 61-90 DAYS	PAST DUE 91 DAYS TO 6 MOS	PAST DUE OVER 6 MOS	O L	C D
	05	0317		106			03179	0701	403121011			05	172.80			173					
										A/C BAL	SD	05	172.80			173					
										TOTAL	BALANCE		172.80								
L-0260-99													CR LIMIT	D&B	RATING	PAY PR-				X	X
OPEN 01-00		NEW BEDFORD				MASS	ORD-LIM		$99,999				01-00	01-00		HAB CUR-					
	05	0408		31			04089	0509	404031025			05	298.80					299			
	05	0414		78			04149	0701	404071059			05	316.80			317					
	05	0416		31			04169	0517	404111058			05	110.25					110			
	05	0605		31			06059	0706	405291021			05	518.40			518					
	05	0804			98033	76	07259	0725	730477	0000	0000	03	24.50		25						
										A/C BAL	SD	05	1268.75		25	835		409			
										TOTAL	BALANCE		1268.75								
L-0264-99													CR LIMIT	D&B	RATING	PAY PR-				X	X
OPEN 01-00		WICHITA				KANS	ORD-LIM		$ 200				01-00	01-00		HAB CUR-					
	05	0515		47			05159	0701	405141048			05	267.30			267					
	05	0516		46			05169	0701	405141049			05	18.00			18					
										A/C BAL	SD	05	285.30			285					
										TOTAL	BALANCE		285.30								
L-0267-99													CR LIMIT	D&B	RATING	PAY PR-				X	X
OPEN 01-00		AURORA				COLO	ORD-LIM		$99,999				01-00	01-00		HAB CUR-					
	05	1016					12178	1217	387797			03	114.40						114		
	05	1030					04039	0403	951486			03	110.46					110			
	05	1014					03129	0312	936032			03	24.00					24			
	05	1029					03249	0324	423535			03	54.00					54			
	05	1014					12048	1204	377530			03	52.80						53		
	05	1014					12068	1206	380117			03	26.40						26		
	05	1105					02069	0206	401418			03	220.85						221		
	05	1106					02069	0206	401418			03	16.50						17		
	05	1107					12068	1206	875254			03	28.65						29		
	05	1031					12268	1226	888982			03	33.00						33		
	05	1114					01279	0127	908267			03	23.10						23		
	05	1125					02259	0225	927323			03	40.42					40			
	05	1206		30			12068	0105	312041002			05	105.60						106		
	05	1212					02069	0206	401418			03	230.17						230		
	05						01079	0107	896												

Figure 3.2 Weekly status report (courtesy of Clairol, Inc.).

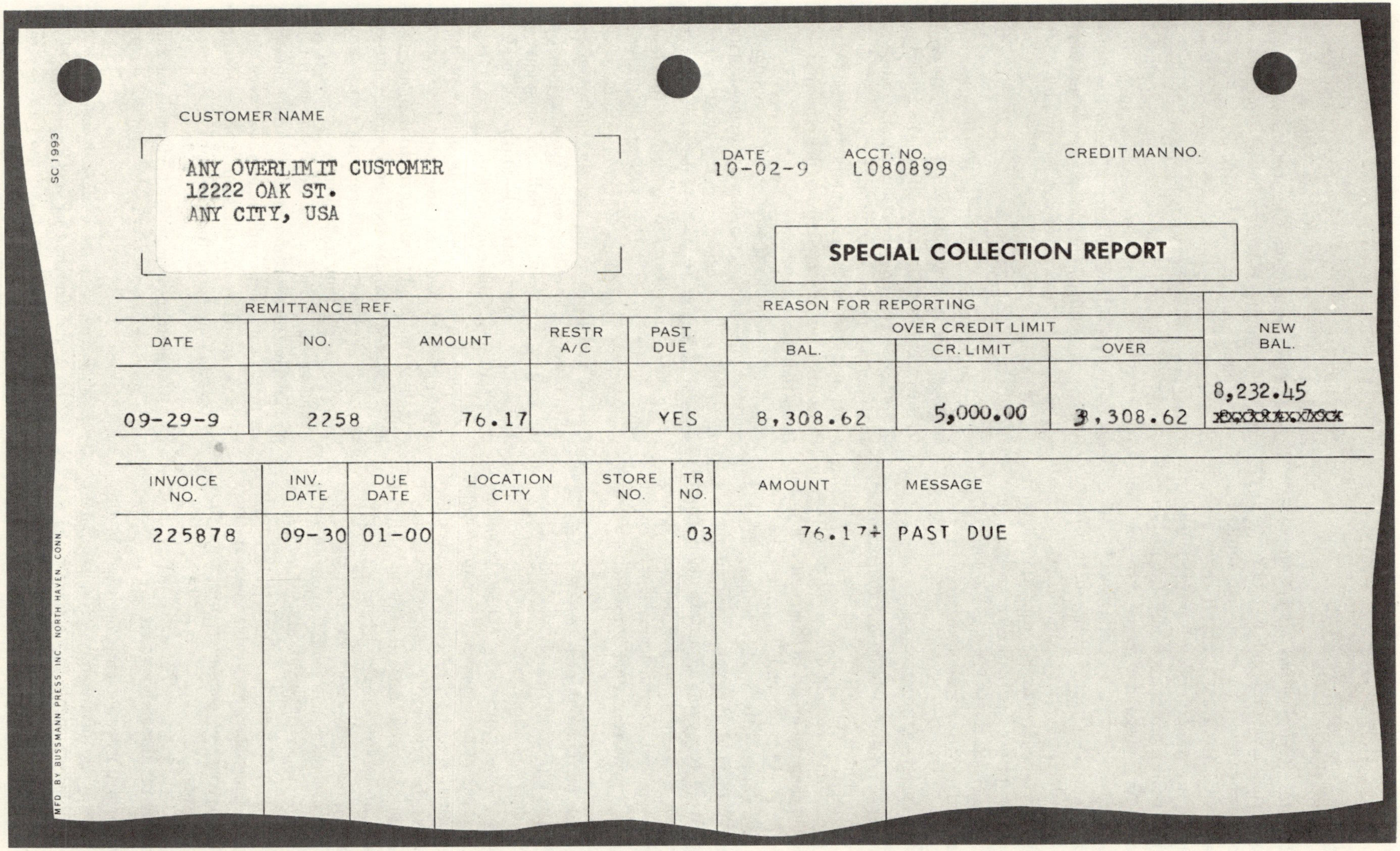

SC 1993

CUSTOMER NAME

ANY OVERLIMIT CUSTOMER
12222 OAK ST.
ANY CITY, USA

DATE 10-02-9 | ACCT. NO. L080899 | CREDIT MAN NO.

SPECIAL COLLECTION REPORT

REMITTANCE REF.			REASON FOR REPORTING					
					OVER CREDIT LIMIT			
DATE	NO.	AMOUNT	RESTR A/C	PAST DUE	BAL.	CR. LIMIT	OVER	NEW BAL.
09-29-9	2258	76.17		YES	8,308.62	5,000.00	3,308.62	8,232.45

INVOICE NO.	INV. DATE	DUE DATE	LOCATION CITY	STORE NO.	TR NO.	AMOUNT	MESSAGE
225878	09-30	01-00			03	76.17+	PAST DUE

MFD BY BUSSMANN PRESS, INC. NORTH HAVEN, CONN

Figure 3.3 Special collection report.

Customer Ledger Record

Chapter 14, "Application and Control of Cash," describes five different methods for applying cash when the open items are kept on a computer-posted receivables file. Two of these methods require some type of printed ledger record for visual identification and for marking paid items for subsequent removal from the account as a result of cash application.

One of the earliest and still one of the most successful cash application methods is the use of a printed customer ledger record. The ledger record may be printed periodically, or each time a check is received. Some firms use a copy of a customer statement for cash application.

USEFUL FOR CREDIT REFERENCE

In several computer installations the customer ledgers are printed weekly for cash application bookkeepers. Under certain operating conditions it is possible that the credit department can perform their credit approval functions by referring to a copy of the weekly ledgers. If this procedure is adopted, then the systems designers should provide for printing information from the customer data bank on the bottom section of the ledger records for the benefit of the credit department. Please refer to Figure 3.4.

It should be pointed out that printing a weekly status report, in lieu of providing a copy of these ledgers to the credit department, is a better approach because the status report is usually an exception report. It includes only certain selected accounts; by contrast, customer ledgers may be printed for all accounts on a periodic basis, or new ledgers may be printed on a basis of recent activity. The criteria for printing ledgers may not coincide with the criteria for accounts that should appear on the weekly status report. On the other hand, if a copy of the ledger records will serve the credit department functions effectively, there are savings both in terms of computer operating time and forms costs.

OTHER CREDIT DEPARTMENT REPORTS

The reports illustrated and discussed in this chapter are by no means the only ones potentially available to a credit department when the receivables are computerized. For example, Chapter 2 illustrated a monthly Credit Guide being used by the Wolverine Tube Division of the Hecla Corporation. Chapter 4 shows the Collection Summary History printed from the computer data bank at M. Lowenstein & Sons on a quarterly basis for the benefit of the credit men. Other chapters cover various special reports designed for reference or for account reconstruction. All of these reports serve a purpose and should be considered as part of the overall group of reports required for the efficient operation of all phases of a computerized receivables system.

INTERFACE WITH CUSTOMERS

The chief credit executive is not only vitally interested in the working tools to be provided by the computer for internal use, he is also concerned with customer relations at all times. Now, the general public has in recent years become very irritated with computers because of the difficulties encountered in communicating with firms that use computers.

It is a common experience for a customer to respond to a computer-printed statement or dunning letter by writing a letter that provides specific information as to cash remitted at a prior time, merchandise returned, the reason for a deduction, etc. The customer logically expects recognition of his communication by some type of action taken, or a reply. Unfortunately, quite often nothing happens. After repeated letter writing or telephone calls the customer becomes angry and frustrated—and tends to blame the problem on the computer.

Obviously it is ridiculous to blame an inanimate piece of hardware; the fault lies with receivables or credit management. Many firms have fostered the idea that everything that goes wrong is the fault of the computer by running advertisements that state this!

The credit manager should be aware of this possible breakdown of communications between his firm's customers and the credit or receivables department. Here are the steps that he can take to forestall or solve the problem:

1. Designate the adjusters to perform as the human interface between customers and the computer system.
2. Make sure that the personnel budget provides for a sufficient number of adjusters to handle normal adjustment functions, plus the rapid

CUSTOMER LEDGER RECORD

ACCOUNT NO. 387-809-7

FASHION CENTER BOUTIQUE
ARCADE SHOPPING CENTER
DALLAS, TEXAS

D & B RATING	D & B DATE	CREDIT LINE AMOUNT	CREDIT LINE DATE	SOLD SINCE	DATE LAST AFFECTED	LEDGER DATE
				02-22-7	05-23-7	05-25-67

POSTING DATE	INVOICE TERMS DISC. OPT. %	DISC. OPT. DYS.	TYPE	DUE DAYS	EXTRA DYS.	EXTRA 1	FINAL DUE DATE	STORE NO.	BATCH NO.	INVOICE OR EFFECT DATE	INVOICE OR EFFECT NUMBER	MEMO AMOUNTS	TR. NO.	AMOUNTS DEBITS	AMOUNTS CREDITS	AGING CURR.	1-30	31-60	61-90	91-120	OVER 120	ENTRY NO. CLNT. NO.	SER. NO.
G AND W	SPTW																						
02-16-7	000	010	04	010	000	0	06-10-7		163	02-15-7	02655		200	330.00		X						0074	0005
03-09-7	000	010	04	010	000	0	09-10-7		137	03-07-7	02860		200	195.00		X						0074	0007
03-16-7	000	010	04	010	000	0	06-10-7		106	03-14-7	03051		200	261.00		X						0074	0010
03-23-7	000	010	04	010	000	0	07-10-7		089	03-20-7	03114		200	120.00		X						0074	0011
03-24-7									CK#	03-10-7	13080		320	1.12		X						0074	0012
03-27-7	000	010	04	010	000	0	09-10-7		323	03-23-7	03205		200	360.00		X						0074	0013
03-31-7	000	010	04	010	000	0	07-10-7		026	03-30-7	03298		200	82.50		X						0074	0014
04-06-7	000	010	04	010	000	0	10-10-7		176	04-04-7	03370		200	370.00		X						0074	0015
04-11-6									CK	03-15-7	13-11-0	25.00										0074	0017
04-20-7	000	010	04	010	000	0	09-10-7		062	04-17-7	03668		230	852.00		X						0074	0018
04-20-7	000	010	04	010	000	0	09-10-7		062	04-17-7	03661		230	186.83		X						0074	0019
04-20-7	000	010	04	010	000	0	09-10-7		062	04-17-7	03662		230	717.50		X						0074	0020
04-24-7	000	010	04	010	000	0	09-10-7		168	04-18-7	03682		230	1,284.00		X						0074	0021
04-28-7	000	010	04	010	000	0	07-10-7		184	04-26-7	03797		230	60.00		X						0074	0022
05-04-7	000	010	04	010	000	0	08-10-7		086	05-01-7	03944		200	225.00		X						0074	0023

CASH ON A/C	TOTAL OPEN CREDITS	TOTAL D/RISK	AGING CURRENT	1-30	31-60	61-90	91-120	OVER 120	TOTAL PAST DUE	FUTURE DUE 1-30	ACCOUNT BALANCE
0	.00	3,100.33	5,045	0	0	0	0	0	0	591	5,044.95

INTEREST RECORD OPEN	PAID THIS YEAR	CHARGE TO CLNT.	C - R THIS YR.	C - R LAST YR.	EXCESSIVE DISCOUNTS & SHORT OPEN	PAID THIS YR.	CHARGE TO CLNT.	C - R THIS YR.	C - R LAST YR.	HIGH BALANCE CURRENT 6 MOS.	LAST 6 MOS.	PAY HABITS % EARLY %	PRMPT %	LATE %	AVER. DYS LATE	DATE OF LAST CASH	DATE LAST SOLD
1	0	0	0	0	0	0	0	0	0	5,070	0	100	0	0		04-25-7	04-11-6

Figure 3.4 Customer ledger with credit department data included.

handling of special receivables problems of all types originating from customer correspondence. Not only should they be able to handle the internal research and paper work promptly, of even greater importance is a fast and satisfactory reply to the customer. This group should also respond promptly when notified of internal changes and adjustments as directed by the General Credit Manager, or the credit executives.

Summary

The combined experience gained from a considerable number of computerized receivables installations in business firms provides a positive basis for reaching several important conclusions:

- The reports as described and illustrated in this chapter bring to the credit man all the data required for the efficient functioning of a modern credit department.
- These new reports not only replace functionally the old, conventional machine-posted ledger records, they provide more information presented in a more concise, useful format than has ever before been possible.
- Availability of these special reports to the credit men has eliminated the conflicts between the various groups of people who, in the past, found it necessary to take turns working with the customer ledgers. Through the use of these specially designed reports, each department or operating group has its own forms and reports to work with.

CUSTOMER DATA BANK

You may have noted the variety of credit data printed as part of the various reports. How this data is developed and where it is stored are topics covered fully in Chapter 11.

CHAPTER 4

Automatic Credit Checking by Computer

Credit checking is a continuous, vital function in any credit department controlling the extension of credit to trade accounts. The past decade has seen a constant increase in the number of orders handled by the average credit department, as well as a large increase in the total dollar volume. As of today, order approval represents a volume operation in many medium-size to large firms and is largely responsible for a major share of the total credit department operating costs.

Traditionally, order checking has been handled by a multilevel credit group. Junior credit men or trainees might handle orders up to a stated amount, with large orders being referred to a senior credit man working with a group of juniors. Regardless of the functional division of responsibility for credit checking, it represents a costly paper-work problem that deserves special attention in any busy credit department.

ATTEMPTS TO STREAMLINE CREDIT CHECKING

Over the years before computers were in the picture, the credit fraternity adopted various methods for streamlining credit checking to reduce the time required and overall costs. One method was to approve all orders under a stated amount, such as $50, without calling for the credit folder. Another approach was to identify top rated accounts and to approve all orders from these accounts up to a predetermined amount such as $1000—$2000—or $5000.

The purpose behind these methods was to free experienced credit men from routine paper work and minor problems so that they could concentrate their time and attention on controlling marginal or risk accounts, or working with customers or the sales force. Moreover, even though the various shortcuts adopted reduced the work load as planned, the quantity of orders that still required the credit man's personal attention continued to be large. For example, orders from marginal accounts frequently represent 25% to 35% of all orders, or more, in many firms. The rule usually followed in most firms is that these orders require the personal approval of the credit man assigned to the account. In turn, this may require that the credit man pull the credit folder for the account before passing credit. As part of his review and account evaluation procedures, the credit man usually will want to know the current receivables balance and the status of the account. Now, in a large firm where the number of people involved in credit and accounts receivable functions is large, obtaining the credit folder and ascertaining the account status are costly and time-consuming operations.

FILING COSTS

Maintenance of credit folders and filing documents in the credit folders from day to day represent a substantial expense in many firms. One large firm in New York City has 18 credit men handling about 50,000 accounts; they are supported by 14 file clerks who maintain the credit files and carry them back and forth, to and from the desks of the credit men.

REVIEW OF MANUAL METHODS

In retrospect it appears that attempts made in prior years to reduce the work load involved in credit checking were well intentioned but not really effective on a broad scale. Too much paper work still remained that required personal handling by credit men which effectively chained them to their desks and precluded the use of their knowledge and experience along more constructive lines.

AUTOMATIC ORDER CHECKING

As alert credit managers in recent years learned how computers function, they began to wonder if a large part of the credit-checking burden could be safely delegated to the computer. If so, this would make it possible to apply uniform rules and tests to all orders at high speed and would help reduce the work load in a department generally faced with a constantly increasing volume of orders.

Today automatic order checking has moved swiftly from the theoretical stage to reality in many firms across the nation. Like any other computer application, however, it requires long and careful planning to implement—and after installation it requires continuing management control.

Automatic order checking is a form of *credit management by exception.* Building the criteria for order approval into an electronic computer is a major step toward mechanizing the routine aspects of credit management to free experienced credit men for more constructive, profitable work in building a sounder customer base and credit controls for increased future sales and profits.

CRITERIA FOR ORDER APPROVAL

A computer is not capable of exercising judgment, but it can make specified comparisons and tests at tremendous speed, based on criteria built into the program in the form of instructions. Therefore, credit checking must be based on rules carefully formulated by the credit executives and fed into the computer for the credit-checking function.

The primary test in wide use requires that each account be assigned a credit limit. The computer first adds the current order under review to the total of other open and unshipped orders—then it adds the total of all orders to the present account balance. If the total exposure is *less than* the credit limit, the order has passed the basic and first test. Other tests that are made are explained on subsequent pages.

The phrase "credit limit" is more apropos than credit *line* because it is considered as being the maximum amount that the credit manager is willing to invest in the account.

SETTING CREDIT LIMITS

Traditionally credit limits are assigned by each individual credit man who applies whatever rules and criteria he thinks appropriate to determine the amount for each customer. However, assigning a credit limit represents an extension of credit. Therefore, credit executives should give considerable thought to formulating a set of rules and guidelines for all credit men to follow when setting credit limits . . . to achieve uniformity and to protect the firm's investment in receivables. Because of the importance of setting a credit limit that will not unduly inhibit sales but also will protect the creditor from undue loss, methods for *automating* the calculation of the credit limit for each account are receiving considerable attention today in the credit field. PPG Industries, Inc., in Pittsburgh has done an outstanding job in this new field and reports successful results from calculating credit limits based on a formula. The specific formula that they have developed and are currently using is explained in detail in Chapter 5.

The impetus for this vital, pioneering type of project came into being because of Robert Howells' firm belief that "the credit man of today cannot resolve his over-extended position by merely adding to the payroll. The solution must come from methods and procedures changes, some of which may not have been thought of at this time" (Mr. Howells is General Credit Manager of PPG).

ORDER APPROVAL BY EXCEPTION

From the standpoint of an ideal situation, automatic credit checking requires that all orders be routed into a central processing point. Also, the computer should accumulate the grand total of all open and outstanding orders for each account. In addition, the credit-checking system requires storing the latest account status information and an analysis of the past due situation if any.

An order may be referred by the computer for a variety of reasons that are based on specific tests programmed into the order-checking run for this purpose. For example, an order may fail to meet the first test, which compares the total account exposure with the assigned credit limit. Or, the account currently may have past due items that represent a substantial percentage of the credit limit. Or, the amount of the order being tested may exceed a specific *order limit* built into the account's data bank.

Caution. A small past due amount should not be allowed to cause an order from a large, well-financed account to be referred. Rules for past due situations should be carefully formulated in order to hold the number of referred orders to the minimum and yet not lose control of past due accounts.

ORDERS FOR FUTURE DELIVERY

Future orders pose a special problem where the total of open orders is routinely added to the account balance for comparison with the assigned credit limit. Suppose an order specifies shipment from three to six months in the future, rather than as soon as possible? Should the order amount be included in the total of open orders, which increases the total account exposure immediately? Many credit analysts express the conviction that such orders should be ignored until they mature, since they represent a future obligation of the customer rather than one that must be met within terms. They suggest that the order amount put on the order file should be included in the total exposure only when the estimated shipping date enters the current time period.

APPROVAL BASED ON D & B RATING

If a firm does not use credit limits, an alternative criterion might be the Dun & Bradstreet rating. This requires the credit manager and his credit men to prepare a schedule of amounts which represents the total exposure acceptable for each D & B rating. This could be further modified by dividing the accounts into categories such as manufacturing, wholesale, and retail. That is, the total exposure could vary for each D & B rating according to the account category.

USE OF ACCOUNT BALANCE AS GUIDELINE

If a large firm has branches or distribution centers scattered over a large geographical area, or located all over the nation, accumulating and approving orders at a central point may not be feasible. Some method of order approval at the decentralized locations must be devised. PPG Industries, Inc. (located in Pittsburgh), uses an ''Over Credit Limit Report'' for negative order approval. That is, any customer whose name is *not* on the computer-printed list is currently acceptable as a credit risk.

Assuming that accumulating the grand total of all outstanding orders at a central control point is not possible, then the account balance becomes the key criterion for a comparison with the assigned credit limit. Therefore, the computer prepares an ''Over Credit Limit Report'' as a by-product of updating the customer open item file. As implied, the credit limit amount is compared to the latest account balance during the updating run; any account balance that exceeds the credit limit causes the account name and status information to be printed on the special exception-type report. This report is distributed immediately to all branches and distribution centers where sales orders are processed.

If the sales department or a retail store manager wants to sell merchandise to an account appearing on the ''Over Credit Limit Report,'' PPG requires submission of a special credit approval request form that is illustrated below (see Figure 4.1).

INTEGRATING A BILLING SYSTEM INTO THE CREDIT AND COLLECTION OPERATIONS

Automatic credit checking at a central order processing point leads very logically into producing the invoices on the computer. Let us review the procedures that take place after the computer credit checking has been accomplished.

One large firm with automatic credit checking goes ahead and prints the shipping order forms

Figure 4.1

Local Credit Approval for Account over Limit (Courtesy of PPG Industries, Inc.)

Date ____________

REGIONAL CREDIT OFFICE

From Unit ____________ ____________

EDP number Unit name

1. Account Names ____________

Customer code number ________ : Order limit $________ : Credit limit $________

2. Latest Daily Over Credit Report on hand is dated ________ Shows Balance $________

3. An order for approximately $________, register number ________
was released to this account today under the conditions as described in 4A, B, or C.
(To be completed by Shipping Unit)

---

4. CHECK below—A, B, or C to indicate your reason for approval:

A. *Up to $1000.* Limited to the amount of *payment,* but not more than $1000, received within the last 10 days and not reflected on the Daily Over Credit Report.

____

____

Amount of payment received $________ Date received ________

B. *Accounts with limits from $100 to $500.*

1. *Up to $200.* Limited to the amount of *promised* payment that is expected to be received within 5 days on this account.

____

____ Amount of payment promised $________

(1) A second release should not be made until promised payment has been received.

2. *Up to $100.* Limited to the judgment of the Servicing Unit or Salesman.

____

____ (1) A second release should not be made until payment is received.

C. *Accounts with limits from $600 to $5000*

____ 1. *Up to $1000.* Limited to the amount of promised payment that is expected to be received

____ within 5 days on this account and restricted to not more than the order limit.

Amount of payment promised $________

(1) A second release should not be made until promised payment has been received.

2. *Up to $200.* Limited to the judgment of the Servicing Unit or Salesman.

(1) A second release should not be made until payment is received.

---

5. Remarks:

---

for all orders, even though some have been referred for credit department attention. The shipping papers for such orders, however, are routed to the credit department instead of to the warehouse. This enables the credit men to hold all flagged orders until they make a decision on each one.

Shipping papers for approved orders are routed to the warehouse for immediate handling and shipping of the products ordered. When the annotated shipping papers are returned to central billing, the changed information and other data are fed into the computer for each order. Then the computer prints the invoice documents, and inscribes the accounts receivable information on a reel of magnetic tape for input later to the accounts receivable customer master file.

Each time the customer master file is updated by the posting of new sales, or the application of cash a work tape is created which is fed back into the credit checking runs. This tape brings into the computer the latest account balances, and the past due situation for each account.

Case History of Automatic Credit Checking

An article written by the eminent credit executive, Morton Reitman, appeared in the July 1968 issue of *Credit and Financial Management.* entitled ''How a Computer Works for Credit Management,'' the article dealt with an on-line credit checking system and explained in detail the concepts behind the system and the procedures followed at that time by the New York City-based firm of M. Lowenstein & Sons, Inc.

PROCEDURES

The following procedures were outlined in the article; they may be considered as being reasonably typical of what is required for automatic credit checking in any computerized firm.

Step 1. Batch incoming customer orders after sorting them by credit-man groups.

Step 2. Type the customer account number, order amount, and estimated delivery date, utilizing a typewriter that punches paper tape as output.

Step 3. After routinely processing all orders in a batch, insert the punched paper tape in a "read station" located on the side of the typewriter. Flipping a "start" switch instructs the sending device to transmit the order data to the computer, which may be located close by—or hundreds of miles away.

Step 4. The computer receives and stores the order messages, then starts searching its files for the customers involved in the group of orders. It makes all programmed tests and sends the results back to the same typewriter terminal that transmitted the order information to it.

Step 5. The receiving typewriter, actuated by the computer, types a brief message about each order submitted for credit checking.

Step 6. Order clerks attach the computer messages to the order copies. Orders which failed to meet the tests are separated from other orders and sent to the various credit men along with the computer-based data typed on the receiving typewriter.

CRITERIA FOR ORDER APPROVAL OR REFERRAL

Each firm implementing credit checking with a computer should develop its own list of rules and guidelines. However, it will be interesting to examine the tests that were built into the system as described by Mr. Reitman:

- Compare credit limit to the sum of the latest account balance—plus total open unshipped orders, including the order now being tested.
- Determine if the account has one or more past due items. If so, add the amounts and compare the total to the credit limit, then calculate the percenttage of past due to the credit limit. (Based on the type of account, the percentage figure, if high enough, would cause the order to be "referred.")
- Compare the date of the last financial statement received with the current date; calculate the number of months since the receipt of the last statement. Then relate the type of account to the number of months. (This may trigger a rejection of the order as explained below.)

Customers of M. Lowenstein & Sons, Inc. are in the volatile soft goods business, engaged in manufacturing, distributing, or in retailing. It is well understood in this field that the financial strength of the customer is of the utmost importance and can change rapidly in a short time span. For this reason the computer was programmed to refer any order if the latest financial statement obtained from a manufacturer is more than 16 months old. For a retailer the latest financial information must have been obtained within the past six months.

QUALIFYING A PAST DUE CONDITION

To assure that orders from well-rated firms will not be routinely rejected merely because of small past due amounts appearing on the account, the computer is programmed to ignore past dues less than seven days old. If more than seven days old, then other tests are applied. If the account fails to meet the tests shown in Table 4.1 below, the computer refers the order.

Special consideration should be given to open items that have been disputed (and, therefore, remain unpaid), or are in process of adjustment.

Table 4.1
Table of Past Due Tests (Dollars)

Credit Limit	Total Past Due Allowable
Accounts under 5000	Up to 500
5000 to 10,000	Up to 1000
10,000 to 25,000	Up to 3000
Over 25,000	Up to 5000

That is, such items should be flagged and the program should be written so that the computer ignores these special items when making the prescribed past due tests.

If an account has no credit limit assigned, then the order will be rejected automatically if past due items appear on the account. Also, the removal of a credit limit from an account is a popular control device in wide use to enable a credit man, in effect, to remove the automatic order approval for certain accounts from time to time.

OTHER FEASIBLE TESTS

Edward Frank, a dynamic young General Credit Manager, has had many years' experience with computer systems as applied to credit functions. One of his control devices is what he calls the "Early Warning System." One of the tests made by the computer that he installed on automatic order approval was a determination of the length of time the account had been on the books. If less than six months—and the current test revealed that the account had past due items older than 60 days that exceeded $500—the computer was programmed to print a special report which required immediate attention by a credit man.

Then, the credit man was required to set up a credit folder on the account, in addition to reviewing the account for the purpose of approving or rejecting the order at hand. The reason for this was that Mr. Frank had instituted a policy of not setting up a credit folder for any account—until circumstances like those described above made it necessary. This policy reduced credit department costs substantially in several ways. For example, during a recent one-year period his department paid for only 1100 Dun & Bradstreet reports covering a customer file of 55,000 accounts!

HOW COMPUTER REPLIES

When the paper tape data representing information on about 50 orders has been read into the computer, it starts replying almost immediately. For each order in the batch it causes the receiving typewriter to type the following information.

- Customer name and address extracted from the customer's data bank.
- Order amount, followed by symbol "R" or "A" (rejected or accepted).
- Latest ledger balance and aging status of open items in summary format.
- Credit-man number assigned to account.
- *Reason* for referral—if referred.

The receiving typewriter types the information on unit sheets of paper so that, in the event of order referral, the operator can tear off the message and *attach it to the order form* for further review and personal handling by the credit man.

Experience has shown that, on the average, the computer will refer about 25% of all orders in a typical batch at M. Lowenstein. These orders are then routed to the credit men for processing. Of the 25% personally reviewed, credit can be passed on about one half of the orders without pulling the credit folders. This means that credit folders are pulled for only about 12 ½% of all orders received.

CREDIT MAN CAN OVERRIDE COMPUTER

Computer referral of an order merely alerts the credit man to the fact that minimum computer tests were not satisfied when the computer analyzed the latest account data in the data bank. The credit man can easily approve an order referred initially by the computer, since the system provides for a forced acceptance for this purpose.

The computer accumulates all orders reported to it, whether initially approved or referred, and the ones approved by the credit man after special analysis. All approved order amounts are added to the total of approved but unshipped orders. When a new order is then submitted to the computer, it adds the total of unshipped orders to the account balance and then compares the total exposure to the credit line. If the total is still less than the credit line—and all other corollary tests are met satisfactorily—the computer will approve the order.

FINANCIAL DATA PRINTED ON CUSTOMER STATEMENT

With the objective of reducing the credit man's dependence on memory and to eliminate the continuing reference to credit files, financial data is printed routinely on the top of each computer-printed customer account statement that is provided monthly to the credit department at M. Lowenstein and Sons (see Figure 4.2 below).

Observe that two lines of information appear across the top part of the statement shown in Figure 4.2. Current data taken from the latest financial statement received from the customer prints on the top line; prior financial data appears on the lower print line. Notice that the box headings on the top line are for retail accounts; headings for manufacturers are *beneath the lower line* of account information.

The numbers and letters printed on the statement as shown represent a combination of dates and specific financial information, for instance, net worth, merchandise on hand, working capital, current liabilities, net sales, gross profit percentage, credit limit—and the basis (see letter B) on which the customer borrows bank funds.

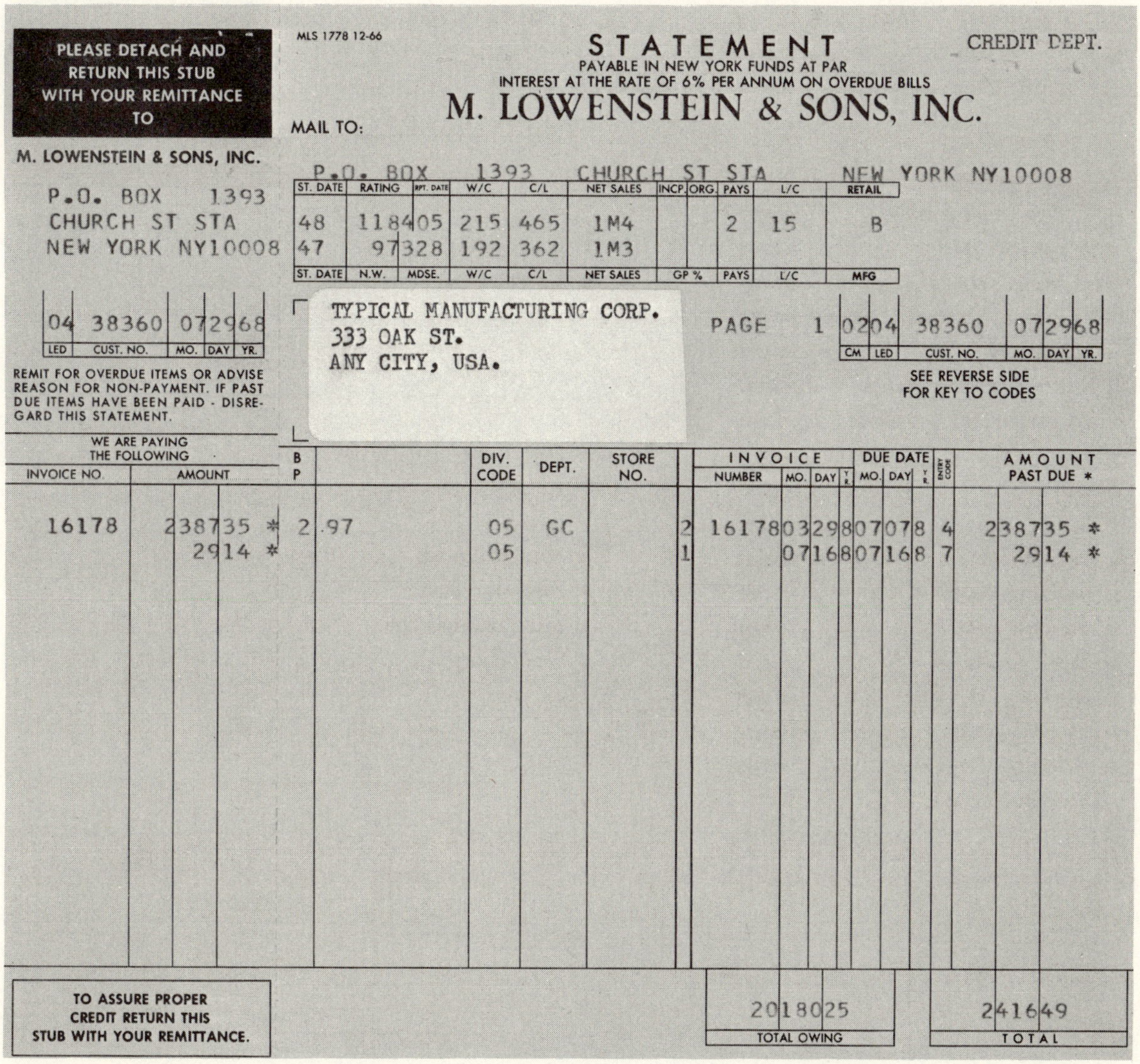
PLEASE DETACH AND RETURN THIS STUB WITH YOUR REMITTANCE TO

M. LOWENSTEIN & SONS, INC.

P.O. BOX 1393
CHURCH ST STA
NEW YORK NY10008

MLS 1778 12-66

STATEMENT

CREDIT DEPT.

PAYABLE IN NEW YORK FUNDS AT PAR
INTEREST AT THE RATE OF 6% PER ANNUM ON OVERDUE BILLS

M. LOWENSTEIN & SONS, INC.

MAIL TO:

P.O. BOX 1393 CHURCH ST STA NEW YORK NY10008

ST. DATE	RATING	RPT. DATE	W/C	C/L	NET SALES	INCP.	ORG.	PAYS	L/C	RETAIL
48	1184	05	215	465	1M4			2	15	B
47	97	328	192	362	1M3					
ST. DATE	N.W.	MDSE.	W/C	C/L	NET SALES	GP %		PAYS	L/C	MFG

LED	CUST. NO.	MO.	DAY	YR.
04	38360	07	29	68

TYPICAL MANUFACTURING CORP.
333 OAK ST.
ANY CITY, USA.

PAGE 1

CM	LED	CUST. NO.	MO.	DAY	YR.
02	04	38360	07	29	68

REMIT FOR OVERDUE ITEMS OR ADVISE REASON FOR NON-PAYMENT. IF PAST DUE ITEMS HAVE BEEN PAID - DISREGARD THIS STATEMENT.

SEE REVERSE SIDE FOR KEY TO CODES

WE ARE PAYING THE FOLLOWING INVOICE NO.	AMOUNT	B P		DIV. CODE	DEPT.	STORE NO.		INVOICE NUMBER	MO.	DAY	YR.	DUE DATE MO.	DAY	YR.	ENTRY CODE	AMOUNT PAST DUE *
16178	2387 35 *	2	97	05	GC		2	16178	03	29	8	07	07	8	4	2387 35 *
	29 14 *			05			1		07	16	8	07	16	8	7	29 14 *

TO ASSURE PROPER CREDIT RETURN THIS STUB WITH YOUR REMITTANCE.

TOTAL OWING	TOTAL
2018 025	2416 49

Figure 4.2 Sample customer statement showing financial and sales information for credit man (courtesy of M. Lowenstein & Sons, Inc.).

DATA ON RETAIL ACCOUNTS

The credit information considered essential for retail accounts is somewhat different. Consider the following information printed on a retail customer's statement:

17 AAA1 28 14M 6M2 1HM 9 C 1 R

Again, these letters and numerals represent a combination of dates and financial data:

17—date of last financial statement was January (Month No. *1*, 196*7*)
AAA1—Dunn & Bradstreet rating
28—credit report dated February 1968
14M—working capital is $14 million
6M2—current liabilities: 6 million 200 thousand
1HM—net sales are $100,000,000
9—in business 9 years
C—firm is organized as a corporation
1—pays on discount basis
R—Credit Limit is "requirements"

QUARTERLY REPORT OF CUSTOMER LEDGER HISTORY

In addition to the financial data available to the credit man by reference to the customer statement form, he can also refer to a quarterly report that shows the aged accounts receivable status for a period of time. Notice that one print line represents a month; this report shows the past payment performance of the account at a glance (Figure 4.3).

PRINTED CREDIT GUIDES

Printed credit guides are another method of bringing account information to the credit man in a systematic manner. This is a specially designed report that presents the latest account

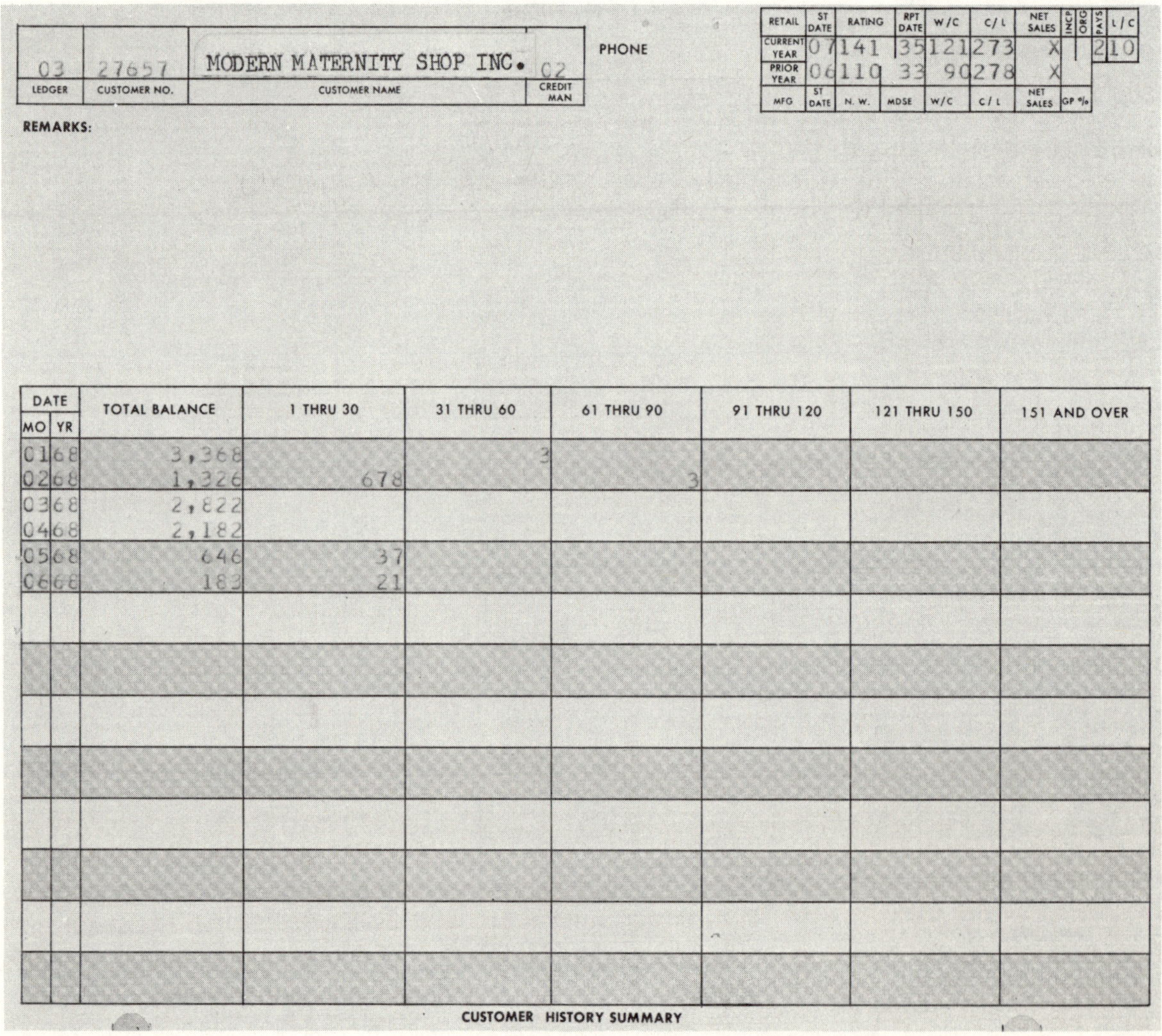

LEDGER	CUSTOMER NO.	CUSTOMER NAME	CREDIT MAN
03	27657	MODERN MATERNITY SHOP INC.	C2

PHONE

RETAIL	ST DATE	RATING	RPT DATE	W/C	C/L	NET SALES	INCP	ORG	PAYS	L/C
CURRENT YEAR	07	141	35	121	273	X		1	2	10
PRIOR YEAR	06	110	33	90	278	X				
MFG	ST DATE	N. W.	MDSE	W/C	C/L	NET SALES	GP %			

REMARKS:

DATE MO	DATE YR	TOTAL BALANCE	1 THRU 30	31 THRU 60	61 THRU 90	91 THRU 120	121 THRU 150	151 AND OVER
01	68	3,368		3				
02	68	1,326	678		3			
03	68	2,822						
04	68	2,182						
05	68	646	37					
06	68	183	21					

CUSTOMER HISTORY SUMMARY

Figure 4.3 Customer history summary (courtesy of M. Lowenstein & Sons, Inc.).

data accumulated and stored in the customer's data bank. The credit guide may be printed in the form of a ticket, a full page to place in the credit folder—or it may be a label that can be glued to an account history or on the outside of the credit folder.

Coding Financial Reports

Bringing customer financial information from storage in a computer device to the desk of the credit man is a big step forward in scientific credit management. This is one method of eliminating the need for calling for credit folders.

The first few firms that set up procedures for bringing financial statement data into a computer placed a trained accountant in charge of statement review and coding for input. Shortcuts have since been developed, such as encouraging the customer to fill out a simple, precoded statement form for submission to the creditor form. This has made it possible for people with little accounting training to process incoming statements, and to route them to keypunching.

EXTRACTING DATA FROM AGENCY REPORTS

One large firm solved the problem of extracting data from agency reports by designing a simple three-part form. The credit man fills in the customer name and account number, then reviews the agency report. He circles the financial figure facts he wants taken from the report and stored in the customer's data bank. He then passes the report to a secretary who copies the data to the three-part form for easy keypunching. The credit man retains one copy; two go to the input department.

SPECIAL CUSTOMER FINANCIAL STATEMENTS

To properly handle special customer financial statements, PPG Industries routes them to a trained accountant who reviews each report, codes each item to identify it for input and processing, and then sends the statement to the keypunch section.

BENEFITS OF CODING FINANCIAL DATA

Since the coding and entry of customer financial data is surprisingly easy, this enhances the many benefits to be derived from this modern technique. For example, the computer can calculate all desired ratios and percentages at very high speed. Furthermore, it can compare the latest figures with the ones taken from a prior statement—and report significant changes or TRENDS immediately to the interested credit executive.

The utilization of a computer in this way represents a very logical method of harnessing the power of an electronic computer to serve the requirements of a modern credit department effectively.

REVIEW AND EVALUATION OF AUTOMATIC ORDER CHECKING BY COMPUTER

Automatic order checking with a computer is a method for handling large volumes of orders on an exception basis. By permitting the computer to make all prescribed tests and routinely to approve orders from firms that are good credit risks, or have nothing past due, approximately 75% of all orders will escape manual handling, research, and processing.

Orders that are initially referred by the computer are brought to the personal attention of the credit men for review and appropriate disposition. This is truly *management by exception.* It enables credit men to concentrate on problem accounts and to do a more effective job.

GAIN SUPPORT OF SALES DEPARTMENT

Rejection of an order always carries with it the possibility of a negative reaction from the sales department, which understandably is striving to make as many sales as possible. Installation of credit checking by computer may create the impression among the sales people that the computer itself has the power to reject orders. It is important to explain to the sales group that the computer merely makes a series of programmed tests; if an order fails to meet one or more of the tests, it does not actually reject an order; it flags the order for review and a decision by the credit man responsible for the account from which the order was secured.

A corollary point to stress is that the computer should never be allowed to delete an account, or to flag it as an unprofitable account. However, there is nothing wrong with programming the computer to detect unfavorable conditions within an account and to print special messages for the personal attention of the credit man responsible for the account.

REVIEW CRITERIA PERIODICALLY

Once the criteria for automatic order approval have been established and the new system is in actual operation, the credit manager should not consider the list of tests as a permanent solution to the order approval function. Changing conditions may well require modifications from time to time. As a means of management control, perhaps the tests and the entire system should be reviewed periodically on a scheduled basis.

MINIATURIZING CREDIT FOLDERS

On prior pages various methods were presented for bringing coded financial information and other customer data to the credit man in order to eliminate the need for pulling the credit folder on an account as much as possible. However, there will always be situations that require a complete review of all documents, or selected documents found in the credit folder. All credit managers recognize that maintenance of the usual type of credit folders is quite cumbersome and costly. Furthermore, the time lag between the time a credit man requests a folder and the receipt of the folder may seriously affect the flow of orders from the credit department to the order processing department. Also, it inevitably causes the credit man to waste valuable time.

An ideal solution would be to bring the credit folders representing all of the accounts controlled by a credit man to his desk, ready for instant reference. A thoroughly modern version of file folders makes this feasible now through the use of plastic jackets that hold microfilm document images. This modern solution is explained fully in Chapter 7. Each 4″ × 6″ jacket can hold up to 60 letter-size documents of financial statements in micro-image format.

To illustrate the tremendous reduction in filing space that this type of file makes possible, consider the instance of one credit man responsible for 3000 customers. All 3000 micro jackets can be placed on his desk in a metal box measuring only 12″ × 15″!

To read any of the information in the jacket, the credit man merely pulls the customer's jacket and drops it into a microfilm reader. Each small image is instantly magnified and displayed on a screen in full size.

This modern system should reduce clerical filing costs substantially, and it will save the credit man's time on those occasions when he needs to refer to a credit folder.

OVERALL BENEFITS FROM AUTOMATIC CREDIT CHECKING

It has been proved that automatic order checking can reduce order processing costs substantially. This may not necessarily mean a reduction in the present staff because of other pressing duties, which the credit men are not able to handle under manual order approval methods. Certainly, it makes it possible for a given group of credit men to handle substantial increases in order volume.

Morton Reitman mentions in his article that this new approach to order checking enabled him, as General Credit Manager of his firm, to reorganize the credit department after the installation of the computer system. He eliminated the categories of junior credit men and trainees completely. He assigned collection responsibility* for each group of customer accounts to the credit men and eliminated the separate collection department. Morton Reitman sums up his experience with computer credit checking by saying: "This streamlining of the credit department could only be accomplished by harnessing the power of the computer. Order processing departmental efficiency, and overall job satisfaction must be added to the list of benefits."

* Thomas Edick, the progressive young Assistant General Credit Manager for the Stanley Works in New Britain, Connecticut, stresses the fact that combining the credit and collection functions greatly aids the credit man when making credit decisions on orders requiring approval.

CHAPTER 5

Formulized Credit Limits: A Modern Tool for Controlling Credit Granting

Credit executives today are eager to find new tools for handling the increasing paperwork volume, for reducing costs, and for improving the efficiency of credit operations. The climate for change and acceptance of new techniques has never been better.

Mr. Clinton Eckstrom, Jr. (Credit Manager for PPG Industries in Pittsburgh), states in his essay on formulized credit limits: "If credit managers are to achieve status as members of a profession, they must be forward-looking, adopting those new tools which will be responsive to handling the ever-increasing receivables load."

APPLICATION OF CREDIT LIMITS

The use of credit limits as a credit control device is not universally accepted. Various questionnaires distributed to credit managers in the past have uncovered the fact that many credit departments operate without credit limits, or with only a limited use of this device.

Various definitions of credit limits can be found in texts about credit management. For example:

- Credit limits represent a dollar-control device for granting credit.
- They control the amount of investment in a customer.
- The credit limit represents the maximum amount the credit man is willing to risk in one account.
- A credit limit is a tool to expedite the order approval function.

Any research on the topic of credit limits leads to the realization that there is surprisingly little source information available other than the routine definitions found in standard textbooks. In past years the subject has not been explored to any great depth except in the area of terminology. Many credit men use the phrase "credit line" in preference to "credit limit." Some have reached the conclusion that the use of credit line is preferable in dealing with people outside the credit department; namely sales personnel and customers. Internally, the use of the phrase "credit limit" is preferred because credit men should think in terms of restricting the investment in one customer's receivables to the amount assigned as the credit limit. In the remainder of this chapter the two terms will be used interchangeably.

BASIC VALUE OF CREDIT LIMITS

Without established credit lines a company's exposure or investment in an account is undoubtedly subject to the whims and personal opinions of the individual credit man assigned to the account. A corollary problem is that each customer's account must be reviewed *each time* an order is received from the customer.

By contrast, the use of credit limits provides many substantial benefits. Fundamentally the installation and use of a formal credit limit system makes it possible to *establish a uniform, overall corporate credit policy controlling the extension of credit.* As one authority stated: "Setting credit limits *is an extension of credit* . . . determined in advance, and based on certain factors which are evaluated by the credit man in determining the amount assigned to each account."

As we have seen in Chapter 4, automatic order approval requires the comparison of overall account exposure to some type of limit amount. An established credit limit provides the most definitive method for credit checking insofar as controlling the exposure resulting from the approval of new orders.

SAVES CONSIDERABLE TIME

The credit man, using credit limits as a guide, will pass the majority of daily orders without spending much time on them. This enables him to follow marginal accounts more closely, and to provide personal counsel from time to time to help build them into more profitable customers for the future.

OTHER CHAPTER TOPICS

After one accepts the basic premise that credit limits are not only desirable but are necessary to protect the investment in receivables, the related subjects listed below then become meaningful:

- Calculation of credit limits by the application of *standard formulas* applied to a list of facts and figures about an account.
- Application of a computer to the task of calculating the credit limit.

These are very timely and important topics. Mr. Clinton Eckstrom has ventured the educated guess that most corporate credit staffs will be operating with credit limits as a basic control device, determined by a computerized credit-limit formula in the next few years.

Credit-Limits Formula and Its Application

Several years ago two credit executives at the Pittsburgh Plate Glass Company (now known as PPG Industries, Inc.) began to discuss the possibility of calculating credit limits by the use of a formula. These intermittent discussions led to research which revealed that there was no information available in print on the subject of a formula useful for calculating a credit limit for a business firm on a uniform, scientific basis. Believing that such a formula, if developed on a sound and practical basis, would be a valuable tool for any credit department, these two dynamic and progressive credit executives moved ahead within their own firm to develop, apply, and experiment with various formulas.

In recent years these two men have made widely-acclaimed presentations of the theories and practice behind their "Formulized Credit Limits" to credit groups, to credit convention audiences, and at special seminars on credit, for example, those sponsored by the American Management Association. They are:

- Mr. Robert Howells, General Credit Manager of PPG
- Mr. Clinton Eckstrom, Credit Manager of the Industrial Coatings-Fiber Glass Division of PPG.

All of the material presented in this chapter came from an essay submitted by Mr. Eckstrom in 1966 to the Dartmouth Graduate School of Business entitled: "Formulized Credit Limits—A New Tool for Today's Credit Manager." The originators of the credit formula named above made all of their material and experience available to me for inclusion in this book.

BASIC PREMISE BEHIND FORMULA

These two credit executives began their research into the development of a formula with the belief that the formula must produce a credit limit that would reflect the customer's ability to pay, and also must reflect the customer's requirements for the merchandise of the seller. They reasoned that, if the customer does not have the ability to pay his bills, based on his cash flow, then the receivable amount will remain unpaid and eventually will develop into a bad debt loss. They also knew in advance that customer requirements become the primary factor with AAA-1 accounts in the establishment of a credit limit because there is no problem with the paying ability of these accounts.

CONTRIBUTING FACTORS IN THE FORMULA

The formula eventually developed through extensive trial and error for use at PPG is composed of 13 factors:

- Basic Allowance
- Customer Requirements
- Pay Habits
- Years in Business
- Profit Margin
- Current Ratio
- Quick Ratio
- Current Debt to Inventory Ratio
- Inventory to Working Capital Ratio
- Net Worth to Debt Ratio
- Quality of Receivables
- Inventory Turnover
- Judgment Factors

Each factor in the formula was determined by assigning percentages to data on the basis of the relative weight of each factor. The percentage allowances were then adjusted by trial and error until the end result produced a credit limit that met the following tests.

- The credit limit equalled approximately 100% of the net worth for customers in excellent financial condition.
- The credit limit was a reasonable or prudent amount for the average account—much less than the total net worth.
- The credit limit developed by the formula was zero or a minus quantity for customers with major financial problems.

The percentages eventually selected for calculating the credit limit are shown in Figure 5.1, "Work Sheet for Establishing Formula Credit Limit."

It is important to note that liquidity of the financial statement dominates the weighting of the contributing factors involved in the formula.

FIRST FOUR FACTORS

1. *Basic allowance—10% of net worth.* This is the basic amount of credit extended to any customer. The net worth may be determined by reference to the customer's financial statement, or it may be reflected by his Dun & Bradstreet rating. If no statement is available, the information is gathered from other sources and used to estimate the net worth. Deduct intangibles such as goodwill from net worth before applying the formula if the amounts are large.
2. *Customer requirements.* The amount of contribution to the credit limit is based on the percentage of the customer's total purchases to be supplied by the creditor firm. For example, the customer will purchase under 25% of his total requirements, from 25 to 50%, or more than 50%.
3. *Pay habits.* This refers to the customer's paying habits with the creditor firm or with other trade suppliers, or both.
4. *Years in business.* The number of years in business is an important rating factor, since business failure statistics show that the possibility of failure sharply decreases as the length of time in business increases.
5. *Profit margin (before income taxes).* Defined as net income before income taxes as taken from the profit and loss statement.
6. *Current ratio (current assets divided by current liabilities).* This indicates the available working capital in the business and the *liquidity condition* of the business. The rule of thumb commonly applied is that a business should have a 2 to 1 current ratio in order to pay suppliers' bills within terms. The ratio also reveals the value that current assets have to liquidate current debts and represents the margin of protection for current creditors.
7. *Quick ratio (cash plus receivables divided by current liabilities).* This is the acid-test ratio and is a qualitative measure of working capital —and indicates the extent to which current debt can be paid before relying on inventory as a source of funds.

Figure 5.1

Work Sheet for Establishing Formula Credit Limit

Description of Factor	Rating	Contribution to Credit Limit
1. Basic allowance—10% of net worth	10%	
2. Requirements	Under 25%	0
	25 to 50%	5% of net worth
	Over 50%	10% of net worth
3. *Pay habits*		
Discounts or pays promptly net terms	High	10% of net worth
Pays promptly where discount terms available	Good	5% of net worth
Pays per agreed, special terms	Neutral	0
Occasionally late	Fair	−2½% of net worth
Considerably late	Poor	−5% of net worth
4. Years in business	Under 3 years	0
	3 to 10 years	2½% of net worth
	Over 10 years	5% of net worth
5. *Profit margin.* For each 1% of profit margin, add 2/10th of 1% of net worth as contribution to credit limit. Deduct same percentage for LOSS		
6. *Current ratio.* Indicates margin of protection to current creditors	2 to 1 or higher	10% of net worth
	1.25 to 1 up to 2 to 1	5% of net worth
	.75 to 1 up to 1.25 to 1	0
	Under .75 to 1	−5% of net worth
7. *Quick ratio.* Measures extent to which current debt can be liquidated without relying on inventory.	2 to 1 or higher	15% of net worth
	1 to 1 up to 2 to 1	10% of net worth
	.80 to 1 up to 1 to 1	5% of net worth
	.50 to 1 up to .80 to 1	0
	Under .50 to 1	−5% of net worth
8. *Current debt to inventory ratio.* Indication of reliance on unsold inventory to meet current obligations	.65 to 1 lower	10% of net worth
	.65 to 1 up to 1 to 1	0
	1 to 1 or higher	5% of net worth
9. *Inventory to working capital ratio*	.50 to 1 up to 1 to 1	5% of net worth
	.25 to 1 up to .50 to 1	0
	Under .25 to 1 *and* over 1 to 1	5% of net worth
10. *Net worth to debt ratio.* Measures soundness of overall capital structure and margin of protection to all creditors	Over 2 to 1	10% of net worth
	1 to 1 up to 2 to 1	5% of net worth
	Under 1 to 1	5% of net worth
11. *Quality of receivables.* (Gross trade receivables divided by average daily sales)—test of credit and collection policies and liquidity of receivables. *Minimum standard.* Net selling terms plus 30 days	For each 10 days under the minimum standard, add 1% of net worth	
12. *Inventory Turnover.* Measures control and quality of inventory and, to an extent, sales capacity	10 to 30 times	10% of net worth
	5 to 10 times	5% of net worth
	Under 5 and over 30 times	0
13. *Judgment factors.* Includes in the category marketing, security, growth potential, and other factors not specifically covered previously		

8. *Current debt inventory ratio (current liabilities divided by inventory).* Indicates reliance on available inventory for funds for payment of debts.
9. *Inventory/working capital ratio (inventory divided by net working capital).* This represents the amount of working capital tied up in inventory.
10. *Net worth/debt ratio (net worth divided by total debt).* This is a quantitative ratio showing the degree of control by management and the degree of dependency on borrowed capital and on other creditors. It measures the soundness of the total capital structure.
11. *Quality of receivables (days' sales outstanding).* This measures the quality of receivables and is a test of the credit/collection policies of the customer and of the liquidity of receivables.
12. *Inventory turnover (cost of sales divided by inventory).* This is the inventory turnover rate that measures manufacturing efficiency, inventory control, merchandising capacity, and quality of inventories.

The last eight components of the formula represent financial information; five are ratios calculated from financial data extracted from the customer's financial statement or from other sources. Notice that items No. 11 and No. 12 measure the quality of two major assets on the balance sheet.

THE JUDGMENT FACTOR

The inclusion of the judgment factor builds flexibility into the formula. If there are elements present that have not been considered to this point, the credit manager can give them weight so as to establish a credit limit in line with the customer's needs. For example, the final credit limit amount developed through application of the formula may be above or below the customer's requirements. No further analysis is necessary if point No. 12 produces a credit limit *above* requirements. However, if the formula produces a credit limit considerably below requirements, the credit manager can then make two further approaches:

- One, he can apply the judgment factor. That is, he can give weight to elements present but not considered by items Nos. 1 to 12.
- Two, the credit manager can negotiate with the customer as to personal guarantees—or work out arrangements to secure the credit advanced to the customer beyond the formula-produced credit limit.

DOLLAR AMOUNTS RESULTING FROM APPLICATION OF EACH FACTOR

The work sheet shown in Figure 5.1 lists the various elements that produce a contribution toward the total credit limit—which is the net sum of 13 components that, together, make up the formula.

The work form illustrated in Figure 5.2 shows exactly how a credit limit amount is calculated—based on the following sample facts and figures:

Net worth shown on customer balance sheet:	$93,000
Profit margin	2%
7 years in business	
Good pay habits	

Note that the first 12 factors in the formula developed a credit limit of $22,227. However, the credit man deducted $2000 because information developed from comparative statements revealed a slight decline in all major financial statement ratios.

A thoughtful review of how the application of the formula produces the credit limit reveals the fact that most of the factors are based on financial data. Since the credit limit amount resulting from the use of the formula indicates the customer's ability to pay, the credit limit actually represents the amount the firm is *willing to invest* in the customer. The formula method reduces guesswork to a minimum.

FORMULA FULFILLS THE THREE C's OF CREDIT

Over the years one has heard a great deal about the three C's of the credit field: *C*apital, *C*apacity, and *C*haracter. Now, it is interesting to realize that the formula can be directly related to these three C's:

Capital (liquidity)
Current Ratio
Quality of Receivables
Quality of Inventory

Figure 5.2

Analytical Procedure For Establishing a Credit Limit

Work Form

Customer ______________________

Statement dated ______________________

Net worth ______________________

Basic Information	Rating Used	Contribution to Credit Limit
1. Basic allowance—10% of net worth		$ 9,300
2. Requirements	30%	4,650
3. Pay habits (circle appropriate symbol)	H G N F P	4,650
4. Years in business	7 years	2,325
Subtotal 1 to 4.		$20,925
Financial Statement Analysis		
5. Profit Margin	2.01%	372
6. Current Ratio	1.74 to 1	4,650
7. Quick Ratio	.96 to 1	4,650
8. Current Debt/Inventory Ratio	1.28 to 1	(4,650)
9. Inventory/Working Capital Ratio	1.06 to 1	(4,650)
10. Net Worth/Debt Ratio	.96 to 1	(4,650)
11. Quality of Receivables	52 days	930
12. Inventory Turnover	6.6 times	4,650
Subtotal 1 to 12		$22,227
13. Judgment factors *Trend of comparative statement* *Shows decline in ratios*		(2,000)
	Maximum credit limit	$20,227
	Actual credit limit assigned	$20,000

Capacity (ability to pay)
Net Profit on Sales
ROI—return on invested capital
Character (integrity)
Pay habits
Years in business

IS CHARACTER GIVEN TOO LITTLE WEIGHT?

During the trial-and-error developmental stage of the formula, it was thought that, perhaps, the formula did not give enough weight to the character of the customer's management. To find out the relative importance of this factor in bad debt losses, PPG credit personnel pulled the customer folders on bad debt losses covering a period of several years. They analyzed the common factors present in the debtor firms that resulted in bad debts and grouped them under seven headings:

- Sluggish receivables—60 days or more
- Too little or too much inventory
- No working capital
- Small net worth
- Poor pay habits
- Less than three years in business
- Operating at a loss

The significant thing is that none of these common factors are directly connected with personal character. There were no cases of dishonesty, living beyond income, excessive drinking, or not devoting enough time to the business.

RELEVANT FACTORS IN A FORMULA

The PPG formula was the end result of a pioneering venture into the realm of the scientific calculation of credit limits based on certain selected factors. A questionnaire was sent to credit managers in scores of firms. It informed them of the project and requested them to think about the problem and then provide the factors that they thought should be included in a master check list of credit-granting elements that should be considered when developing a formula. The factors listed below were the ones mentioned most frequently by credit managers; the list is in priority sequence.

1. Financial-statement ratios
2. Dun & Bradstreet ratings—agency reports
3. Bank reports
4. Trade references
5. Paying experience
6. Personal visits—major accounts
7. Customer requirements
8. Salesman's opinion
9. Major supplier
10. Profitability of product
11. Competitive conditions
12. Degree of need for the customer's business
13. Customer's reputation
14. Character of management—the appraisal of management ability
15. Years in business
16. Growth potential of customer
17. Source of disposing of off-specification material
18. Seasonal factors
19. Area and industry economic conditions

These items include both financial and sales factors. Therefore, it seems that the most acceptable formula would include elements from both areas so as to arrive at a credit limit that would not unduly inhibit the sales of the company's products.

The originators of the PPG formula recognize that virgin territory is being explored in this credit field. There is a great need for credit managers in other firms to work along the same lines and to develop and test their own formulas. Then, an exchange of information on a broad basis would be mutually beneficial and would move credit management techniques one step forward toward the ultimate of efficiency in operation.

Problems Found in Utilization of Credit Limits

The use of credit limits to control the investment in receivables is not without its problems. Credit management should be fully aware of certain requirements that must be recognized and met through internal control and special procedures as listed in the following paragraphs.

PERIODIC REVIEW REQUIRED

Credit limits require constant and continuing review. They should not be considered as being static. Financial statements should be obtained on a regular basis and should be reviewed along with salesmen's call reports. Credit men should visit major accounts from time to time, especially those classed as marginal risk accounts.

When a new order moves the account over the credit limit, both the account status and the credit limit will be reviewed. The review of other accounts can be handled on a scheduled basis; one approach is to review all marginal accounts quarterly and all regular accounts annually.

CUSTOMER REACTION TO CREDIT LIMIT

If customers are notified of the assigned credit limit, some accounts will feel that the credit limit is too low and is a reflection on their financial position and responsibility. If a competing supplier is willing to extend a higher limit, this may cause a problem for the salesman of the firm offering the lower limit.

EXCESSIVE CREDIT LIMIT

Some customers may accept a high credit limit as an invitation to delay payments of invoices beyond their due date merely because the total owing is still less than the credit limit. Credit personnel should be on guard against this development.

LOW CREDIT LIMIT

If the credit limit is considerably below the customer's requirements, this may cause him to look to a competitor for a major part of his purchases. For this reason, the credit manager should make every effort to work out a mutually acceptable arrangement with the account that will make it possible to sell the necessary merchandise to the customer—but also obtain security for the credit extended in excess of the formula-derived credit limit.

CUSTOMER GOODWILL

Credit men and salesmen should be given special briefings on the ways and means of explaining ''credit lines'' to customers so as not to lose customer goodwill. This is a good subject to cover at sales meetings also.

USE OF IMPROPER FORMULA

When selecting the various factors that enter into the overall formula, credit management must not lose sight of the basic ingredient that is so essential in any formula for calculating credit limits—the determination of the customer's *ability to pay*. Factors that tend to obscure or distort the final result should be analyzed carefully and either modified or dropped from the formula.

Other Aspects of Credit Limits

The credit executives at PPG Industries believe that the customer should be notified of the assigned credit limit amount. They use it as a sales promotion tool. Notification frequently results in an increase in orders from a customer where the credit limit is greater than what the customer anticipated. Notification also eliminates any possible repercussions later when the customer places an order and is then told that his order is being held because his account is ''over the limit.'' Informing the customer of the credit limit amount also carries a potential benefit to the customer. His awareness of the credit limit may prevent his buying an excessive amount of merchandise, thereby tying up working capital in inventory.

It also has been shown that credit limits provide guidelines for salesmen to increase the efficiency of their calls and overall sales efforts. For example, if a salesman knows that a certain account is using only a fraction of the assigned credit limit, he may direct his efforts toward cultivating the account. On the other hand, if the salesman knows that a certain account is perpetually on the verge of being over limit, he may prefer to make calls on customers offering a greater potential.

IMPROVES COLLECTIONS

The use of credit limits has a valuable byproduct; it improves collections and minimizes the number of days' sales outstanding. This result is obtained because the credit limit acts as a control device; when a customer has reached his credit limit, he is required to make a payment before the further shipment of merchandise can be authorized. Credit limits, therefore, tend to reduce or restrict marginal accounts and to upgrade receivables by keeping such marginal accounts closer to selling terms.

ORDER LIMIT

Many firms use an order limit in addition to a credit limit. An order limit provides control over releasing shipments to customers and is a part of the overall credit limit. The value of this control device is that any order for an unusually large amount must be cleared by the credit man.

PPG procedures allow an initial order from a new customer up to $500 to clear automatically. This policy gives the sales department the opportunity to make a quick sale that can be serviced promptly, thereby making a good impression on the new customer.

MANAGEMENT BY EXCEPTION

It has been well established that credit limits make it possible to handle order approval on an exception basis to speed the flow of orders through the credit department. This technique, in turn, can be tied into a computer system that generates an ''Over Credit Limit Report'' on a scheduled basis. This is especially valuable for a firm with many decentralized selling and shipping points. PPG sends such a report on a daily basis to all the retail and similar outlets, and to the shipping warehouses where orders for an area are filled.

Order approval is automatic if the customer's name does not appear on the latest Over Credit Limit Report. This same report is also used by the general credit office personnel for reviewing the credit limits of each account that appears on the report (see Figure 5.3).

Figure 5.3

Daily Over Credit Report 04-01-66 Page 01

Account Number	Customer Name	Credit Limit	Balance	Past Due
03855-00	A B ADAMS & SON	6,000	8,022.89	3,492.62
07120-00		1,000	153.00	153.00
13342-00		2,000	2,300.00	2,300.00
15982-00		0	2,109.55	00.00
16782-00		2,000	1,975.97	629.17
24406-00		3,000	7,692.55	4,261.32
27581-00		2,000	1,772.30	581.39
31963-00		1,000	1,549.64	1,222.45
49911-00		000	1,028.56	.00
51771-00		1,000	1,771.83	875.84
52860-00		3,000	3,865.87	1,662.20
54965-00		000	462.84	306.01
62898-00		1,000	1,598.21	1,303.59
65110-00		6,000	5,292.88	2,309.87
65565-00		1,000	2,037.84	1,210.65
65656-00		2,000	2,578.02	845.57
69817-00		000	2.58	.00
71750-00		4,000	2,562.30	939.48
72843-00		2,000	2,502.90	.00
74062-00		2,000	2,246.87	1,230.73
77099-00		000	878.72	878.72
77578-00		2,000	8,987.24	5,748.38
83709-14		000	76.30	.00
86926-00		3,000	10,859.38	6,089.43
95356-00		1,000	1,311.47	529.47

Computerizing the Credit Limit Formula

After developing the formula factors, the next step at PPG was to harness the calculating power of a computer and to make it produce the credit limit for all of the accounts fed into it. Since most of the data required for the financial analysis is found on the balance sheet, this requires a method of quickly indicating the desired information so that it can be keypunched for entry into the computer. Each item of monetary data can be identified for processing by introducing a line number or a code number along with the amount. This is all that is required for input. Experience with this step quickly revealed that clerical personnel relatively untrained in accounting or financial statements can be instructed as to how to locate the desired information on a statement and to code it for entry.

On balance, the use of a credit limit plus calculating the credit limit by application of a formula are both particularly adaptable to the efficient use of electronic data processing equipment.

BENEFITS OF CREDIT LIMITS BY FORMULA

When the credit executives at PPG were planning for formulized credit limits they visualized the following benefits.

- The protection for investment in receivables.
- The reduction of collection activity.
- The provision of a basis for routine approval of the great bulk of orders processed daily.
- The freeing of the time of key credit personnel by permitting *management by exception* and the upgrading of the use of that time for more constructive work.
- Making *more uniform* the extension of credit by all credit-department personnel.
- The reduction of bad debt losses by consistent application of the principle of a uniformly-calculated credit limit.

A further objective was to eliminate the wide

variances in credit limits where they are established by individual credit men using any methods or criteria they consider to be applicable. It is a known fact that if a case study is handed to six different credit men for establishing a credit limit, the result would be six different credit limit amounts where no formula or other established criteria is in use.

PPG executives report that all of these benefits have now been realized in addition to others. Standardizing the extension of credit under credit limits that have been developed through a formula based on the customer's ability to pay has achieved control over receivables and uniformity. And, credit personnel has been able to handle an increased volume of receivables with no difficulty.

Conclusions

A review and analysis of the use of credit limits as a working tool plus the scientific application of a formula to calculate the credit limit amount for each customer leads to the following thoughts and conclusions.

- The credit limit formula results in an accurate *prediction of* collection results.
- It predicts and assures the soundness of the investment in receivables.
- It provides the tool by which all credit men are tuned into the same channel of thinking about the extension of credit through credit limits.
- Electronic data processing coupled with the credit limit techniques permits the practice of management by exception by directing credit management's attention to only out-of-line performance and permits performance that is on target to take care of itself.

From the viewpoint of the credit manager the use of these modern tools offers a great many benefits. With credit limits established the credit manager will be elevated in the formal organization chart of his firm, and he will move into a closer relationship with top management. Once he is freed from routine tasks he can do more thinking about establishing policy and will have more time to spend on profitable, constructive work with sales, systems, and other activities.

Once the new management tools and techniques are in operation, he will be able to point to reduced credit operation costs and can test the effectiveness of credit personnel through special reports prepared by the computer.

Review and Recommendations

Based on the results obtained over a period of years by the use of formulized credit limits, the following recommendations are made for the ultimate benefit of the credit management profession and for the personal benefit of each reader of this book:

1. Make full use of credit limits for effective management by exception, and to harness the power of today's computers.
2. Make available to salesmen the assigned customer credit lines so as to establish a close working relationship with them.
3. Explain the benefits of credit limits as a selling tool, and define it as the investment your firm is willing to make in a customer.
4. Computerize a credit limit formula by product line to establish credit management by exception and to enable your firm to adopt uniform policies for credit extension.
5. Work with your systems group to refine and develop computer reports for a more efficient credit department operation.
6. Continue to study any credit limit formula developed for your business with the objectives of constantly refining and improving it.
7. Design special reports for reporting the effectiveness of credit personnel.
8. Inform customers of the assigned credit limit in order to avoid future problems and misunderstandings.
9. Request financial statements from customers and prospects to assist in developing and maintaining a close customer-supplier relationship.
10. Develop methods for storing financial data in the computer so that it can develop and report *financial trends* on each major account.
11. Institute a program to educate all concerned in this concept of modern credit management.

CHAPTER 6

How to Automate the Collection Function

A recent advertisement appeared in the *New York Times* recently featuring the picture of an executive dictating a letter to his secretary. The caption above the ad read as follows: "At $2.54 a letter, can you afford *not* to telephone?"

Now, the progressive credit manager of today charged with collection responsibilities may well ask himself this comparable question: At $2.54 a letter, can I afford to continue dictating and typing collection letters?

PHASES OF COLLECTION ATTEMPTS

Collection activities in connection with trade receivables generally follow a pattern involving the use of statements and collection letters. Based on the collection status of the oldest past due item on an account, the collector communicates with the customer via a past due statement —or by sending collection letter No. 1, 2, or 3. Some firms stop routine communications with the past due customer after sending collection letter No. 2 and set up the account for personal followup. Personal followup usually employs the telephone, a personal letter, or a telegram.

COLLECTION FOLLOWUP CYCLE

Surveys of business practices indicate that two weeks is the average time between collection followup attempts in a trade receivables environment. Some firms, because of EOM or PROX invoice terms or for other reasons, may not follow on unpaid items more often than once each month. A few firms have adopted a 10-day cycle between each collection review. This is especially true in those firms that offer short 10-day invoice terms, or where the product being sold is perishable. For example, firms in the food, cooking oils, or vegetable business are most apt to adopt a 10-day follow-up policy.

AUTOMATIC DUNNING WITH COMPUTER

To determine the feasibility of performing dunning work with the computer, let us review typical, established collection procedures. Collection documents usually consist of statements and collection letters that are preprinted forms designed to convey a routine, standard message to the debtor, depending on the collection status of the debtor's account. Also, as mentioned on the preceding page, most firms allow a definite period of time between each phase of the collection effort. Under these normal conditions, automatic dunning with an electronic computer becomes very feasible. It is not only feasible to program a full-scale electronic computer to print the past due statements and collection letters at high speed, it is actually being done today by an ever-increasing number of firms that have computerized their receivables.

BASIC REQUIREMENT FOR AUTOMATED DUNNING

The basic data required for automatic dunning is the final due date of each open invoice. To obtain this due date in each invoice record requires that invoice terms be appropriately applied to each invoice taken into the computerized receivables system. This subject is covered as a special topic in Chapter 12.

A final due date is calculated by applying the invoice terms to one of two base dates:

- The invoice date *or*
- An "as of" date when it appears as part of the invoice terms.

Note the examples that follow.

Invoice Date	*Invoice Terms*	*Final Due Date*
6/14	N30	7/14
6/15	2% N30 as of 9/01	10/01

The invoice on the second line was subject to two-option cash discount terms—with an as of date included in the terms. This date becomes the base for applying the terms to determine the final due date.

GRACE PERIOD

Most firms include a grace period when determining which open invoices are past due and eligible for dunning. The grace period is provided to cover the time that it takes for a customer to prepare and mail a check, and for the seller to receive, apply, and process the check. Because of this time lag, it may be unwise to print a past due statement for an account simply because an invoice was one or two days past the final due date. By including a grace period ranging from five to nine days in the past due determinations, those items that have just turned past due may be ignored until the next review cycle.

DUE DATES SHOULD APPEAR IN EACH INVOICE RECORD

When trade receivables are computerized, each unpaid or open invoice record, which constitutes the customer's file of receivables, is kept in coded format on data storage devices that can read account information into the computer at great speed. The three common ways of storing receivables records for computer processing are:

- Punched cards. A card represents each invoice or credit, plus other miscellaneous debit or credit entries, kept in tub files for easy access.
- Open-item records kept on reels of magnetic tape. Each record or block of records includes the customer's assigned account number for instant identification and processing. The records are invisible to the eye but can be read into the computer and rewritten on a new tape under the control of a set of programmed instructions.
- Records stored on some type of random access or direct access data storage device. A popular type consists of disks that resemble phonograph records; each disk surface is divided into numbered tracks for data storage. Receivables information is recorded on each track and can be quickly retrieved by means of moving a reading head over the face of the disk record until it finds the track on which the customer's invoices and other records are stored.

Because of the extreme importance of the final due date, each invoice or credit memo record stored as part of the customer file should include the final due date in addition to the usual indicative information about the invoice. Storing the discount due date and the discount amount is also recommended for use when the item is eventually paid.

The calculation and storing of these data entities take place during an initial edit-entry run in which the keypunched invoices representing sales are fed into the computer in batches for testing and formatting. After the computer tests the data contained in the punched card representing an invoice or credit, it constructs a complete invoice record in memory. At this time the invoice terms are automatically applied to each invoice through the use of an internal terms table; the due dates resulting from terms application are written into the invoice that is being constructed for subsequent addition to the customer receivables file (Figure 6.1).

Other Requirements for Automated Dunning

As stated on previous pages, the most important single requirement for automated dunning is the accurate mechanization of invoice terms —and the storing of the resulting due dates in each invoice record as an integral component of that record.

COLLECTION STATUS CODE

Another requirement is that each invoice record include a code number that represents the collection status code. This code does not represent the age of the item as much as it indicates the *number of times* the invoice amount has appeared on some type of dunning document.

EXAMPLE

Dunning Document	*Collection Status Code*
Past Due Statement	No. 1
Collection Letter No. 1	No. 2
Collection Letter No. 2	No. 3
Collection Letter No. 3	No. 4

DEFINITION OF A PAST DUE INVOICE

Establishing a definition as to what constitutes a past due invoice requires some thought. This task is the responsibility of the general credit manager. Let us examine some of the considerations that are involved in establishing policy for controlling the automatic printing of dunning documents.

Q. If an invoice is only one or two days past the final due date—and *no other invoices* are past due—should the computer print a past due statement for this one item?

A. Most firms vote "no."

Q. Suppose that one old past due invoice is still on the account under review with collection status code 1, 2, or 3—and that a new invoice only one or two days old is found on the account also?

A. The credit manager probably will want the computer to produce a statement or collection letter showing both past due items.

PAST DUE TESTS

Identifying an item as past due implies a comparison of the invoice's final due date with some base date, for instance, the date of preparing the dunning documents. Using the preparation or run date as the basis for determining past due items is a common procedure. The table below indicates which items would appear on a computer-prepared dunning form.

Customer Number	Batch Date	Invoice Date	Invoice Number	Invoice Terms						Discount Due Date	Final Due Date	Discount Amount	Invoice Amount
				As of Date	Percent	Days	T p	Due Days	Extra Days				
1234567	101570	101270	14456		2	10	N	30		1022	111270	20.00	1000.00

Figure 6.1 Data contents of a typical invoice found in a trade receivables file.

DECISION TABLE

Final Due Date in Invoice Record	*Grace Days*	*Adjusted Final Due Date*	*Run Date*	*PAST DUE?* *Yes*	*No*
6/15	5	6/20	6/15		X
6/14	5	6/19	6/15		X
6/10	5	6/15	6/15		X
6/09	5	6/14	6/15	X	
6/05	5	6/10	6/15	X	

DO NOT USE RUN DATE

It is inappropriate to use the run date as the key date for comparison with final due dates. The *date of the last cash processed* to the account should be the key date for determining past due items for dunning purposes. The reason is that it is not good practice to dun a customer for an item that is apparently past due—but is still open on the account possibly because cash has stacked up and *has not yet been applied.* To avoid this awkward possibility, use the *batch date* of the LAST CASH applied to the accounts for all comparisons.

CASH BATCH DATE

If a firm uses a bank's "lock box" for remittances, then the lock box deposit date stamped by the bank on the end of each check copy is the batch date in most instances. To see how the use of the batch date of the last cash processed affects the dunning process, let us assume that the cash application bookkeepers in a firm are currently behind in their work on the fifteenth of the month. The firm has adopted a review cycle of 15 days or twice each calendar month. Since this is the fifteenth of the month, the computer is scheduled to examine all open invoice records today to determine those accounts that require the preparation of a dunning document.

The actual date of the computer run is the fifteenth—however, the last cash processed was dated the *twelfth*. Therefore, this is the comparison date fed into the computer for use in today's dunning work. Let us see how this date affects the determination of items to appear on dunning documents.

DECISION TABLE

Final Due Date	*Grace Days*	*Adjusted Final Due Date*	*Date of LAST CASH Applied*	*Run Date*	*PAST DUE?* *Yes*	*No*
6/15	5	6/20	6/12	6/15		X
6/14	5	6/19	6/12	6/15		X
6/10	5	6/15	6/12	6/15		X
6/09	5	6/14	6/12	6/15		X*
6/05	5	6/10	6/12	6/15	X	

* Notice that the item on this line is now considered as NOT being past due because the adjusted final due date is later than the date of last cash, which is 6/12. However, the last item is truly past due because the adjusted final due date of 6/10 is earlier than the date of the last cash applied. There is no doubt that this item properly belongs on a past due statement because the final due date is 6/05. Allowing 5 days as a grace period, the check should have been in the batch of checks deposited in the bank's lock box dated 6/08 to 6/09, or 6/10 at the latest. The bookkeepers have applied all cash through the batch date of 6/12—the invoice remains unpaid—therefore, it should be included on any dunning document prepared for the customer's account.

SIGNIFICANCE OF COLLECTION STATUS CODE

The necessary rules for changing the status code of each item record may seem confusing when they are first studied. A key point is that the code does not represent the age of the item, but the number of times the unpaid invoice item has appeared on some type of dunning document. Notice the changing status code of one invoice record examined during each of three automatic review cycles 15 days apart as shown below:

COLLECTION STATUS CODE

Review Date	*Invoice Due Date*	*Grace Days*	*Adj Final Due Date*	*Date of Last Cash*	*Print on Past Due Statement? Yes*	*No*	*Collection Status Code*
6/15	6/05	5	6/10	6/12		X*	Blank
6/30	6/05	5	6/10	6/28	X		1
7/15	6/05	5	6/10	7/13	X		2

* This item met the test of being past due but, since it was the only item on the account past due only two days, it did not trigger the printing of a past due statement. Therefore, the status code remained blank. When the next review cycle of 6/30 found the item still past due, it was printed on a collection document for the first time; the collection status code is then changed to "1."

DETERMINING TYPE OF DUNNING FORM

All credit managers realize that the universal rule in collection procedures devised for trade receivables is that the status of the oldest past due item determines the collection effort to be made. If an account has received a past due statement two weeks ago, and the computer finds the past due item still open, it will then print collection letter No. 1 for the dunning effort. If an account already has one or more items flagged as being in collection status 2, then a No. 2 collection letter will be prepared, since it represents the third level of collection effort.

Obviously the collection status code is one of the keys to a successful automated dunning systems with a computer. The stored program that instructs the computer as to which document to print hinges on a determination of the highest-value collection status code presently found in each account reviewed. Because of this, it is necessary for the computer to examine all open items for an entire account before it begins to print a dunning document. Systems analysts should be aware of this basic requirement, since it directly affects computer procedures in connection with implementing an automatic dunning program.

Designing the Dunning Forms and Letters

The systems team assigned to the project involving computerizing receivables, credit, and collection functions will design all the dunning forms, letters, or reports. As described in a previous chapter, the best results overall will be obtained if the credit manager and his staff work closely with the systems team at all times. This cooperation and teamwork is especially vital when it comes to designing the dunning forms.

In order to prepare for the series of group meetings necessary for resolving the rules for dunning, identifying special problems, and designing the forms, the systems group should make an effort to secure as many sample statements and collection letters used by other firms as possible. One obvious source for this material, often overlooked, is the firm's own accounts payable department. Here, one will find a cross section of statements and dunning letters received from the firm's vendors and suppliers. The credit men also can contribute by visiting other firms that have mechanized their receivables and by accumulating sample forms in preparation for the forthcoming meetings with the systems group.

Credit and collection personnel who participate in the systems design meetings should always feel free to make any suggestion that appears to be pertinent. After all, the eventual users of the computer output are the credit and collection people.

Several group meetings are usually necessary; the systems group needs time to review their notes resulting from each meeting, then they will draw the statements or other forms in rough draft format and will present them at the next meeting. This process continues until the users are ready to give their final approval to the latest in the series of hand-drawn forms.

SEVERAL TYPES OF STATEMENTS

Even among credit people there is sometimes confusion as to the intent and purpose of the two primary types of customer statements:

- Full account statement
- Past due statement

The full account statement is a listing of

every open item on the customer's receivables file at the time the statement is printed. This type of statement is generally considered as being a means of communicating to a customer how his account stands according to the receivables records. However, retail businesses and others consider this statement as a basis for paying their account in full. They first use it for their own accounting purposes, and then consider it as a dunning document and will write checks based on the statement balance.

Traditionally this type of statement is solicited by retail business firms—and by firms of almost any type where the seller's terms are EOM or proximo. The very nature of these terms make it desirable to submit a complete statement of the current month's purchases to the buyer because they become due and payable on the 10th of the month following purchase—unless the invoice date is the 25th or later.

If the business environment requires the sending of full account statements at monthend, then collection letters used as followup may refer to the account balance instead of listing specific past due items.

PAST DUE STATEMENT

By contrast with the full account statement, which shows every open item on the account, a past due statement usually shows only the specific invoices that are now past due. It is specifically designed as a collection device instead of as a statement that is submitted to the customer for informational purposes. For this reason it rarely includes current items in addition to the past due amounts.

It is debatable whether a past due statement should show open credits. Many credit managers will insist on this. Those in the textile and soft goods trade usually adopt a policy of not showing credit memos. Their attitude is that the use of credits is under the control of the customer; it is up to him to clear the past due items from his account by remitting cash—or by indicating the application of open credits to clear the past due items.

If a policy is adopted to show all open credit memos on a past due statement, in addition to past due items, be sure and show all *open unadjusted deductions also.* The reason for stressing this is that roughly 50% of all open credits issued by a typical firm are prepared to cover prior customer deductions and claims originating from remittances. The showing of open credits on a customer statement, therefore, opens the door to confusion and profit losses.

Suppose that a recent credit memo of $100 has been posted to an account to cover a *prior deduction* of $100—but the bookkeepers or adjusters have not had time to apply the credit against the appropriate open debit amount. Any statement to the customer that includes the $100 credit sets up the opportunity for the customer to use this credit again. This places the seller in the position of defending himself against a duplicate deduction of $100 that will be a direct profit loss unless his bookkeepers notice it, track down the situation, and prove to the satisfaction of the customer that it really is a duplicate deduction situation.

If the credit manager insists on showing open credits on a statement, and is wary of creating the situation mentioned above, one way of setting up protection is to show on the statement only those credits that are 60 days old or older. The theory is that the adjusters have had sufficient time to apply credits to remove offsetting deduction debits; the credits remaining are available to the customer to use in settling invoice items coming due.

A much better method is to set up a procedure that flags any credit memo issued to cover an open deduction or claim. This type of credit would never appear on a statement; all other credits could be safely printed on the statement.

DESIGN OF PAST DUE STATEMENT

The design of past due statements varies from one firm to another. The simplest type merely shows the customer the necessary details of the past due items. A carbon copy may be routed to the credit department for their use (see Figure 6.2 below).

Another type really consists of two different statements prepared as one. The original copy for the customer may show the basic information as displayed in Figure 6.2, but a copy designed for the collection department may be wider in order to convey information solely for use by the collector (see Figure 6.3). The left side of this form went to the customer; the part that is to the right of the perforation is the extended section with special information for the collector.

JAMES TALCOTT INC.

FOUNDED 1854

FACTORING

P. O. BOX 754, RADIO CITY STATION

NEW YORK, NEW YORK 10019

PAST DUE STATEMENT

CUST. NO. 0006372

D

DATE 04-22-6

PAGE 1

PLEASE RETURN UPPER PORTION WITH YOUR REMITTANCE TO INSURE CREDIT

ENTRY CODE
1 INVOICE
5. INTEREST

PURCHASED FROM	STORE NO. OR POST. DATE	INVOICE		DATE DUE	ENTRY	EXTRA DAYS WITH INTEREST	PAST DUE
		NO.	DATE				
OWJORGES	02-33	04133	02-21	03-10-6	1		5.92
AFFLDIST	11-29	1C704	11-22	02-03-6	1		90.39
AFFLDIST	01-13	01157	01-07	03-18-6	1		367.95
OWJORGES	03-03	04192	02-23	03-10-6	1		5.92

PLEASE DISREGARD THIS STATEMENT IF PAID 470.18

INTEREST AT 6% PER ANNUM IS PAYABLE ON PAST DUE ITEMS

Figure 6.2 Computer-prepared past due statement (courtesy of James Talcott Factors, Inc.).

DATA FOR COLLECTOR

If open credits are shown on the customer's copy, they should also appear on the collector's copy. Further, the efficiency of the collection effort can be improved by showing invoices *coming due within the next few weeks.* This information enables the collector to discuss with the customer his plans for paying major amounts coming due in the near future.

The batch date and batch number should be printed on this part of the statement. If the invoices are filed by batch date, this data makes it easy to find a specific invoice when the collector receives a request from the customer for a copy of the past due invoice.

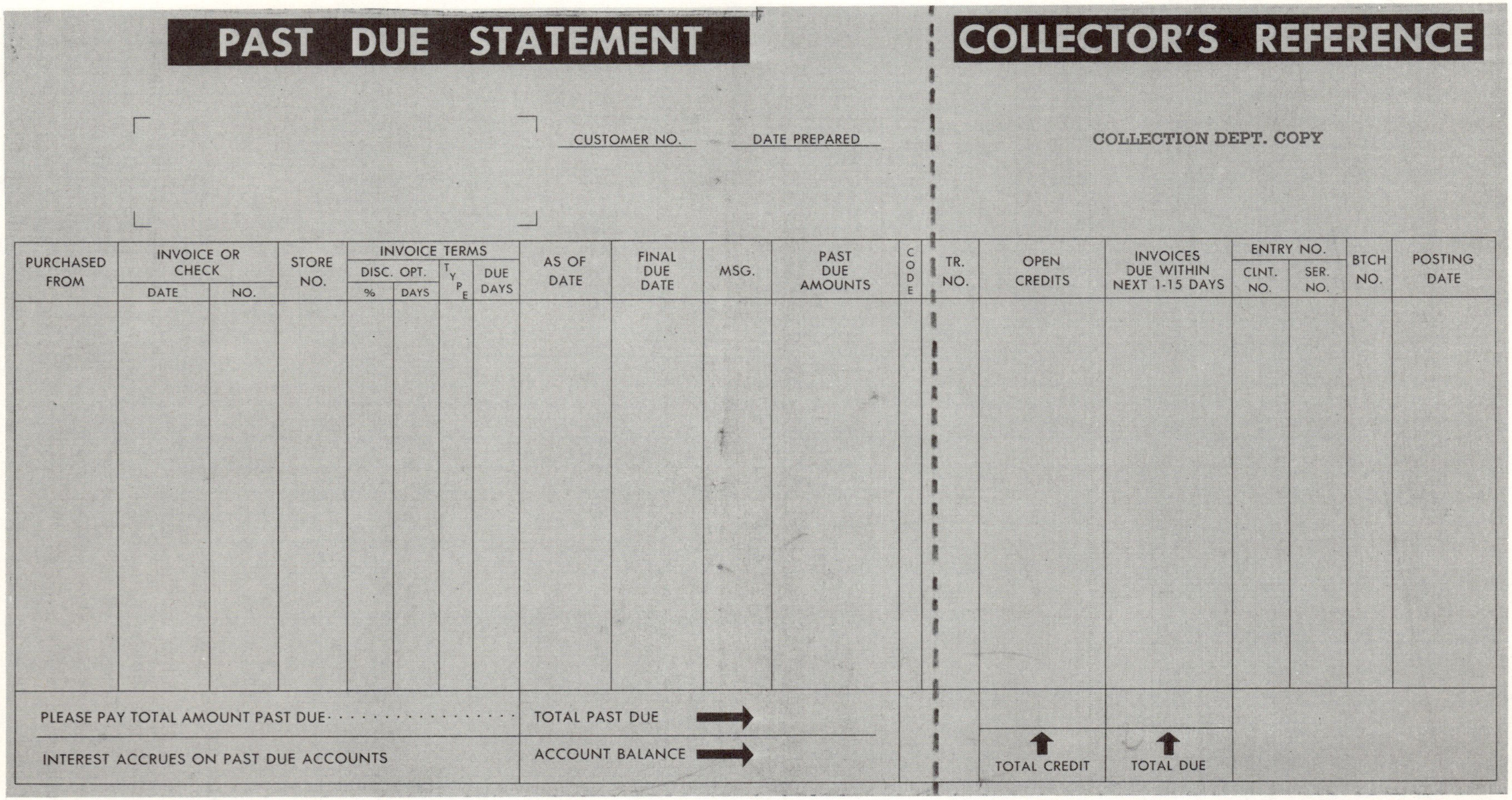

Figure 6.3 Specially-designed past due statement.

Design of Collection Letters

The collection letters that are designed for computer printing may be the regular $8\frac{1}{2}$ in. × 11 in. letter size. Or, they may be reduced to check-size documents for convenience in stuffing and mailing. One large corporation uses check-size past due reminders very effectively. There is space to print up to 12 past due invoice amounts on the remainder. Because the past due notice forms do not have to be folded, this firm uses a Pitney Bowes mailing machine that automatically stuffs the forms into window envelopes at high speed for mailing.

As a matter of policy the first two notices are mailed without referring them to the credit man. However, the third reminder is routed to the credit man who is responsible for personal handling and subsequent followup for the account.

SPECIAL MESSAGES

Often the only difference between a series of collection letters is the primary message printed in the body of the letter for the benefit of the customer. Since it takes several minutes to stop a computer run for the purpose of changing printed forms, it is advisable to design one collection letter, and leave the message section to be filled in by the computer. After the credit manager has prepared the various messages to be included in collection letters No. 1, No. 2, No. 3, etc., the programmers will include these messages in the program written for automatic dunning. This way, the computer can print several different types of collection letters at one machine run.

Special Problems Encountered in Automatic Dunning

Several special situations should be anticipated and a decision should be reached and documented for the guidance of the programmers who are involved in writing the computer instructions for an automatic dunning system. Some of the considerations to be resolved are listed below.

1. Should received-on-account cash credits be printed on a past due statement?
2. Suppose that the total of open, unused credits on an account exceeds the total of past due invoices—should the computer print a statement for the account? If so, should it print the form solely for the information of the collector?
3. If the total of received-on-account cash exceeds the total of past due invoices, should the computer print a statement for either the customer or the collector?
4. Suppose an invoice suddenly appears on an account that is more than four weeks past due but has a blank collection status code? Should the entire account be flagged and referred to the collector for special handling?

(This situation can easily occur because of a routine reinstatement of an invoice that had been removed from the account for some reason several weeks ago. Since the invoice record was absent from the file during the periodic dunning procedures, the collection status code has remained dormant.)

Summary

When pondering the advisability of implementing the concept of automatic dunning, a credit manager may question whether the mechanization of the dunning work decreases the status of the individual credit man. In reply to this question, experienced credit managers who have already mechanized this function state that, on the contrary, it increases the value of the credit man, since it relieves him of a monotonous, time-consuming chore, which the computer can handle much faster and at a lower cost. This gives the credit man time for more creative work with customers or with the sales department.

Experience also indicates that automated dunning definitely reduces the overall clerical costs by eliminating typing pools or the individual typists who laboriously type statements and collection letters under a manual dunning system.

In conclusion we can safely state that automatic dunning is not only feasible, it has been implemented successfully in dozens of firms throughout the nation in recent years. It is one way to assist a busy credit department in keeping up with the constantly increasing volume of paper work encountered in recent years. For all these reasons, mechanization of collection procedures makes sense—and *saves dollars and cents.*

CHAPTER 7

"Instant" Customer Information for the Credit Man

In recent years an increasing attention has been devoted to the ways and means for bringing needed account information to the credit man as required. It is now generally recognized that a modern credit department requires access to the customer receivables file on a random basis. If a systems environment fails to provide this information routinely, then the functions of the credit department will be handicapped to some extent.

ON-LINE CREDIT INQUIRY

One of the concepts born of the computer age is the ''on-line'' credit inquiry capability. This is considered by many in the credit profession as the ultimate in credit tools to solve the problem of quick reference to any desired customer account when performing the credit-checking or collection function. For this reason, many large firms are planning to provide on-line credit inquiry to the credit department as fast as the system can be programmed, tested, and implemented.

HOW IT WORKS

On-line means that the credit man, seated in front of an information display screen, is able to use the computer directly as a means of finding and displaying any desired account instantly. The display device is connected to the computer and resembles a small television set. This is known as a ''CRT'' unit because it is a cathode ray tube with a small screen that can display formatted lines of account information, such as the name and address, open items, account balance, statistical information, and the like.

The device has a keyboard for communicating with the computer. For example, suppose that a credit man wants the latest account status on Henry L. Johnson & Co. If he knows the unique account number, he keys this in through the keyboard of the terminal; the account information will appear instantly on the display screen in front of him. Suppose that he does not know the account number; most on-line systems of this type provide an internal dictionary ''lookup'' capability that centers around the first five letters of the customer's last name. For example, the credit man—not knowing the account number—may type ''JOHNS'' as the input to the computer. It makes a rapid internal search and finds an account . . . which may not be the one wanted. If this occurs, the credit man merely calls for the next account, which may be the specific account he wanted to see in the first place (see Figure 7.1).

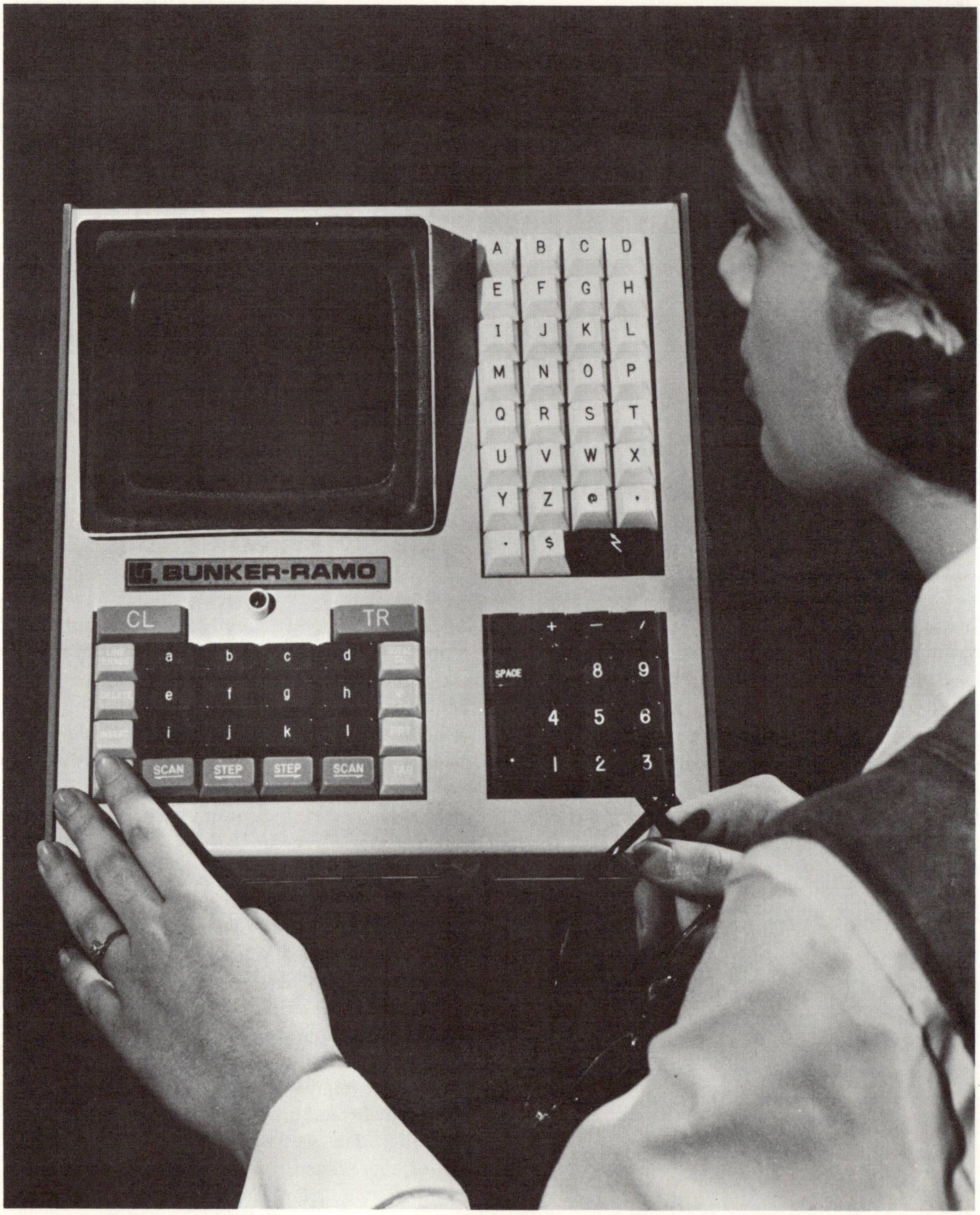

Figure 7.1 Cathode ray tube (CRT) information display terminal (courtesy of the Bunker-Ramo Corporation).

VALUE OF ON-LINE ACCOUNT INFORMATION

On-line account information is of value when checking credit and performing collection follow-up work. This capability makes it possible for a credit man to review the latest account status when pondering about the approval of an order. Before computers were widely available, it was necessary for the credit man to leave his desk quite often and walk over to the receivables department, find the account ledger, review the account status, make pencil notes, and then return to his desk. For this very reason it has been common over the years to find credit men keeping their own memo accounts receivable records in their desks. These ''bootleg ledgers'' represented extra time and work on the part of each credit man, but the working environment frequently caused practices of this kind to emerge. For example, in many instances the credit department was located several hundred feet away from the receivables department. And when the credit man took the time to walk to the area where the customer ledgers were kept, often he could not quickly locate the ledger because of the different groups of people working with the accounts during the day.

Collectors can make good use of on-line account data display when telephoning or corresponding with a delinquent customer. Being able to scan the open items on the screen has value because the collector can question the customer about his plans for paying large invoices not yet past due, but coming due in the near future. He may also note the presence of unearned discount charges, late interest charges, and other items that he may want to call to the customer's attention.

FORMER METHODS OF INFORMATION RETRIEVAL

Many successful receivables systems have been installed on computers over the years—with no random access capabilities included in the hardware configuration. We solved the information retrieval problem by scheduling the printing of specially-designed reports (described below) for the credit men.

Aged Trial Balance. For approximately the first week of each month the latest account information could be quickly obtained by reference to an aged trial balance printed at month-end. Depending on the quantity of account information built into the customer's data bank and printed on this report, a credit man could easily obtain information for credit approval, for credit interchange replies, and for collection follow-up.

Weekly Status Report. This report, in effect, was a weekly updating of account information on an *exception basis*. Typically, this report included the latest account status for only three categories of accounts:

- Those over credit limit
- Those with past due items
- The restricted or marginal accounts

Daily Special Collection Report. This simple but effective report stems from cash application and subsequent processing. Its purpose is to inform the credit and collection department of cash received that:

- Paid one or more *past due items*—to halt unnecessary collection activity.
- Was applied to an account that was *over credit limit*.
- Reduced the balance of a restricted or marginal account.

This exception-type report not only provides the very latest account status but is also a vehicle for clearing sales orders previously placed in a ''hold'' file because of an overlimit condition or because of a past due situation.

LEDGER REQUESTS

In addition to the scheduled reports described above, we usually provided the capability of ledger printouts on request. This feature meant that the credit man had to fill out a request form and to submit it for keypunching. During the next accounts receivable file updating run, the computer would print a complete customer ledger for the requester. It is true that this meant a delay of several hours, but it was the best answer possible without an on-line hardware configuration.

HARDWARE REQUIREMENTS FOR AN ON-LINE SYSTEM

There is no doubt that the concept of an on-line credit inquiry system is quite appealing and has a practical value as well. However, like many other desirable objectives, the costs of such a system are substantial.

There are two distinctly different costs involved in planning and installing an on-line inquiry system: one-time costs and operating costs.

The one-time costs are the ones connected with systems analysis and design, followed by extensive programming time and costs. Because of the complexity of an on-line system, the combined one-time costs may represent a very substantial budget item ranging into the hundreds of thousands of dollars. The time span for such a project may also be quite discouraging to a credit manager, since some pilot installations have required from two to three years to develop, test, and install.

Operating costs consist of machine rentals, supplies, support personnel, and the like. The equipment required to implement an on-line system is of several different types:

- The random access information storage devices connected to and controlled by the computer. The most common version of this device uses disks for recording receivables file information for random access, and resembles a phonograph.
- Larger or additional computer working memory units to accomodate the larger programs required for handling on-line inquiry operations.
- Electronic control boxes that operate and control the data display terminals which are located in the user department.

TYPICAL RENTAL COSTS

Rental costs vary substantially from one installation to another. In order to obtain some idea as to operating costs, consider an actual case history. We prepared a detailed operating-cost estimate for a large industrial firm with 15,000 accounts and roughly 100,000 open items on the accounts receivable file. Since there were seven credit men in the department, we added into our estimate the cost of eight CRT display terminals for the on-line data display, providing one to the credit manager in addition to those for the credit men who also handle collections.

The monthly rentals for all the additional equipment for an on-line credit inquiry system utilizing a Model 360/40 computer added up to $5400 per month or $64,800 per year. This was in addition to the regular computer costs, since the computer had been installed within the firm for several years.

SUMMARY AND REVIEW

There is no doubt about the potential operating value of an on-line credit inquiry system to a busy credit executive faced with a constantly increasing volume of orders and paper of all types, accompanied by rising personnel costs. However, a review of the time required for preparatory installation work, plus the cost figures involved in the usual computer hardware approach to an on-line system, brings out these discouraging facts:

1. The credit manager may have to wait up to three years to see any results.
2. The investment in systems design work and programming and testing is usually a very large budget item.
3. The continuing operating costs after installation are also apt to be a very substantial budget item.

What is the answer? Is there an acceptable alternative to a true on-line credit inquiry system? Fortunately, because of some recent technical developments in the field of computers and microfilm, there *is* an acceptable alternative to an on-line system. The length of time required to plan and to install the system can be reduced to weeks; the operating costs incurred after installation are reasonable and minimal.

Computer-Output to Microfilm: Known as "COM"

In today's business environment new technological developments appear on the scene rapidly and in large volume. One of them that is receiving increasing attention from government, education, and the business world is the device known as "Com"—Computer-Output to Microfilm. The device is actually a small computer that "prints" on microfilm. It accepts, for example, a report appearing on a reel of magnetic tape in print-format (ready for printing on paper by a computer-printer) and converts the report information to visible lines on a reel of microfilm at tremendous speed. This is known as "Micromation."

SPEED OF PRINTING

A typical computer-operated impact printer operates at speeds up to 1000 lines per minute.

In terms of the production of pages, consider this: the impact printer will turn out roughly 1000 report pages in one hour. The microfilm printer can produce 20,000 pages per hour, and it operates independently of the computer. When the reel of microfilm is subsequently placed in a microfilm reader, the report appears on the view screen exactly as though it had been first printed on paper and then photographed (Figure 7.2).

This device was originally invented at the insistence of the Social Security Board in Baltimore, which is swamped with millions of payroll reports each year and is inundated with up to 30,000 requests for account information each working day. The board officials foresaw the time when the overwhelming volume of paper records simply could not be handled, processed, and retrieved economically or within a reasonable time frame. Something had to be done. This brought about the birth of the original "micromation" device; now there are more than 30 different manufacturers of this type of equipment.

This new high-speed device has entered the business scene at the right time. Many computer installations are beginning to bog down simply because of the ever-increasing number of major applications being added to the computer's work load. Also, consider the fact that the primary method of communication between the computer and the user is printed reports. Up to now, each new application or job put on the computer immediately has increased the demand for more printed forms and reports. (On-line applications alleviate this situation to some extent.)

Because of the scheduling problem that is prevalent today in the computer rooms of both

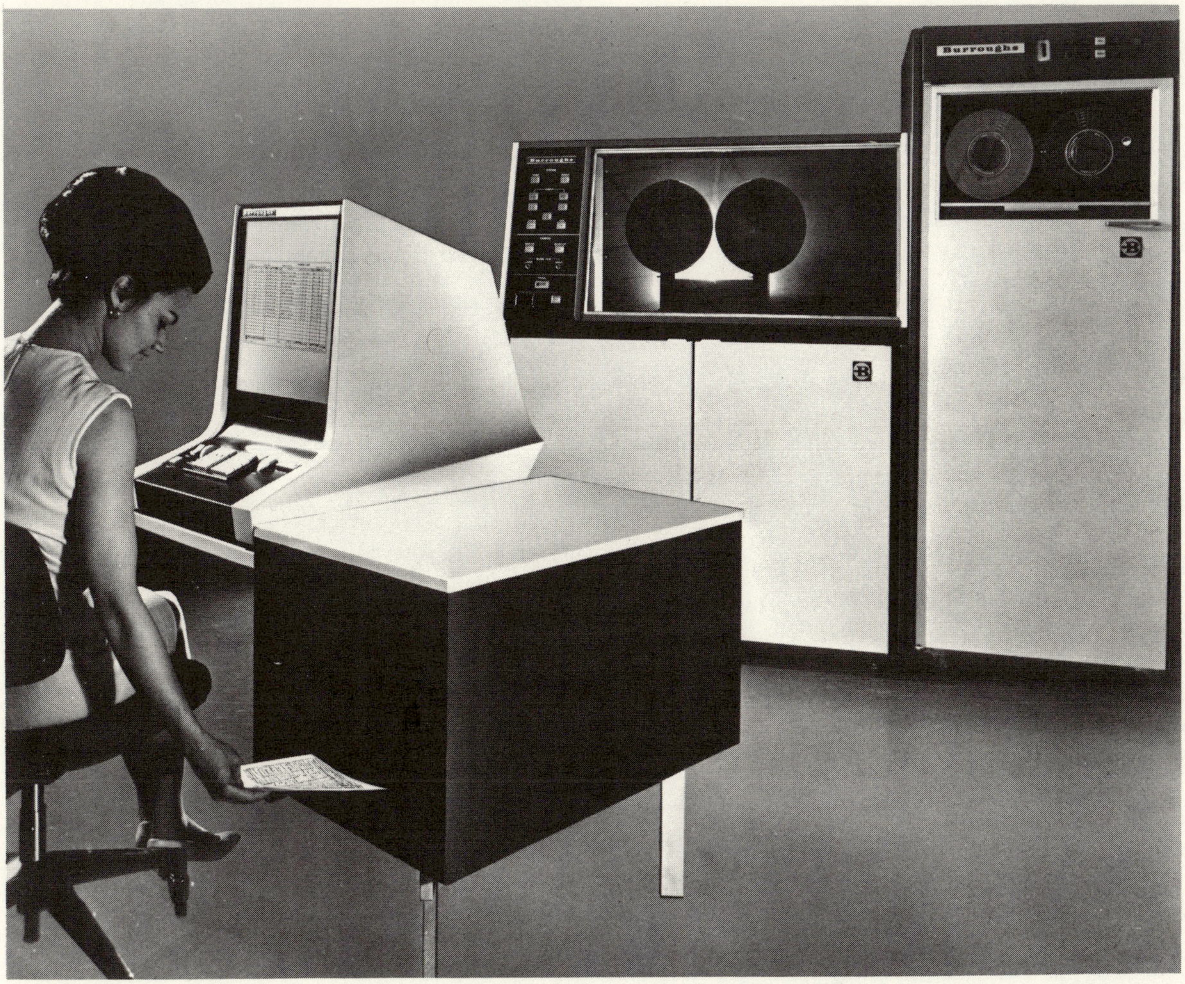

Figure 7.2 Computer output to microfilm: a microfilm printer (courtesy of Burroughs Corporation).

large and small firms, I have seen a credit department working with customer account data updated only once a month—even though the department was physically located next door to a large room with two computers working two or three shifts each day. And, as indicated above, this scheduling problem results largely from the mass of printed reports that must be produced daily, weekly, and monthly. The explanation for this is that the printing operation, which seems very fast to a layman, is actually a very slow operation compared to the other computer capabilities such as reading or writing magnetic tape or disk records. The speed of sorting or merging data is fantastic. The computing function is unbelievably fast. The problem lies in the fact that the impact printer is an electronic-mechanical device that can operate only at a limited rate.

REAPPEARANCE OF HAND POSTING

When a busy credit department is denied its key reports on time, its efficiency begins to suffer. A further development is the reappearance of "bootleg ledgers" maintained in the desks of the credit men. Or, various people begin to hand post information to the old computer report—to provide some of the current information that should be provided by a new, updated, computer report.

MICROMATION CAN BENEFIT THE CREDIT DEPARTMENT

Every credit manager involved with data processing should be aware of the fact that micromation devices can not only save his company money by reducing operating costs but can also help bring the scheduled reports into his department on time. It does this by providing, in effect, a high-speed printer that operates *independently of the computer*. Therefore, the computer will no longer be held back by the relatively slow impact printers found today in all computer installations.

A further benefit is that certain voluminous reports, such as a Customer Paid History File, can be placed on compact film records at low cost. Reference to such a file is on a random basis; since this file is nearly always in customer account number sequence, it is easy to find the account in question on the microfilm reader screen (see Figure 7.3).

Possibly the best feature of the use of computer-output-microfilm techniques to obtain credit department reports is that the information can be placed at the point of use more often, and on time more consistently. Many credit departments suffer from the usual scheduling bottleneck that is connected with a computer operation: statements, account status, and aging reports so vitally needed by the credit executives may be unavailable for long periods of time.

The "On-Time" System: An Alternative to an On-Line System

Industry leaders predict that more than 1000 firms will have COM devices installed by the end of 1971. The number of service bureaus offering computer-output-to microfilm services is increasing almost daily; some of them are appearing in smaller cities as well as in the large metropolitan areas.

All this recent activity is causing systems analysts and credit managers who are aware of what can be done in this new field to reevaluate the usual computer approaches to solving operating problems and information retrieval methods.

THE "ON-TIME" SYSTEM

At my firm as we began to work more and more on microfilm-based information retrieval systems, we pondered over the resemblance between a CRT display unit and a microfilm display screen. From an objective viewpoint, considering each device as a means of displaying information, the microfilm reader/printer is a more efficient device—and represents a very small investment, and low operating costs. Consider the facts shown below for comparison purposes:

	CRT Display Device	*Microfilm Display Screen*
Number of characters	960	8408
Number of lines	12	64
Display complete computer report?	No	Yes
Obtain hard copy?	No	Yes

Of course, the offsetting features of the CRT are that it has an input keyboard for communi-

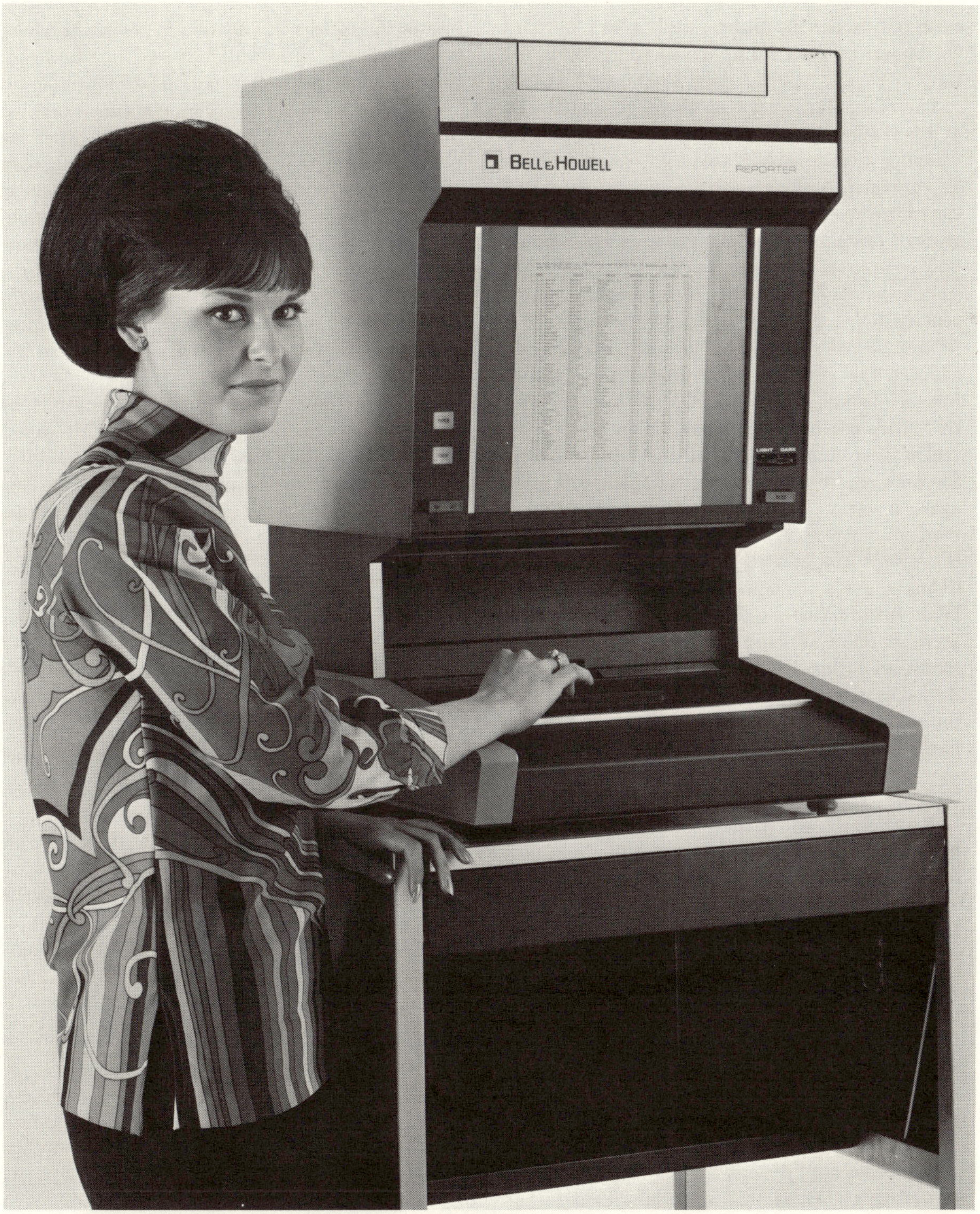

Figure 7.3 Microfilm display screen (courtesy of Bell & Howell Micro-Data Division).

cation with the computer—and it can be used as an information input device since, it is on-line.

The resemblance between the microfilm reader and a CRT unit led us to think in terms of developing a set of procedures that would provide an equivalent on-line credit inquiry system to a credit group—without paying the usual high costs of systems design, extensive programming, and computer hardware rentals. The basis for such a system is the ability to take the most current customer file—updated by the computer by processing sales, cash, and journal entries—and convert the entire set of records to a visible format through the use of COM. After obtaining the entire receivables records file on one master reel of microfilm tape, we can then obtain a copy for each credit man and one for the credit manager—at very low cost. Now, by providing a reader or a reader/printer to each man, he has the means for locating any desired account—displaying all the open item details and data bank information on the screen—and he can leave it there as long as necessary for review, study, dictating letters, etc. Or, if the display device is a reader/printer the credit man can push a button and obtain in seconds a full-size hard copy print of the ledger account or page.

LOW PROGRAMMING COSTS

A system based on the use of COM, followed by information display on microfilm readers, seldom represents much of a programming problem. The reason is that the basic requirement for using COM is that the computer has already "printed" the report or ledger data on a reel of magnetic tape—ready for printing on paper in the usual format. The COM device takes this print-formatted data directly from the reel of computer-prepared magnetic tape and prints the report on film in lieu of paper.

BASIS FOR CRT OR ON-TIME SYSTEM

The basic requirement for any type of credit reporting system is that sales be added to the customer receivables file periodically—and cash should be applied as soon as possible. One of the rules here is that no cash should be taken in on account if it is at all possible to apply it to specific paid items. A buildup of unapplied cash in a trade receivables environment gradually degrades the collection function to the point where it becomes of little value if the buildup continues unchecked over a period of months.

In other words, the account status provided to the credit men in the form of printed reports—on-line display on CRT units—or display on microfilm screens should reflect, as far as possible, the very latest account information. An interesting point here is that the on-time system, using low-cost microfilm display units, provides customer account information *equally as current as the true on-line method*—unless the application of cash is truly handled on-line all during the day.

The basis for making this statement is that customer data displayed on a CRT unit comes from the same data base used for the COM process—which is the complete customer file. This file is only as current as the information last processed to it by the computer.

COM APPROACH TO IMPLEMENT THE ON-TIME SYSTEM

After all preparations have been made, here are the simple steps that are required to implement on a scheduled basis an on-time credit inquiry system:

1. Send the latest customer receivables file "printed" on reels of magnetic tape to an outside service bureau equipped with the COM machines.
2. The service bureau converts the data on magnetic tape to printed customer "ledgers" on a master reel of microfilm. They will return the magnetic tape to you.
3. The service bureau makes as many additional copies of the master reel of microfilm as specified by you, the user.
4. The service bureau returns all reels of film to you, ready for immediate use.
5. Distribute one reel of film to each credit man—and possibly also provide one to the collectors.
6. The credit man now has either the entire customer file—or just his group of accounts, ready for instant reference on a random basis.
7. The credit man inserts the magazine of film in his electric reader; the reader automatically threads the film leader into the receiving spool, ready for any account reference.

Usually, the customer master file is kept in

account number sequence—which may also be in alphabetic sequence. This means that the credit man can find any account in which he is interested either by name or by account number within a few seconds.

ON-TIME SYSTEM COST ELEMENTS

Here are the cost elements involved in implementing and operating an on-time system:

- The cost of converting the customer file to microfilm through COM.
- The cost of additional film copies, and placement in magazines.
- The depreciation cost of microfilm readers, or reader/printers.
- The supplies required for reader/printers.

EQUIPMENT COSTS

The very best electric microfilm reader/printer, equipped with automatic film threading feature, rotating image head, fast printing of a hard copy on depression of a print button and able to display an entire page of computer-prepared printouts, represents a one-time investment of roughly $1600. If depreciated over a period of 84 months, the monthly depreciation cost per reader/printer is only $19 per month. If the display device is placed under the manufacturer's maintenance service, the annual costs represent an additional cost of operating the system.

SPECIAL COST STUDY: A CASE HISTORY

For comparison purposes, let us go back to a discussion of the actual case history connected with the large industrial firm in the Northeast that had 15,000 active customers and roughly 100,000 open item accounting records on the computer file at any given moment. As explained previously, we developed the cost of computer hardware rentals to implement an on-line credit inquiry system, using eight CRT display terminals to serve the eight key people in the credit department. The monthly rentals for all the necessary hardware, including a larger working memory for the computer plus the random access devices required (and the monthly rentals for the CRT devices plus an electronic control unit), added up to $5400 per month or *$64,800 per year*.

ESTIMATED ANNUAL COSTS FOR EQUIVALENT ON-TIME SYSTEM

Based on converting the entire customer file from magnetic tape to microfilm through COM twice each week, the following annual costs would be incurred to operate an "on-time" credit inquiry system utilizing COM techniques and equipping the credit department with one reader/printer plus seven electric microfilm readers:

	Weekly Costs	*Annual Costs*
Service bureau charges for COM	$114	$5928
Film copies for credit men	42	2084
Depreciation on readers and reader-printer on 84-month basis		1560
		$9572

RELATED PROGRAMMING TIME AND COSTS

As indicated, one of the big advantages of considering the on-time system is the speed and relative ease with which you can plan, program, and install an on-time microfilm credit inquiry system. A realistic time span for implementation from date of completing your planning is about two months. It takes this much time for a firm to assign a technician from the systems group to work with the credit manager and the outside service bureau, and for the technician to learn the special codes tied in with programming the computer-prepared print format tapes to control the preparation of page images on microfilm, which is the output from the microfilm converter device we have referred to in this chapter as the COM device.

OTHER USES IN A CREDIT DEPARTMENT

After you have installed the microfilm readers, other uses for the COM technique and the readers will occur to you. For example, the *Customer Closeout Report* (a monthly report of all accounting records removed from the customer file because of journal entry or cash application) is typically a bulky, expensive printout from the computer at the end of each month. This type of reference report is much more efficient when displayed from microfilm—and costs much less to produce.

Other reports that may be considered for film display instead of paper are the Monthly Aged

Trial Balance, the Weekly Status Report, credit memos processed for the week or month, and the like.

ANOTHER METHOD FOR OBTAINING FILM DISPLAY

Suppose that your firm is far removed from a service bureau equipped with a COM device. And, we shall assume that your total volume of reports could not justify installing your own COM device at a monthly rental ranging from \$1500 to \$4000 per month. What is the next best answer to the objective of ''on-time'' credit inquiry system through the use of microfilm?

Consider the use of a special camera device that is designed for the high-speed photographing of computer-printed report pages in continuous form. This unit has one or two microfilm cameras in it that can picture 10,000 computer-printed pages per hour, or more. The operation of the camera unit is largely fully automatic.

Now, this approach requires that the computer print the customer ledgers to be displayed on the screen of each credit man's microfilm reader. However, print only ONE original copy on paper. Then, take the original printout to the photographing device, and feed it into the automatic feeding device. This produces one original (or two) reels of microfilm, with up to 3000 full-size report pages (customer ledger records would not require a full page; therefore, you will get considerably more than 3000 individual customer ledger records) on a roll of microfilm 100 ft. in length.

Then, send the original role of film out for processing—and request the required number of copies. From this point on the procedures are the same as for the COM approach.

The high-speed photographing device is available from Bell & Howell and Recordak Corporation. The device sells for roughly \$4100; therefore, the monthly depreciation costs would be nominal. In addition to using the camera for implementing an on-line credit inquiry system, it has the potential for reducing paper costs on many other computer reports up to 60%! (Multiple-copy paper forms used on computers are expensive.) (See Figure 7.4).

Figure 7.4 Continuous-forms microfilm camera (courtesy of Bell & Howell Micro-Data Division).

BENEFITS OF ON-TIME SYSTEM TO CREDIT DEPARTMENT

The advantages and benefits to be gained from the low-cost on-time microfilm system are many:

- Customer account status and all related account information are brought to the credit man's desk on a consistent, planned basis—while the information is current.
- It provides instant access to any account on a random basis—without the credit man leaving his desk.
- It enables the credit man or the collector to discuss the details of all unpaid items with a customer while on the telephone.
- The system can be planned, programmed, and installed—in a short time and with a minimum of one-time installation costs.

OVERALL BENEFITS OF COM TO YOUR FIRM

Up to this point in this discussion we have concentrated on determining how the use of COM plus microfilm readers can aid and assist the credit department in its daily operations. Now, there are obviously many worthwhile benefits that can be gained by your company through the use of COM for many other departments and reports. Some of these known savings and benefits are:

- It breaks the computer scheduling bottleneck.
- It improves service to all computer users who depend on printed forms or reports from the computer.
- It eliminates the need for pencil notations on reports that are caused by new updated reports not being received often enough.
- It possibly save hundreds of hours of computer-print time—in a firm that uses the computer on more than one shift for printing.
- It saves *up to 60%* on computer forms costs.
- It sets up compact, efficient information retrieval centers at each major point of reference—and eliminates the present bulky, heavy computer printouts usually kept in binders.
- It saves valuable floor space through record retention on film to replace paper files.
- It reduces the costs of distributing reports by a substantial amount. One small reel of microfilm can hold up to 3000 report pages—and can be mailed for about 10 cents. (One 100-ft. reel of film weighs only 6 oz.).

Modern Micro-Systems and the Credit File

This chapter would be incomplete without mentioning the possibilities for improving the credit file situation—reducing personnel costs—saving large areas of floor space—and bringing the credit files to the fingertips of the credit men.

Credit files are typically bulky manila folders kept in metal file cabinets. The documents found in these files represent a variety:

- Financial statements from customers
- Bank reports
- Agency reports
- Correspondence

Reference to the files is frequent; maintenance of the files is a problem. The ability to find, hire, train, and keep efficient file clerks is becoming more strained as time marches on in the 1970's. There is no foreseeable reversal of this long-term trend.

Fortunately, the answer to this overall problem is here now; it is being installed by more and more progressive firms as the executives familiar with filing problems learn about micro-systems and film jackets.

MICRO-SYSTEMS

This new word refers to the use of microfilm cameras, readers, and utilized film formats in an integrated systems approach to implement an Information Retrieval System. Currently in use are four different versions of film records; however, the film jacket is the one that relates most closely to modernizing credit files.

FILM JACKETS

As hinted at in the preceding paragraphs, the film jacket is the file folder of the future. It represents a unit method of filing film images that permits the constant and intermittent addition of new document images to an existing file that has been set up for a customer, vendor, policyholder, and the like.

The jacket consists of two layers of thin plastic sealed at the top, bottom, and on the left edge. However, the left-hand edge is open for the insertion of film strips or single images—which corresponds to filing a sheet of paper into an ordinary manila file folder. See the illustration below of a film jacket, frequently called a "microfiche jacket" (Figure 7.5).

Notice that the jacket is structured with five individual channels that hold document images or groups of images. This jacket will hold up to 60 letter-size documents!

One hundred jackets require only 1 in. of filing space—this means that up to 6000 documents can be filed in 1 in. of space. This incredible compactness makes it possible for an insurance company to file 60,000 jacket files in one rotating metal wheel; the jackets can conceivably contain more than 3,600,000 individual document images kept in less than 12 sq. ft. of space!

THE READER-FILLER MACHINE

A special device called the "Reader-Filler" makes this unitized micro-image approach to filing documents easy and practical. It was in vented by the NB Jackets Company in Woodside, Queens, New York. This device coupled with use of the five-channel jacket makes it possible to mechanize all routine filing with a

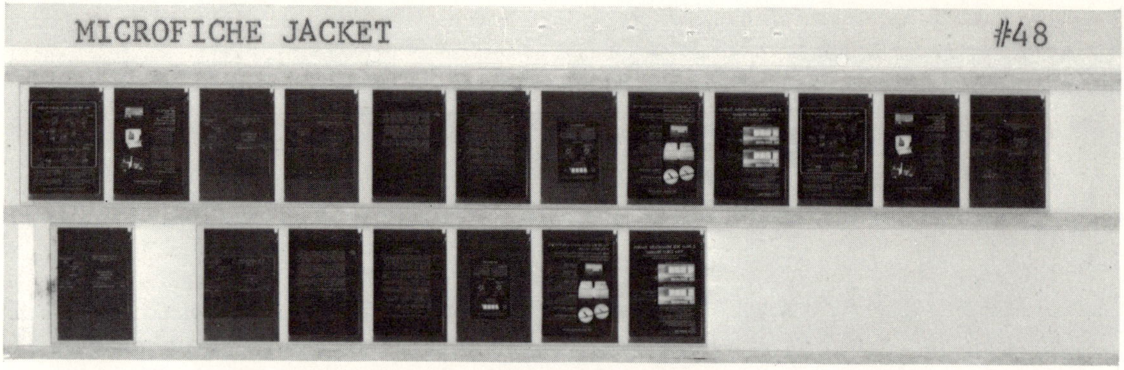

Figure 7.5 A typical 4 in × 6 in microfilm jacket (courtesy of N. B. Jackets Corporation, Long Island City, N.Y.).

Figure 7.6 The reader-filler machine.

small investment in equipment. The file operator remains in a comfortable, seated position and handles the selective filing of all documents after they have been filmed and the film strips brought to the reader-filler machine (see Figure 7.6).

By merely pushing a button, the operator causes the film strip to move through the inserter unit and into the selected jacket channel. A full-size image of the document about to be interfiled is projected onto the screen in front of the filing operator for verification of filing. Depression of another button cuts off the image or string of images that are now inside the jacket.

BENEFITS OF FILM JACKETS FOR CREDIT FILES

Many credit managers are impressed with the many potential benefits to be gained from replacing the old, clumsy credit folders with the film jackets:

- They save large areas of floor space because of the compactness of jacket files.
- They possibly reduce personnel costs by speeding up the interfiling operation—or by bringing the credit files to the desk of each credit man.
- *Rapid Retrieval.* Jackets are well indexed with fully visible titles for quick location and selection.
- *Logical grouping of filed records.* The typical jacket provides five channels or filing areas for storing the film images. This means that financial statements can be kept separate from bank reports, or agency reports. It means that general correspondence can be segregated from collection correspondence, etc.
- *File Protection.* One or two people can be put in charge of all credit files in a very compact area, easy to control.
- *File Mobility.* The jackets weigh very little. This makes it possible to place the customer jackets needed by each credit man right on his desk in a very small area. Or, the jackets may be maintained in a central area; when the credit man asks for a particular file, the file operator can pull the jacket and route it to the credit man. Or, the operator can *duplicate the entire jacket file in seconds at a cost of only 5 cents.*
- The rapid updating of jacket files. As indicated, the interfiling operation is a seated function, and can be accomplished at a higher rate of speed than filing paper documents into four- or five-drawer metal file cabinets.
- The reduction of investment in filing equipment normally required for bulky paper files and file folders.

CHAPTER 8

Special Reports for the Money Manager

The computerization of trade receivables offers a unique opportunity to accomplish a great deal more than merely mechanizing the posting of sales, the application of cash, and the production of credit department reports and dunning documents. This project opens the door to the planning and development of several special reports with great potential value for top management in general and for the *money manager* in particular.

The analysis of the contents of the reports covered by this chapter reveals that none of the key data is extracted from the customer data bank that has been developed especially for credit reporting. Instead, these reports focus on analysis and evaluation of the open-item accounting records found on the customer master file (the first three reports). Another special report, *Hidden Financial Costs Revealed by Remittances,* captures valuable data as a byproduct of the computerized audit of remittances. The last report *Determining True Costs of Credit Sales,* includes the concept of private factoring which develops, through special techniques applied to sales invoices, the *average due date* of all sales for an entire month—for each division or subsidiary—and reports financial losses through disallowed customer deductions, remittance differences, and the like.

I. Analysis of Investment in Receivables

In today's business environment the investment in receivables may represent the largest asset on a firm's balance sheet. Furthermore, receivables deserve special attention from money managers because, unlike the investment in inventories, receivables are only one step away from cash. It is increasingly recognized by alert businessmen today that operating cash is difficult to obtain and that the interest and other financial costs involved in bringing in debt capital add to the difficulties of operating a business at a profit.

The special report, *Investment in Receivables,* enables management to review and to evaluate the receivables investment several different ways. For example, the report may show summary aging totals for each subsidiary or division—and for each region within the subsidiary or division. One line of data per marketing unit indicates the makeup of the receivables asset—and the age of the open invoices outstanding that were generated by the marketing unit (see Figure 8.1).

The preparation of such a report is based on the assumption that each open item found in the receivables file includes the necessary basic in-

INVESTMENT IN RECEIVABLES

Month of:

DIV.	REG.	Total Outstanding Receivables	Total Regular Invoices	Total Disputed Invoices	Open Credits	On–Account Cash	Unadj. Deductions		INVOICE AGING SUMMARY					
							Total $	%	Current and Future Due	1–30 Past Due	31–60 Past Due	61–90 Past Due	91 Days and Over	

Figure 8.1 Investment in receivables.

dicative source codes, such as company or division number, and region number. (Determining the necessary indicative codes properly requires a careful study of the organizational and reporting structure of a firm.)

EVALUATE COLLECTION EFFICIENCY

Another version of the report groups all open items by credit group number—and provides a one-line summary for each credit group that shows:

Credit group number
Total open receivables outstanding
Number of past due accounts
Aging status: 1 to 30, 31 to 60, 61 to 90, 91 to 120, 121 or over

The primary purpose of this report version is to evaluate the collection efficiency of the credit groups.

ANALYSIS BY CREDIT RISK CATEGORY

A fundamental requirement for this report is that the credit manager has classified and coded each customer according to the credit risk category. A typical breakdown is as follows:

- Accounts rated AAA1 are coded as risk-type "A."
- Accounts with substantial financial backing but which are not AAA1 are rated as "B-risk" accounts.
- Marginal accounts or those rated as more risky than the A or B account are coded as "C-risk" accounts.

During the computer scanning run that produces the data for the analysis of investment in receivables, the computer simply stores the open items in counters or accumulators set up internally for each credit risk category. On completion of the scanning run the computer prints the *total investment* and the number of accounts in *each credit risk category*—and ages the investment for analysis and review.

Lloyd Sinnickson, the very progressive and able General Credit Manager for the American Cyanamid Corporation located in Wayne, New Jersey, developed and applied this concept to his computerized trade receivables several years ago. The data obtained monthly enables him to evaluate and protect his firm's investment in receivables and to indicate to the various sales departments, from time to time, possible desirable shifts in sales and promotional efforts to correct *an imbalance* in the current investment revealed by the credit risk category totals.

That is, the totals obtained from the computer run may well be utilized for planning marketing strategy. Suppose that the most recent figures indicate a high concentration of investment in the A and B risk categories, with a corresponding small investment in high-risk Class C accounts. If the selling price of the firm's products includes a substantial gross profit, and capital is available from internal sources to finance an increase in receivables, it may be advisable for sales management, working closely with credit management, to plan a campaign with the deliberate intent to increase sales to Class C accounts.

II. Monthly Report of Aged Open Deductions

As part of the cash application process, many unadjusted deductions and claims amounts will be set up and added back to the receivables file, awaiting internal research and final disposition of the deduction or claim. The cash applier creates paper work for this purpose, which is routed to the department or departments required to check on the validity of the deduction or claim.

The people assigned the task of filing deduction papers and following up on credit memos that are eventually issued to cover the deduction or claim—if it is allowed—are called ''adjusters'' or ''customer correspondents.'' One of their primary duties is to follow open deduction papers until a decision is reached and reported as to the disposition of the customer's claim. When an adjuster receives copies of credit memos, issued from time to time, the adjuster matches the credit to the open file of deductions—finds and removes any matching documents if the credit fully covers the original deduction amount.

Frequently, however, credits will be issued without a copy being received by the adjustment section. Therefore, a special report, produced on a scheduled basis by the computer is indicated. Such a report is shown in Figure 8.2, ''Division report of unadjusted deductions and open credits.''

The adjusters use this as a working report—

DIVISION REPORT OF UNADJUSTED DEDUCTIONS
AND OPEN CREDITS

For Division Credit Manager
Copy for General Credit Dept.

Division or
Subsidiary: LESTER CHEMICAL

Report Date: 5-31-66

CUSTOMER NAME City/State	ACCOUNT NO.	POSTING DATE	D/N DATE	D/N NO.	DUE DATE	D/M NO.	DISC. %	NO. DAYS	DEDUCTION AMOUNT	OPEN CREDIT AMOUNT	C/M NO.	DUE DATE	TERMS	ENTRY NO.
ROBERT ABLE & SON		4/12	4/12	1286	5/12	385	2%	49	38.20					12-017
NEWARK, N.J.	024-600-3	4/28								38.20	687	4/15	2%	12-024
		4/29								112.40	800	5/20	3%	12-030
THOMAS ABLEMAN STORES, INC.														
DOVER, DEL.	024-612-6	4/09								77.65	1215	5/12	5%	12-050
ALBERT BROWN SHOPS		5/08	5/08	1450	6/08	442	2%	23	16.80					12-104
OYSTER BAY, N.Y.	024-810-4	5/12								16.80	1490	5/15	2%	12-108
CHARLES MEN STORES														
ALBANY, N.Y.	025-012-7	3/21								15.00	1060	4/17	3%	12-009
		3/28								44.20	1115	4/28	3%	12-014
HAROLD DAVID & CO.														
SYOSSET, N.Y.	025-610-6	5/02	4/02	1622	5/02	514	N	59	150.00					12-030

Figure 8.2 Division report of unadjusted deductions and open credits.

to find open credits on the receivables file which clears an offsetting deduction. The adjusters pull the deduction papers from their files and dispose of them according to established record retention schedules.

VALUABLE REPORT FOR MANAGEMENT

This report has potentially *great value for management* at various levels:

- Financial management can review the divisional status of all open deductions, since the report is usually organized by operating division. Notice that the report shows the number of days that each deduction has been outstanding.
- Divisional managers and sales managers will be interested in reviewing this exception-type report to detect problem situations and *overage adjustment situations*. Note that the report includes each customer's name and address for convenient follow-up by field salesmen or sales management.

III. Monthly Report of Disputed Invoices

Over a period of time, certain invoices will become disputed items for various and sundry reasons. They will remain open on the file for long time periods, until they are eventually paid or charged off. These items represent a special type of problem and should be reported monthly to management for special attention.

This requires that the computer system provide a means for bringing in a special, indicative code, which is stored in the actual invoice record. This makes it possible to control these items when printing past due statements or collection letters, since most credit managers would not want these known, disputed items to appear on dunning documents. The code also makes it possible to produce this report as a by-product of any computer run that reads the entire customer master file into working memory of the computer as part of the computer run.

This report should show the customer's name and address, the details of the disputed item—and the amount in dispute *aged*. This can be done by printing the amount in one of the usual four or five aging columns, similar to the design of an aged trial balance report.

IV. Hidden Financial Costs Revealed by Cash Remittances

There are indications that top management people tend to think of the turnover of receivables in terms of an equivalent amount of cash being received. Unfortunately, this is far from being the case. Money managers involved in periodic cash forecasting have become painfully aware of the surprising difference between the amount of expected cash—and the amount actually deposited. The unique report shown here was designed specifically for the purpose of reporting the noncash items that are inevitably part of the offset to gross amounts credited to receivables as "paid."

SOURCE OF SPECIAL REPORT

All of the information required for this report is captured as a by-product of the computerized audit of cash remittances and held on a work file that is built up for a period of one month. This work file may easily represent many thousands of individual checks from customers in each of many divisions—yet the financial cost data and cash flow figures are data presented as a one-line summary.

The computer techniques required to capture the basic data and to calculate the use of capital are quite technical and will not be explained here; preference is given to analyzing the end product, the report itself.

NONCASH ITEMS INVOLVED IN REMITTANCES

The spread between the gross invoice amount removed from the receivables file and the amount of actual cash consists of:

- Discount effectively allowed
- Unadjusted deductions and customer claims
- Remittance shortages revealed by audit of remittances
- Remittance differences absorbed as expense

One purpose of this special management report is to reveal the amount of each of these noncash items in the aggregate for each division (see Figure 8.3).

DISCOUNT ALLOWED

The amounts charged to this account include many expense factors. For example:

REPORT OF PROFIT DILUTION THRU CASH REMITTANCES

Month of: OCTOBER 1971

DIV.	GROSS CREDIT to Accounts Receivable	TOTAL Cash Received	NONCASH AMOUNTS							Use of Capital			
			Disc. Allowed		Unadj. Deductions	Remit Shorts	Remit Diff Abs	Tot NON– CASH AMTS	% to Gross	Terms Days	Actual Days	Var. Days	Interest Value
			Amount	%									
DIV 1	2,000,000	1,849,960	46,217	2.3	84,620	12,845	6,358	150,040	7.5	35	45	10	5,556
DIV 2	5,674,000	5,336,726	70,388	1.2	230,960	23,112	12,914	337,274	5.8	30	18	12–	18,912CR

Figure 8.3 Report of profit dilution through cash remittances.

- The discount earned by customers who paid according to discount terms.
- The unearned discount taken—and allowed by the receivables people or by the credit department.
- The excess discount taken, over and above the correct amount earned.
- The discount taken erroneously by customers on the amount of freight and taxes added to the merchandise amount to create an invoice total.

Because of these hidden extra financial costs, it is not unusual for the percentage of discount allowed to gross sales to exceed any of the discount rates found in the official list of invoice terms offered by the sales department.

UNADJUSTED DEDUCTIONS

Trade customers nationwide are accustomed to arbitrarily deducting amounts from remittances for a wide variety of reasons. The magnitude of the deductions problem and the amount of money involved has been increasing for years. Now, in the era of tight money and high-cost capital, customers are taking even more deductions, since they reduce the amount of cash to be disbursed. This topic is of major importance in the overall planning and implementation of a computerized receivables system; therefore, it is covered in detail in Chapter 17.

REMITTANCE SHORTAGES

Careful audit of a large number of remittances usually reveals many unexplained shortages—and a few overpayments as well. Moreover, these shortages may or may not be unadjusted deductions, since they are not mentioned by the remitter. Some receivables managers adopt the attitude that a major, unexplained short amount is a ''hidden'' deduction and will handle it accordingly by creating deduction work papers for subsequent research.

Other firms will code the difference as a remittance shortage and will bill the customer at once for the amount short.

REMITTANCE DIFFERENCES ABSORBED

The total amount shown on the illustrated report represents the net total of all ''small'' over and short amounts developed when auditing thousands of checks. The distinction between a remittance difference on the short side and a remittance shortage charged back to the customer is the amount involved. Suppose that your firm has adopted a policy of absorbing any difference amount up to $4.99 but will bill the customer for a shortage of $5 or over. The computer would ''absorb'' any amount from 1 cent up to $4.99 into the account total, ''remittance differences absorbed.''

Many firms add the small differences, such as the $4.99 into the discount allowed account. I do not recommend this, since it distorts the figures presented by this report as discount effectively allowed. There is much value in keeping these two types of financial costs separated for reporting purposes.

TOTAL NONCASH AMOUNT

By adding the four noncash amounts together, the computer then prints the total noncash amount involved in the thousands of checks represented by the monthly summary figures. Then, it divides the total noncash amount by the related gross credit to receivables amount and prints the *percentage figure*. This is the key figure for money managers to watch; it is, in effect, a significant *trend indicator*.

ANALYSIS OF USE OF CAPITAL BY CUSTOMERS

When net invoice terms are offered to customers, there may be a substantial difference between the invoice terms-days offered to customers and the number of days they use the seller's capital before remitting. By contrast, attractive cash discount terms, such as 2% N30 offers a financial inducement to pay 20 days before the final due date. Under these conditions the majority of customers may pay 10 to 15 days from invoice date in order to earn the cash discount.

Through the use of weighted average techniques the computer can easily capture the data for each and every check received from all customers in a division for an entire month—and present the figures as to use of capital for management analysis as illustrated in the special ''Profit Dilution'' report.

Term-Days Offered. This number represents the weighted dollar-day value of all the invoice terms offered to customers. The calculation is based on the number of days from the invoice date to the final due date; this way, it picks up the time period resulting from ''as of'' dating included in invoice terms.

Actual Days Outstanding. Figured from the invoice date to the effective date of receipt of cash, for each and every invoice. Again, the number shown on the report has been weighted with the dollar value, to present accurately the financial implications behind customers' use of our capital.

Variance Days. This is the number of days (minus or plus) indicating the average number of days paid *before* (minus days) the final due date—or the number of days (plus) *paid after* the final due date.

Interest Value. To calculate the interest value of the amount of capital involved, multiply the total gross amounts paid by the number of variance days, then by the prime rate or some other applicable interest rate; the result is the interest value of the aggregated early or late payments.

Note: If nearly all customers are paying on a discounted basis, the variance days will be a minus number. And, the interest value will be a negative amount, indicating an income amount. However, consider the fact that the price paid for this is the amount of *discount effectively allowed.* It is a thought-provoking exercise to compare the financial cost of discount allowed to the apparently offsetting interest credit amount. Usually, the financial price paid as discounts allowed is far too high in relation to normal or even abnormally high interest costs.

V. Private Factoring: A Method for Determining True Cost of Credit Sales

Many multidivision firms in the past two decades have instituted *profit center accounting.* This is an excellent management approach to obtaining profitability figures for each operating division. A monthly Balance Sheet is prepared for each division, showing the investment in the division's assets and its liabilities. A companion Profit and Loss Statement gives the division credit for all sales generated, less cost of goods sold. Then, all operating expenses are deducted and the net profit or loss is shown.

Operating expenses usually include interest charges for the home office investment in the division's fixed and current assets—including an estimated amount of capital tied up in receivables.

THE BLIND SPOT

The usual approach to profit center accounting as briefly covered above is reasonably accurate and adequate in every respect except one. If the home office has taken over all receivables, credit and collection functions, and has set up a centralized department in the home office for cash application and all other functions related to receivables and credit management, the true costs of handling the credit sales for each division are obscured and seldom known to any of the home office money managers.

PRIVATE FACTORING

There are several definitions and explanations for private factoring:

1. It is a financial reporting method which determines and allocates all financial costs involved in receivables administration to the devision that originated the sales.
2. It develops the financial costs in detail and provides special reports to division managers of the cost of discounts allowed—remittance differences absorbed—interest value of late payments—unadjusted deductions not allowed and not collectible—interest value of changes of terms—cost of extended sales terms and future dating, and the like.
3. The ultimate application of private factoring is seen when a parent firm sets up a separate financial corporation to handle credit, receivables, and collection functions for all of the divisions. This new corporation charges its "clients" a fee for services rendered, based on gross or net sales submitted to the factoring corporation. In addition, interest is charged against cash advances to subsidiaries—if the net income from monthly sales is drawn on by a subsidiary.

CREDIT DEPARTMENT BECOMES A PROFIT CENTER

Quite often when the factoring concept is implemented organizationally, the credit department becomes the nucleus for the new operation and, in effect, becomes a *profit center* in its own right. Typical fee arrangements with its ''clients'' may range from 1½% to 2% or more of monthly gross or net sales. The services rendered by the new financial corporation to earn the fee are:

- Maintains professional credit group and passes credit on all orders.
- Handles all the receivables accounting and overall administration, including cash application and disposition of major differences.
- Handles the adjustment function.
- Performs the dunning and collection work for all divisions.
- Advances operating cash to subsidiaries that request advances against factored sales.

FACTORING SALES STATEMENT

Figure 8.4 below illustrates a typical factoring-type, monthly sales statement prepared at monthend for each division or subsidiary. Notice the following reported facts referenced by line numbers on the statement:

- Line No. 1 Net sales factored.
- Line No. 2 Discounts applicable to each group of sales.
- Line No. 3 Service fee rate (percent of net sales).
- Line No. 4 Average due date of sales—based on first option found in invoice terms.
- Line No. 5 Discounted interest.
- Line No. 6 Net amount due the operating division or subsidiary.

WEIGHTED AVERAGE DUE DATE OF SALES

The weighted average due date of all sales is determined by the application of "dollar-day" techniques to sales figures. It represents the average, composite date when the cash is expected to be received based on the short term or discount due date of each invoice entered into the receivables system. This date is not an actual calendar date because the number of terms days involved in the invoice terms have been *weighted* by multiplying the days by the invoice amount.

Focal Date	*Invoice Date*	*Invoice Terms*	*Discount Due Date*	*Invoice Amount (Dollars)*
5/31	6/01	2% 10 N30	6/11	2000
5/31	6/10	2% 10 N30	6/20	5000

Dollar-day calculations produce a weighted average due date of *6/17*. Notice that, if each of the two customers pay exactly on time, the cash flow will be as follows:

$2000 received on 6/11

$5000 received on 6/20

The weighted average date of 6/17 reflects both the actual due dates and the *amount of money* involved. Therefore, this composite due date will not serve the purpose of accurate cash forecasting.

CUSTOMER PAY HABITS A FACTOR

A more direct approach to cash forecasting is for the computer to scan the discount due date for each open invoice on the customer file and store the invoice amount in an accumulator for each 10-day calendar period. The final totals represent mathematically accurate predictions as to the cash that *may* be collected in accordance with invoice terms. However, the customer's accounts payable departments may not elect to pay certain items, or they may elect to pay on the basis of the final or long-term invoice terms because of a cash shortage.

It is a well-known fact that business accounts payables policies and payment methods usually follow a reasonably consistent pattern. A well-designed computer system for receivables will include the automatic calculation and storing of *pay habits*. When variable invoice terms are offered to business accounts, pay habits are usually based on whether the customer pays "discount, prompt or late." If he pays an invoice on the basis of the first option (because of a discount) the payment is classified as paid "early" or on a discount basis. If he pays on the basis of the long-term option, and is not late, the payment is classed as being prompt, etc.

Pay habits, if developed by the computer system when cash is being processed against the customer receivables file, data are stored *for each account*. With this data available for each account being reviewed, it would seem that the computer could first determine the invoice amounts due to be paid within certain time periods for this customer—and then modify the results in accordance with *past pay habits*. For example, the pay habits data may indicate that the customer's account under review seldom pays on a discounted basis. In that case the computer would be programmed to note the final

MODERN FINANCIAL CORPORATION
STATEMENT OF FACTORED SALES

To LESTER CHEMICAL DIVISION
1899 PEACHTREE ST.
ATLANTA, GA.

Month of: MAY 1972

Line No.		Sales	Credits	Net Sales
1		$2,580,000.00	330,000.00	2,250,000.00
	Discount %	Net Sales	Discount	Net Sales less Discounts
2	NET 1% 2% 3%	515,618.00 754,382.00 895,700.00 83,850.00 2,250,000.00	 7,543.00 17,914.00 2,515.50 27,972.50	2,222,027.50
	Service Fee %	Net Sales less Discounts	Service Fee	Net before Interest
3	1½%	2,222,027.50	33,330.00	2,188,697.50
4	Average Sales Due Date: JUNE 30, 1972			2,188,697.50
5	Interest to Due Date			18,239.90–
6	NET DUE YOU			$2,170,457.60*

Figure 8.4 Factoring sales statement.

due dates found in each open invoice record and to store the invoice amounts in the calendar time period indicated by the final due dates—rather than predicting payment on the basis of the short term due dates.

Summary

Financial managers increasingly require sophisticated, modern tools for evaluating and controlling the constantly growing receivables asset. The special reports presented in this chapter are intended to provide the necessary facts and figures for management review and appropriate action.

The unique *Report of Profit Dilution Thru Cash Remittances* deserves special attention, since it reveals data on hidden financial costs never before available as a by-product of receivables administration.

Managers of multidivision firms should investigate the very significant benefits and profit improvements to be gained from the implementation of the ''private factoring'' method of operating and controlling centralized receivables and credit functions. A growing list of ''Fortune 500'' industrial firms are now operating as factors for their subsidiaries or divisions.

Section II.

For Systems Analysts and Credit Managers

CHAPTER 9

The Systems Design Phase of a Receivables Computerization Project

Part I. The Basic Review or Feasibility Study: Preliminary Step to Systems Planning

Before beginning the many work phases involved in systems design and development, a thorough basic review project should be initiated, even though top management has authorized and budgeted a project to computerize receivables, credit, and collection functions. In many firms it is established policy to require a complete feasibility study and final report before making a final decision on the implementation of any specified computer application.

The only difference between a basic review and a feasibility study is that the latter is supposed to result in a complete, definitive report that outlines the investment in time and money if the proposed project is approved and begun. This report usually includes other valuable data, such as benefits, disadvantages, manpower staffing requirements, and other important aspects. Management reviews the report and makes a determination either to proceed with the project, or to divert the resources of the firm (manpower, experience, and cash) to other, more profitable projects.

REASONS FOR BASIC REVIEW

A thorough, comprehensive review of what is *currently being done* in each department affected by the new system, or to be served by the new system, is *essential* to provide a sound basis for all subsequent systems planning and design work.

Where there is great pressure from top management to computerize a manual function or application, there is a great temptation to skip the usual basic review steps and to get on with the task of designing and documenting the desired new system. However, by necessity, the burden of developing a complete, efficient system then falls almost exclusively on the systems men; the systems concepts and approaches will be based primarily on assumptions as to what current requirements are instead of on factual information. Designing a system and writing procedures based on assumptions or incomplete information may lead to great difficulties at the time of installation and operation.

If one could interview only a few department heads and obtain the necessary information, a basic review would be greeted with more enthusiasm. Unfortunately, it is usually necessary to work right on the ''firing line'' with people doing the actual work in order to get a feel for what is being done—and to document accurately what the job requirements are.

WORK FLOW DIAGRAMS

During the basic review, take copious notes, accumulate a supply of sample forms (preferably with entries on them), and then prepare a work flow diagram to determine those functions or areas that were not covered completely. Flowcharting existing manual procedures—sometimes frowned on by systems managers—does offer the benefit of revealing weak spots in your documented procedures, and provides the quickest way of proving that you have truly developed a sound understanding of what is being done.

The basic review and interviews with line and staff people in the various departments can also produce many side benefits. For example, if the systems analyst or analysts invite ideas and suggestions from those most qualified to give them, the system when finally developed will probably be much more efficient than it would otherwise be.

AREAS TO COVER

The basic review or feasibility study should cover all of the following areas in order to obtain the necessary information for your receivables project.

- Credit authorization policies and procedures
- Collection Policies and Functions
- Order processing and billing
- Invoice batching, posting, and proving
- The analysis of sales invoice terms and arrangements
- Cash application, remittance audit, and related procedures
- The handling and control of unadjusted deductions and claims
- Journal entries; methods of application to receivables and internal control procedures

In addition, the following work steps should be accomplished to round out the fact-finding aspect of the basic review.

- Determine the overall number of trade customers on the books, and establish the number of active accounts.
- Ascertain the various types or groups of customers being sold. For example, are they in retail, manufacturing, or wholesale?
- Review the overall organizational structure of your firm. (This is important in subsequent planning of distribution of various reports.)
- Review present invoice filing methods and retrieval procedures.

Since automatic dunning is potentially a very valuable aspect that possibly should be designed into the new system, spend enough time in the collection department to determine the following.

- The types of dunning documents now being used: statements, collection letters, or notices.
- The frequency of the collection followup review cycle.
- The organization of the credit department; On what basis are customer accounts assigned to credit men?

CREDIT DEPARTMENT REVIEW

While reviewing the credit department, the systems analyst should ascertain the criteria in use for credit checking. This is vital because it will indicate the nature and type of information to be stored in the "customer data bank," which is an important segment of the customer master file. He also should inquire as to credit interchange procedures and the document information required for this function.

CUSTOMER PAY HABITS

Discuss with the credit people their understanding and use of "customer pay habits." This discussion will give you valuable clues concerning the information to be developed as cash is applied to open items on the customer file—how the data should be printed for credit men's use—and the time period to be covered by the reported pay habits. For example, the comparative time periods may be three months—six months—or one year. Notice the word "comparative"; it is of little value to build up pay habits experience for only a current time period. The real value of this information is found by comparing one or more time periods in order to detect a *trend* in the customer's pay habits.

STUDY UNADJUSTED DEDUCTIONS AND CLAIMS

The handling, reporting, and controlling of deductions and claims—which originate with the application of cash to customer accounts—is of extreme importance. This phase of the systems study may be considered almost as an entire subsystem. Proper attention to this vexing problem, and the development of special computer-prepared reports for the adjusters and for management use will pay great dividends.

To indicate the magnitude of the deductions/claim problem in today's trade receivables environment, it is not unusual for industrial firms to find that the open, unresolved deductions on the receivables file—at any given time—add up to *4% or more* of the total dollars outstanding. And a count of the individual entries on the receivables file may reveal that the total number reaches into the thousands. In a recent receivables conversion, we found 30 retail chain store accounts with more than 8000 individual deductions and claims entries on them.

INVOICE TERMS AND CONDITIONS

Mechanizing the application of invoice terms to each invoice and credit that enters the new, computerized system is a very difficult and critically important essential work step. Unless this is done properly, there is no real foundation for automatic preparation of past due statements, or for preparing collection letters. Also, the basis for preparing the monthly aging reports will not be present; the aged totals for each account will represent haphazard estimates of the account status.

Reference here is to the fact that invoice terms, when applied to an invoice, create a unique set of due dates: a discount due date and a *final due date*. The latter is the base for all dunning and aging functions and reports.

Do not underestimate the difficulty of ferreting out all the various invoice terms and conditions that are being offered by the sales department or departments; even the credit men may not be as fully aware of the terms being offered as they should be.

Suggestion. Request the general credit manager to undertake the responsibility for developing a complete list of what he considers to be invoice terms and conditions found in your firm. Set up a meeting with all the key credit men present; be sure that the accounts receivable manager is also present. Review and discuss each set of terms with the group. Determine from a group concensus of opinion what the terms actually mean, expressed in terms of available discounts and terms-days. Then prepare a chart showing your understanding of the mathematical equivalents of each set of terms and review the chart in detail with the group once more. Please read Chapter 12, "How to Mechanize Invoice Terms," before you enter into these discussions.

CASH APPLICATION, AUDIT AND CONTROL

As stated before, cash application is one of the most important aspects of the entire systems planning and design project. To compound the confusion in this area, we in the receivables field have now documented five different methods for handling cash application in a computer system:

- Automatic cash application
- Pre-identification methods:
  - Utilizing printed open item ledger records
  - Utilizing interpreted punched cards pulled from tubs
  - On-line display of open items using CRT display units (cathode ray tube terminals)
  - Display of open items on microfilm display screens, based on modern micromation techniques.

As indicated by the listing of the different methods above, there are only two major methods of cash application. One is the so-called "automatic" approach and the other features the pre-identification method. (Both of these major approaches to cash application with a computer are covered in great detail in Chapters 14 and 15).

As a suggestion, you should spend considerable time working with one or more cash appliers as they actually perform their functions. Notice the many different types of deductions taken —the reasons for the deductions—and the fact that, quite often, the check amount seems to represent an error in calculation. That is, it is very often difficult to understand how the accounts payable clerk in the customer's office determined the check amount.

CASH AUDIT

In any trade receivables installation, each remittance should be thoroughly audited. This can be done manually—or the computer can accomplish this vital function. Many computer installations in existence on trade receivables produce worthwhile benefits in many ways—but the systems planning team left the audit of remittances in the hands of the cash appliers, to be done manually, which is both slow and costly.

It is strongly recommended that you invest the necessary time and research in the development of a *fully automated audit* of each remittance. To audit a remittance requires doing the following.

- Comparing the effective receipt of cash date to the discount due date found in each paid invoice. Then you should determine whether the remitter earned the available discount—or forfeited it.
- Calculating the negative amount of discount on each credit "used" in the remittance—for those credits subject to discount terms.
- Calculating the amount of anticipation (early interest) due the customer—or the amount of *late interest* due your firm.
- Determining whether the check amount equals the net amount required to "settle" the items covered by the check; a plus or minus difference may result as part of the summing up audit function.
- Preparing internal paperwork for deductions and claims; preparing notices or statements for unearned discount or major shortages that require communication with the customers.

INVOICE TERMS AND CASH AUDIT

Invoice terms and the resulting due dates serve two different purposes. The final due date is the basis for all aging and automatic dunning. The *discount due date* and the *final due date* are both important in the computer audit of paid items covered by a remittance.

A major factor in developing your instructions for the automatic audit is the determination of the credit department's policies with relation to enforcement or nonenforcement of certain sets of terms. These policies dictate the rules you will build into the complex cash audit program. To explain why requires borrowing some of the material from Chapter 12, which fully covers invoice terms as a topic and explains how to mechanize any and all types of invoice terms.

TWO TYPES OF TERMS

According to industry practice there are two basically different types of invoice terms: cash discount and trade discount terms.

Cash discount terms puts a premium on early payment, thus earning a discount. Trade discount terms have little, if any, relation to the passing of time, the discount offered by these terms are considered to represent a *reduction of the selling price.*

Sometimes, for various reasons and as a matter of policy, either set of terms may be handled as the opposite type when it comes to the remittance audit. For example, what appear to be cash discount terms may be audited as trade discount terms. Occasionally, we find trade discount terms treated, in effect, as cash discount terms where the discount amount is lost when the customer pays late (see the examples shown below).

DETERMINE MANAGEMENT OBJECTIVES

One of the prime requisites for the basic review or feasibility study is to determine and document *management objectives* for the new system. This is done by a series of informal interviews with members of line managements followed by interviews with members of the top management team.

Open the interviews by asking for their ideas and thoughts as to what results the proposed new system should produce, and in what format. Quite often you will be the recipient of very worthwhile suggestions and ideas that can be built into the system.

An effective followup step is to prepare a memo after each interview, and to send a copy to the executive interviewed. This helps to eliminate misunderstandings, and it documents the information received and the suggestions made to you during the interview.

In connection with analyzing notes taken during an interview with a member of top management, it is recognized that the systems analyst has a very difficult job because of the necessity for developing a *double translation* of what the executive has said. He must first translate the executive's remarks as to the information problem into a format that would ideally fill his stated needs. Then he must translate a practical procedure into specifications; a procedure that offers the best compromise between the ideal set of information to satisfy the executive and what can be produced, considering hardware limitations, economic costs, operating problems and the like.

Bear in mind that the principal cause of

Examples of Terms Enforcement Policies

Code	Terms	Terms Type	Invoice Amount (Dollars)	Check Date	Discount Due Date	Discount Allowed
A	2/10 N30	Cash discount	$1000	6/12	6/10	20.00
B	2/10 N30	Cash discount	1000	6/25	6/10	0
C	2/10 N30	Trade discount	1000	6/25	6/10	20.00
D	3/30 N31	Trade discount	1000	7/31	6/15	30.00
E	2/30 1/31	Trade discount	1000	9/15	6/15	10.00
F	2/10 EOM	Trade discount	1000	8/10	7/10	0

Explanations for above coded lines

A The "N" in the terms indicates cash discount terms; the customer paid well within the 5-day grace period; he earned the $20 discount.

B Same terms; the customer paid 15 days late; he lost the discount.

C Same terms—but NOT ENFORCED BY POLICY. The customer gets credit for the $20 discount even though he paid 15 days late.

D Again the "N" in the terms would seem to identify a cash discount; however, it is difficult to equate a loss of 3% with only one extra day. Therefore, the credit manager may specify that any terms with a discount rate higher than 2% ARE TO BE HANDLED AS TRADE DISCOUNTS.

E Even though the remitter paid 3 months late, he earns the final discount of 1% anyway.

F EOM or Prox terms are usually handled as trade discounts terms. However, in this illustration the credit department had rules that any such item paid more than 15 days late forfeited the discount.

management disappointment with the results of expensive and time-consuming computer projects is the failure of the systems analyst to properly carry out the first translation, from the statements of the executive to the analyst's own conception of what information is actually required.

Part II. Introduction to Systems Design and Development

INTRODUCTION

The wide acceptance and use of electronic computers in the business world has covered a time span of less than 10 years. This is a very short time in which to develop a large group of true professionals to support computer applications and operations. Moreover, the shortage of programmers receives continuing publicity and attention. Seldom is it mentioned that there is an even greater shortage of seasoned, professional systems analysts.

It is difficult to produce a capable systems analyst by training alone. And, there are very few training schools or seminars open to him for training. One of the most valuable assets of a systems analyst is a broad business or specific industry experience. He must also be the sales type in the sense that, preferably, he should be equally at ease with the president of his firm as with the computer console operator.

PROJECT FOUNDATION

There are many difficult work phases involved in a successful conversion of trade receivables, credit, and collection functions from a manual system to a profitable computerized operation. None of the work phases can be said to be unimportant; however, the systems planning, design, and specifications represent the foundation for the entire project. Unless the system is thoroughly defined with complete specifications provided for subsequent programming, the project will be handicapped at almost every turn, and it may require several years to overcome the many problems and operational "bugs" that will inevitably develop.

Members of top management with little or no data processing experience quite often regard programming as being the major requirement for implementing a planned computer application. As an educational measure, the systems manager or analysts should explain the nature of their function, the typical time requirements, and the overall significance of systems design and specifications in relation to programming. Apparently, some of this confusion on the part of management personnel stems from the fact that many of today's systems analysts have graduated from the ranks of the programming group.

PROJECT SCOPE AND COMPLEXITY

In recent years hundreds of industrial firms have computerized their trade receivables, credit, and collection functions. Interviews with scores of individuals who have been involved in the actual project work have brought out the interesting fact that there is a distinct tendency to underestimate the complexity of the project, the amount of work involved—and the overall time required for systems planning and design, programming, testing and debugging—and the conversion from manual records and methods to computer processing.

KEYS TO PROJECT SUCCESS

In a trade receivables system, cash application and control of differences and unadjusted deductions represent the heart of the entire system. If cash is not consistently and properly applied to specific invoices or to other types of open items, the collection function begins to lose its efficiency, and it will eventually collapse when the amount of unapplied cash reaches a certain point.

Another key to designing a valuable, successful receivables system is to understand that the *prime user* is the credit department. The system should be designed to serve the requirements of the credit department, first and foremost. The only real reason for maintaining receivables records—is to COLLECT THE MONEY!

To further emphasize the vital role played by the credit department, consider the fact that a receivables invoice begins with an order from a customer. The credit department must first approve that order before it becomes an invoice. Then, the invoice stays on the receivables records until it is paid. If it becomes past due, the collection arm of the credit department is responsible for taking appropriate action to collect the overdue money. Thus we observe that the credit department is involved in each step in the typical order/invoice/cash cycle of business transactions.

In connection with designing the system to aid and assist the credit department, a useful guideline to remember is that it is a fallacy to assume that a computer can replace human judgment and experience. However, the computer can make extensive tests and report the results for further review. The systems analyst should take the approach that the computer is not going to replace the credit executive; instead, the system is intended to help the credit executive become a more effective member of the management team.

COMMUNICATIONS ARE A PROBLEM

Once the scope and magnitude of a trade receivables computerization project are grasped, it then becomes obvious that a *team effort* is the best solution. The reason for stressing this is because the overall system covers these diverse functions and management control aspects:

- Credit policies and functions
- Accounting and control
- Cash application, cash audit, and control over differences
- Collection policies and procedures
- Money management
- Sales terms offered by the sales department

By referring to the list above, it becomes obvious that the best results will be obtained by harnessing the ideas, experience, and best thinking of a TEAM of people, such as:

- General credit manager
- Accounts receivable manager
- Controller, treasurer, or financial-vice president
- Systems analysts
- Programmers and others

THE ADVISORY COMMITTEE

A very successful "team" approach used many times over the years has been to set up an advisory committee to guide, direct, and assist the systems analysts on whom fall the burden of actually doing most of the systems analysis, design, and specifications work. Quite often the general credit manager, when asked, becomes the chairman of the advisory committee. Another key member is the accounts receivable manager. As indicated above, there also may be a representative of the controller's office or someone to represent the financial arm of the company.

IVORY TOWER APPROACH NOT ADVISED

The combined experience of hundreds of firms in the new and fast-changing data processing field in recent years has revealed many lessons as to what to do and what NOT to do in the area of systems design and development. If the goal of the systems group is to achieve a highly successful computer operation on trade receivables, credit, and collection functions, each report and every aspect of the proposed new system must be fully accepted and endorsed by the users at every level and in each department that uses the output of the new system.

It is nearly always a costly mistake for any group of systems analysts to take the "ivory tower" approach when designing a computer system. This refers to the practice of systems analysts working on a project more or less secretively for a long period of time, doing all the planning and systems design alone and *without the participation of the key users* of the proposed new system.

This approach makes the users both uneasy and resentful. They feel that they have something to offer of value to the new system, since they have been doing a job for 10, 15, or 20 years, etc. They naturally want to know what is going on—and feel very strongly that the new system may not provide what they need to run their departments or functions efficiently. Under these conditions, when the new system is finally released and presented to the users, it may be disastrous, since all of the users will have a strong urge to discredit the new system and reports. Unfortunately, they may be at least partially right since it would, indeed, be a rare group of systems analysts who would actually have enough concentrated experience in the complex field of trade receivables administration, plus credit and collection experience, to enable them to know, without outside aid and assistance, exactly what is needed and why.

In summary, consider this interesting admonition: "It must be remembered that there is nothing more difficult to plan, more doubtful of success, nor more dangerous to manage, than the creation of a new system. For the initiator has the enmity of all who would profit by the preservation of the old institutions and merely lukewarm defenders in those who would gain by the new ones."

Who said that? The systems manager of a larger computer operation in today's modern age? No. It was Machiavelli—in the year 1513 A.D.

SELL, DON'T TELL

To achieve superior results in any applications system design work, the systems analyst should strive to attain a high degree of personal, effective salesmanship. Your motto might well be: "Learn to sell, don't tell."

The point is that there is a big difference between achieving your goals by persuasion rather than by abrupt, arbitrary methods. Frequently the one personal characteristic that elevates a man from line or staff management to top management is his proven ability to work in harmony with others, and to accomplish stated objectives without undue personnel problems.

PARTICIPATION OF TOP MANAGEMENT VERY ESSENTIAL

Now that there are several thousand computer installations, an analytical study of successful versus unsuccessful installations brings out the necessity for top management to be involved in a project from its very beginning. If the working team and staff and line people get the impression that the project does not have the full backing and support of top management, the project is in trouble even before it gets underway. For this reason some member of top management should assume the responsibility for an accounts receivable computerization project. The systems analysts and the advisory committee should report progress to the key executive at stated intervals and should obtain his suggestions, guidance, and approval for major decisions made, or policies established in the interim period since the last meeting.

Summary

This chapter has introduced the subject of systems design, documentation and specifications, and has stressed the fact that the prime "customer" of the new system is the credit department. Many projects intended to computerize trade receivables have been relatively unsatisfactory to all concerned because the systems analysts considered the receivables operation as an *accounting function;* they did not adequately realize that the focus of the entire operation should be to backup the credit department operations in every way possible. Although it is true that the posting of sales, the application of cash, and the "posting" of cash are accounting functions, this is only an incidental to the overall objectives of receivables management and of collecting all funds when due.

A well-known expert in the receivables field, James MacLaury, now residing in Dayton, Ohio, pointed out many years ago in various seminars which he chaired that the only real reason for maintaining receivables is to collect the money represented by the entries on the customer accounts. He said: "If every customer paid each invoice exactly when due—never took an unearned discount—never deducted a claim from his remittance—and never made an error in the check amount . . . then there would be absolutely no reason for maintaining detailed receivables records."

CHAPTER 10

How to Design a Computerized Trade Receivables System

INTRODUCTION

The contents of this chapter are almost entirely of a technical nature; the information is structured and presented primarily for the benefit of systems analysts and other members of the Project Team. A basic objective of this chapter is to provide guidelines and specific information that will be helpful in the execution of the systems design and development work. This explains why many different major topics are covered in a seemingly random sequence; however, all of these topics have a vital significance to the systems designers.

Special emphasis is given to discussions of developing Proof and Control totals, because an accounts receivable file may easily contain accounting records that add up to scores of millions of dollars. Also, many of today's systems analysts are recent graduates from the programming staff and may not be fully aware of the overriding importance of maintaining control totals for each and every step involved in the computer processing of receivables.

ACTIVITIES COVERED BY SYSTEMS DESIGN AND DOCUMENTATION

Designing a computer receivables system and preparing the documentation and specifications covers many work phases or steps. The list below is provided as a checklist for the systems analysts—and to inform others connected with the project as to the nature and scope of the massive amount of work required to design and document a complete system thoroughly.

- Prepare a master list of all computer runs and reports.
- Prepare a master list of all transaction codes.
- Prepare unit work-flow diagrams for each computer run.
- Prepare layout sheets for all input/output records in detail.

  (This covers punched cards, magnetic tape records, and disk records.).
- Write narratives for each run covering the purpose of the run, file organization, methods of accomplishment, frequency, etc.
- Write specifications and description of each transaction code to be used in the system.
- Specify all edit tests in detail.
- Prepare a master list of all sales invoice terms—and explain the time periods represented by the terms.
- Write procedures for batching, terms coding and proving sales input.
- Write detailed procedures for cash batching, proving, and for cash application.

- Write comprehensive procedures covering bookkeeper *review and disposition* of major differences developed during the audit of remittances.
- Working closely with the advisory committee, design and draw all reports and working forms to computer-printer scale.
- Again, working closely with the advisory committee, develop the proposed contents of the "customer data bank." (This ties in very closely with determining the contents and format of certain key credit department reports, such as the Aged Trial Balance, Weekly Status Report, and others intended to inform the credit men of the latest account status.)

Prepare a Master Project Schedule

Preparation of a master schedule showing all major activities involved in the receivables project will enable management to control and evaluate progress. The schedule should list each major work phase or action step along with the starting *week number*. (Most work schedules express time in terms of one week, two weeks, or one month.)

Rather than show specific start/stop dates, the schedule indicates the week or month number when the work is supposed to *begin*—and the week or month number when the project phase is expected to be *completed.*

The schedule for a receivables computerization project may include the following work phases or activities.

- Systems design, development, and documentation
- Programming, testing, and debugging
- The conversion of open items, preliminary and final conversion
- The setting up of master customer file
- The setting up of account coding system, and numbering accounts
- The setting up and staffing of special input section
- The ordering of auxiliary equipment and supplies
- The planning and organizing of the library for storage and control of magnetic tape or disk files*
- The computer site preparation*

*These steps will not be necessary if your firm already has a computer installation that utilizes magnetic tape or disk files.

SEQUENCE OF WORK PHASES OR ACTIVITIES LISTED

Preferably the work phases listed on the master schedule should be in priority sequence. However, there will be some overlap of work that is a natural and expected result of an ongoing team effort.

PROGRAMMING, TESTING, AND DEBUGGING

It is debatable whether the master schedule should include the formidable programming work phase. It is probably better to have one master schedule covering all preparatory steps, the general systems design, conversion planning, and auxiliary steps—but not including the programming. Then, when programming is about to begin, set up *another master schedule* designed to evaluate and to control progress on this major work phase.

In addition to the master schedule, the manager of programming will require the usual individual reports weekly or semimonthly from each programmer assigned to the project.

Developing the Master Transaction List

Developing a comprehensive list of transactions for the new receivables system is a vital task; I suggest that this be done as one of the first major work phases. The reason for stressing this is that control of all input/output functions is based on the computer recognition of each transaction code. This code ties in with routines or subroutines that recognize the record format, length, location of all data fields, special action codes, and the like.

FOUR TYPES OF TRANSACTIONS

Four major types of transactions affect a trade receivables file:

1. Sales
2. Cash application and add-back records resulting from cash audit
3. General journal entries of all types
4. General file and data bank maintenance

After developing a tentative master list of transactions—which includes every conceivable type of transaction that can affect the receivables file to be kept on the computer, plus the ones that are required for internal processing purposes, you then are faced with the decisions as to the *code structure* to be utilized for identifying each transaction. Are alphabetic codes satisfactory? If you decide on the use of numeric codes, should the basic code be composed of two digits, three, or even four digits?

ALPHA VERSUS NUMERIC CODES

Alpha codes do not offer the versatility and scope of numeric codes. Also, I have found them to be somewhat confusing from the standpoint of report readability. I recommend the use of numeric codes.

NUMERIC CODE STRUCTURE

A comprehensive trade receivables system processed by a computer will require 40 or more individual transaction codes in most instances. The ultimate total should be somewhat less than 100 codes; therefore, a basic 2-digit code structure will accomplish the desired results.

However, many benefits can be obtained from the use of a 1-digit suffix number or identifier code. This, in effect, changes the 2-digit code to a 3-digit code. To illustrate the value of a suffix digit, consider the problem of *transferring* an open item record or an entire account from its present location on a customer receivables file to a new location. (This is frequently necessary because of misposting, setting up new accounts that are actually a division of an existing account, and the like).

Now, when a record is transferred, the rule is that the basic transaction code should not be changed. Furthermore, the input transaction code itself, which indicates a transfer is to be made, may have several variables:

- Transfer a single open-item record
- Transfer all open-item records as a group
- Transfer the entire account

Through use of the suffix digit, one basic "transfer" code can handle all of these conditions:

No. 66.0 Transfer a single record

No. 66.*1* Transfer all open items as a group

No. 66.*2* Transfer the entire account

REINSTATEMENT PROBLEM

Consider the common reinstatement problem. The basic rule in designing a receivables system is that for any record that is removed—provision must be made for restoring it if necessary. When reinstating records into an input/edit run, it is necessary for control purposes to *identify* those records. Yet, you want to restore the record with its original basic transaction codes, which identify it as an invoice, credit, deduction, or some other type of record. Suppose that the code for an invoice is *01*. To reinstate this item we keypunch the basic record—and assign a transaction code of 01.9. The suffix "9" identifies the record throughout all processing runs as a reinstated record. Whether or not the "9" remains as part of the transaction code once the record has been restored to the customer receivables file is relatively immaterial. The value of the identifier 9 is in the preliminary edit/processing runs.

FILE MAINTENANCE ENTRIES

Many different transaction codes are required for setting up new accounts, and for overall file maintenance. This also refers to maintenance of the customer data bank that is usually a part of the master file. Bear in mind that one code is needed to simply eliminate an unwanted name and address record (and related records) from the active customer file. This situation occurs when the clerk in charge of determining and setting up new accounts establishes a new account, and later finds that it is actually a division of an established customer's organization. When you transfer the group of open item accounting records from the new account to the other ledger account, the customer name and address record (and associated data-type records) will remain on the customer file until removed.

Structure and Organization of Narrative and Specifications

One of the very important work phases involved in systems design, and in the development of all necessary documentation, is the writing of a narrative for each computer run. The narrative should follow a prescribed pattern so that nothing important will be omitted—and for ease of study by the programmer:

I. Introduction and purpose of run

II. Organization of the Run

A. Input files—designate type and sequence.
B. Output files—designate type and sequence.

III. Method of Accomplishment
Description of each job phase—provides formulas, examples, record formats explained, special functions served.

IV. Outline of Internal Controls
Describe lead card or console input requirements.
Describe internal record control or systems checks.
Outline control totals to be developed.

V. Frequency of the Run

DECISION TABLES

Decision tables may, or may not be a part of the material included under Method of Accomplishment, or in addition to the overall narrative. A few firms use decision tables primarily to *replace* the usual narrative. It is true that a narrative is frequently an awkward method of explaining to the programmer the requirements of a complex computer run. It is for this reason that the use of decision tables seems to be on the increase in the more advanced data processing groups.

Develop and Design Reports with Users

Determining report contents and structure is necessarily a fluid situation. Before a report is finalized you will probably have to draw it at least three times. One reason for this is the necessity of getting the ultimate user or users involved in its content and design. The teamwork approach means that you will first sketch out the report in rough shape and review it with the prime user. Ask his opinion of the various data columns, and get his ideas as to the arrangement or sequence of the report information.

Armed with this new information, you then draw the report again. Check it with similar reports obtained from other firms if possible. Then go over it once more with the user or user group if several people will be actively using the report. After the changes that will inevitably result from such a discussion, you can draw the report for the third and (hopefully) the last time. A copy should be submitted to the user as the final step, so that he can study it from time to time and possibly suggest a final change before the system is finally completed and the programming begins.

AUDIT REPORT-DATA SOURCES

A professional systems analyst is always anxious to avoid the embarrassing experience of designing a report and putting it into final shape only to find out later that certain data obviously required for the report has not been brought into any of the input records, nor developed by computer calculations. In other words, the systems designer was guilty of a basic oversight when designing the system and writing the specifications.

One way to guard against this is to carefully review each report column and trace the data to be printed back to the source. Some analysts code each data field on each input record—and correlate this code to a column or print area on the report. However, some of the report data may come from working memory rather than from an input record; this is indicated on the report form for purposes of this cross-checking.

Another useful safeguard for systems analysts is to check out a printed form or report by testing it with many actual examples of information taken from live transactions. This requires a certain amount of time, but it will pay off very well in many instances.

Write Complete Procedures

One of the many responsibilities of the systems design team is to write complete instructions and procedures for use by the "people subsystem" involved in a computer application. Quite often, this aspect of a new application is given insufficient time and attention. It is equally as important as designing the computer runs and specifications, and possibly more important, since it is people who must make the new system work as well as possible.

There is a tendency on the part of systems design groups to postpone the writing of procedures until most of the myriad other work phases have been completed. Through trial and error I have reached the conclusion that procedures should be written immediately and in conjunction with the development of the computer run to which the procedures closely relate. For example, when developing the cash input records and paper forms, plus specifying the initial edit/proof runs—this is the time to write the cash application procedures in detail, since they implement and explain the use of the forms and input records that you have designed for the computer-oriented part of the function.

Writing key procedures should preferably be a team effort. Sit with the accounts receivable manager, for example, and write the preliminary cash handling, batching, proving, and cash application procedures with his aid and assistance. After all, he is the line manager who must eventually make the procedures come to life; they must be well-written and practical.

AREAS OR FUNCTIONS REQUIRING WRITTEN PROCEDURES

1. Cash batching and controls.
2. Cash application and setting up deductions.
3. Review of major differences (Cash Received Journal).
4. Disposition of differences and related proof procedures.
5. Data bank input and maintenance of customer master file.
6. Clearing open deductions and corresponding invoice credits from the open items file. (Handled by the adjusters as "equals.")
7. Journal entries of all types.
8. Identifying new customer accounts and assigning account numbers.

Prepare Outline of Major Functions of Each Run as a Preliminary Step

A complex computer run may necessarily perform from 20 to 40 or more major functions. The writing of the paragraphs to fill in the "Method of Accomplishment" section of an organized narrative for such a run becomes a very difficult operation. The systems analyst will tend to get lost in the maze of details and other information presented for later use by the programmer.

This difficult task will be much easier and much more complete if you will first list all major functions of the run as they occur to you. Then, rearrange the list so that related functions to be performed appear grouped together. Number each function on the outline.

Now, when you are writing the narrative for the "Method of Accomplishment" section of the specifications, you can take one item at a time that appears on your master outline, explain the function, and provide the essential details, formulas, examples, etc. You can include the outline code number as part of your written material for a tie-in between it and the topic on the outline.

To illustrate this approach I have selected an actual outline taken from the specifications for a computerized trade receivables systems design project. See the example that follows.

Outline of Major Functions for Preliminary Cash Audit Run No. 123.0

1. Calculate the number of days EARLY OR LATE for each paid invoice record. Store the number of days with sign in each paid invoice record.
2. Calculate the *total average days* early or late for the entire remittance (covering a group of invoices and credits) by using weighted average method.
3. Calculate the *average due date* by applying the average number of days, early or late, to the effective check date. Store result in Payment Summary Record.
4. Use interest formula, calculate INTEREST AMOUNT, print on cash journal for each remittance.
5. Determine if the available discount was *earned* or *unearned* one invoice at a time. If earned, credit the amount to the customer by placing the discount amount in a discount counter.
6. Calculate amount of cash REQUIRED TO SETTLE the items paid by a remittance. Print in indicated special column on cash journal.
7. Compare the cash required to actual check amount; print DIFFERENCE amount in difference column. If amount is short, apply plus sign; if over, apply minus sign.
8. Punch a difference work card if different amount is $5.00 or over, plus or minus.

9, 10, 11, etc.

After completing the outline of major functions, then proceed to take item No. 1 and prepare the necessary detailed narrative plus illustrations or other material that will be helpful to the programmer who must implement the desired function successfully.

Structure of Open Item Record

Obviously great care should be taken when designing the open item record. These records represent the accounting aspect of the overall customer file. Data carried in the open item record have many uses in the system. I suggest the inclusion of two special-purpose data fields in the open item record:

- Internal sort codes
- General Purpose codes

INTERNAL SORT CODES

In the early days of computer systems design we attempted to use transaction codes for two purposes: record identification and for sorting. This unnecessarily complicated the transaction code structure, and quite often was not a satisfactory solution to sort requirements anyway. The use of internal sort codes is a superior approach to the problem.

The availability of this 2-digit data field makes it possible to have the program handling any given computer run assign 1 or 2 digits or letters to each individual record written on output files. Then, take the output file into a sort run where the records are sequenced in accordance with the sort code values. In the very next run the sort codes may be changed because of subsequent sort requirements. The transaction codes remain undisturbed and do not enter into the sort unless there is some special reason for the use of the transaction codes in the sort specifications.

I will use cash-related records to illustrate the use of internal sort codes. Immediately following the deletion of open item records during the "delete" (cash application and deletion of indicated records) run, we want to audit each remittance and print a Cash Received Journal. For purposes of this run, we want the individual records in the following sequence:

- Customer name/address
- Cash remittance record
- Received on account record (if present)
- Paid item records
- New, unadjusted deductions records

To accomplish this, we go back to the delete run and specify that, as these various records are written out on a DELETED RECORDS WORK TAPE FILE the program is to assign the following internal sort codes:

Sort Code	*Name of Record*
1	Customer name/address
2	Cash remittance record
3	Received on account record
4	Paid item (deleted) records of ANY TYPE (any TR code number)
5	New (flagged) unadjusted deduction records
6	Journal entry-deleted records of any type

By sorting all of these output records on the major code of customer number, then on CHECK NO., then on the internal sort code within check number—the records will line up as indicated above.

GENERAL PURPOSE CODES

The title of this suggested data field provides a clue as to its possible use. Many times it is necessary to assign a temporary flag or special identifier code to one or more records in a particular computer run. Locating and specifying the character position for such flags or codes at random is both confusing and may lead to programming bugs. It is preferable to provide a uniform method for handling this problem and a prescribed group of codes in each and every record. This assists the systems designer and the programmer in detecting and implementing these special codes.

Two characters would be minimal; leave space for four special characters in the general purpose data field.

AUDIT TRAIL REQUIREMENTS

A well-designed system makes it possible to find the original document or source of the open item record. This is very important for several reasons. We refer to it as an "audit trail" because of the insistence of external auditors that the system provide for this back-tracking capability.

Even more significant is the genuine need for

finding the document backing up the record as part of routine operations. Frequently it is necessary to find an invoice that appears on a past due statement—because the customer requests a copy for his payables files. When bookkeeper-reviewers are reviewing the major differences shown on the cash journal, they may want to verify terms appearing on an invoice involved in a remittance. Adjusters may want to work back from an unadjusted deduction entry and may want to look at the original remittance information that was the source or authority for setting up the deduction initially.

BATCH DATE AND NUMBER

Inclusion of a batch date in each open item record provides the major clue as to where to find the original document—if all documents are filed by the assigned batch date. The addition of a *batch number* reduces the volume of documents to be searched within the batch date file. Consider how we usually apply these techniques to cash input, processing, and proof:

1. Rough-sort the checks and place roughly 50 checks in each stack.
2. Assign a consecutive batch number, beginning with 001 each day, to each batch.
3. Add the total check amounts and create a batch ticket that now shows the *batch date, batch number* and total amount of cash.

The batch number serves the purpose of providing proof over the keypunch function by bringing into the initial edit/proof runs the total of each batch; the computer then verifies that the detail records equal this total.

Now, at the remittance review stage, suppose that a reviewer wants to find the remittance voucher and related documents that back up a check amount shown on the cash journal. Since the cash journal shows the check batch date and *batch number,* it is easy for the reviewer to go to the files, select that batch of remittance papers—and find the documents filed with the small batch of 50 documents.

MODERN MICROFILM INFORMATION RETRIEVAL SYSTEMS

The use of a batch date and batch number becomes even more significant and valuable when microfilm equipment and techniques are utilized to set up information retrieval centers. The filmed records replace the bulky invoice and other paper files that require expensive floor space and a large investment in filing equipment.

When an integrated system is developed and installed—integrating the use of microfilm document retrieval methods into the overall system—it is possible for a clerk seated in front of a microfilm reader to locate, find, and display one invoice selected from 1,000,000 invoice images in a total of about 15 seconds! This is made possible by the use of batch dates and batch numbers, which are required anyway for a well-planned system.

CASH APPLICATION IDENTIFIERS

The key to accurate cash application in trade receivables is good communications between the accounts payable department of the customer and the accounts receivable department of the seller. However, the design of your own internal records and working reports is of critical significance in making cash application easy and efficient. For example, there are five keys to identifying a paid invoice:

- Invoice date
- Invoice number
- Store number
- Purchase Order number
- Invoice amount

Seldom will the remitter list all five of these keys on his remittance voucher. Well-designed accounts payable systems require listing the three major identifiers for the benefit of the seller's accounts receivable department: invoice date, number, and amount. Chain stores will usually provide the *store number* in addition to other basic invoice identifiers.

Moreover, a good receivables system will provide for these identifiers internally in each record set up; and the various printed customer ledgers, cash journal, and other reports listing open item records should display this basic information.

Input/Output Files

It is, of course, essential to fully identify each input or output file in all specifications and documents. To use descriptive names is not satisfactory. Some type of numeric coding provides the best answer to the identification problem. Some experienced analysts use the 3-digit coding system explained below.

NUMBER EACH FILE

Assign a basic 2-digit code number to each file of any type—punched cards, magnetic tape, or disk. Then use a suffix digit to indicate changes in the basic file. For example, if a transaction file is sorted, and the base number of the file is 05-0, the sorted output file is then assigned number 05-1. The 05 identifies the basic file; the suffix "1" indicates that this file has been changed to some extent.

In Figure 10.1, which shows the Preliminary Cash Audit Run in which file No. 07-1 is an input file, note that the output file is No. 07-2. The output file has been changed to the extent that the program has assigned a *consecutive audit number* to each record on the No. 07-2 file. Since the records now are not the same as on the input file, the number assigned to the file should not be No. 07-1.

PREPARE LIST OF FILE RECORDS

Programmed instructions which control input and output are based on transaction codes that are keyed into routines and subroutines for processing records of all types into and out of working memory. For this reason, I suggest an addition to the usual systems documentation: provide the programmer with a list of every conceivable type of record that may appear on a specific input or output file.

This not only assists the programmer and tends to eliminate rewriting of certain sections of the run program later, it serves as a valuable checklist for the systems analyst. The reason for stating this is that experience has shown that the time and thought necessary to prepare the list of codes for each file brings out problems and a consideration of special records that otherwise might have remained hidden until the programs were written and tested initially. Then

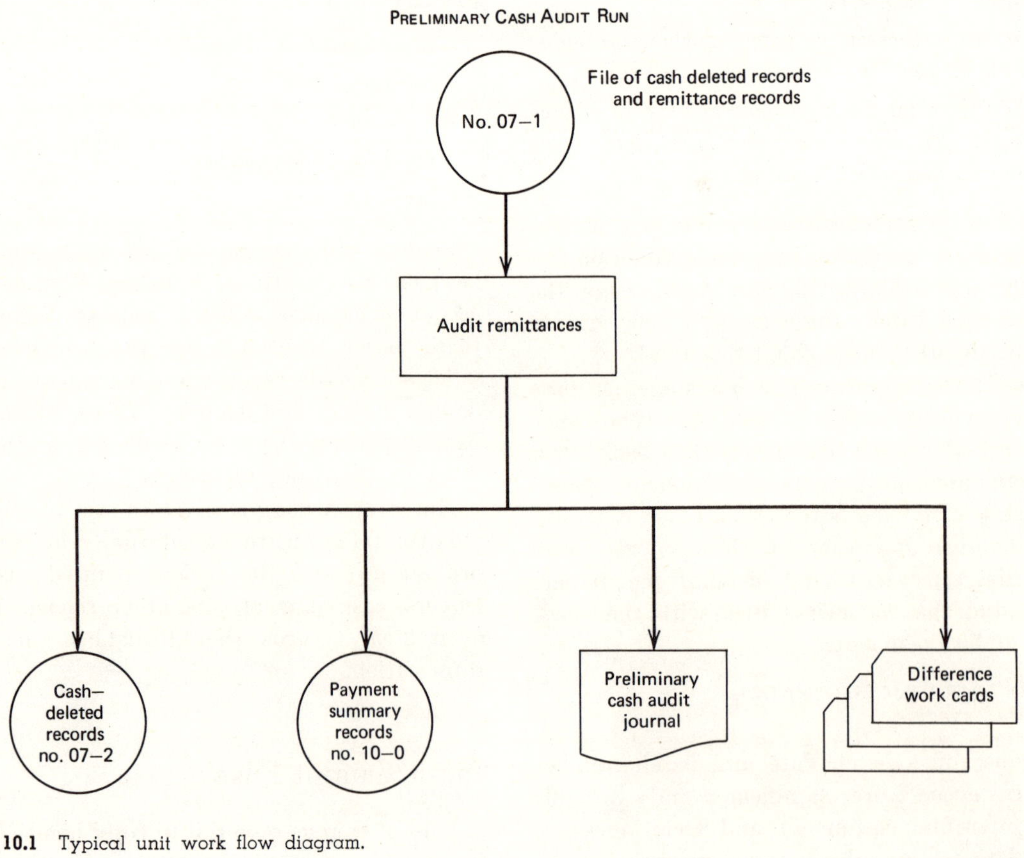

Figure 10.1 Typical unit work flow diagram.

the oversights would have become apparent, with resultant program changes, rewriting, and additional testing.

See the sample list of file contents below, taken from an actual job.

Run No. 123.0 Preliminary Cash Audit Run Contents of Input File No. 07-1

Transaction Number	Record Name
01.0	Customer Name/Address Record
79.0	Cash Remittance Record
80.0	Cash Remittance Memo Record—for Cash-Equals
31.0	Cash Remittance Finder Record—Unmatched
ALL	Deleted Records of any type
40.0	Unadjusted Deduction, flagged (new)
41.0	Internal Charge, flagged
50.0	Received on Account record, flagged (new)
51.0	R/A—Invoices to come, flagged
52.0	R/A—Cannot Apply, flagged

Develop Lists of Edit Tests

The systems designer is better equipped to prepare the list of edit tests than the programmer assigned to the programming work phase.

Beware of making the input edit tests too restrictive. For example, one of the key records brought in is the *cash remittance record.* At first blush you would specify that this record should be rejected by the computer if the cash amount field is blank. This would be a mistake, since we use cash remittance records with blank amount fields when processing ''debits-to-come cash.'' (This refers to cash that arrives for application before the invoices being paid have been received and posted to the customer file.)

Now, when the invoices paid by the check eventually appear on the customer file as open items, the cash appliers must then apply the check to the open items. We call this the ''Cash-Equals'' procedures. One way to obtain the usual cash audit is to prepare routinely a cash remittance record for input that refers to the *original check date and check number*—but the AMOUNT FIELD is left blank.

One of the difficult decisions to be made in connection with edit tests is this: If the basic cash remittance record fails the edit test, and is rejected—should the related group of cash finder records and unadjusted deduction records set up also be rejected? What will be the result if these records are accepted and go into the cash received journal without the basic cash remittance record?

Suspense Accounting and Related Control Problems

One of the first steps that an experienced systems analyst takes when embarking on a systems design project is to determine the computer operating mode that will apply to the proposed application:

- Will the computer be available for edit and proof runs during normal business hours—or does the operating schedule indicate that runs will be made on the second or third shift?
- Is this particular application to be considered as just another application to be processed on a service-bureau basis (processing work for company departments as though they were outside customers on a scheduled basis)—or, will this application be given a high priority status so that the computer can be considered as being dedicated to this prime application?

The determination of the applicable computer operating mode is extremely important, since it dictates, to a large extent, how initial edit/proof runs and related procedures for review and correction of invalid transactions must be handled. A further discussion will clarify this point.

DEDICATED BASIS

Where the edit/proof runs will be performed during normal business hours—and no further processing or updating will be done with the input files until all rejected (invalid) transaction records have been researched, corrected and fed back in—there is no necessity to provide for ''suspense'' accounting and control procedures.

SERVICE BUREAU BASIS

By direct contrast, if the computer department operates on a scheduled service bureau basis, this usually means that all scheduled computer runs will be completed from beginning to end, once started. This approach means that the computer will reject certain input transactions that fail to meet all edit tests—and the valid transactions move on into all subsequent processing and file updating runs without interruption, and without waiting for any corrections and the re-input of rejected transactions of any type.

REJECTED RECORDS MUST BE CONTROLLED

Proceeding with valid transactions, after rejecting certain transactions from an input batch, immediately presents the problem of *control* over the rejected records of all types. Consider this illustration:

1. The 1000 sales input records for today, which were divided into batches of 50 records each for proof and control, are fed into a sales edit run.
2. The computer accepts 990 records and rejects 10 as invalid.
3. The computer calculates the grand total of the 990 valid records and proceeds to handle all subsequent sort, merge, and updating runs based on the 990 valid records.
4. The 10 sales records classified as rejects now must be researched, corrected, keypunched, and fed back into tomorrow's sales run.

The control problem begins with the 10 rejected sales records. This not only changed the original batch totals, but creates the need for a control clerk to record and control the 10 rejected records. This may seem easy until you find from experience that one or more of the *corrected records* fed back into the computer may be rejected—and, a fresh group of rejects will appear from that day's group of sales input.

Thus so far we have referred exclusively to input and control of sales records. The same situation applies also to cash and journal entry inputs. To visualize the scope and extent of the control problem, we now see that a control clerk must maintain separate controls over three types of input transactions—and by batch date groups:

- Sales
- Cash
- Journal entries

TWO POSSIBLE APPROACHES

One way to maintain control over rejected transactions is to develop special programs that create a special *item suspense work file* for each type of input transactions. This becomes, in actual use, a recycling file from necessity, since any group of input items may include a batch of corrected items from prior days—and the new batch of transactions may well include a number of items that will fail the edit tests, and must be added to the item suspense file. Therefore, these specially-written computer programs must be designed to add new rejects to the suspense work file and to delete corrected records that are coded for identification and matching to suspense items on the suspense file.

The concept behind this approach is sound, even though there are certain hidden complications, but the investment in programming is apt to be substantial.

An alternative method that requires a minimum of programming effort places the control responsibility in the hands of a designated control clerk. The computer's role becomes that of simply printing *special lists* of rejected items —and *special lists* of corrected items accepted, or rejected.

This method keys on the original batch date found in each transaction record. The computer can print the totals by individual batch date of all corrected records fed back in. This makes it easy for the control clerk to maintain control records for each batch date for each type of transaction and to record the value of corrected records until the control total reaches zero.

You may want to specify that a separate page of corrected input records be printed *for each different batch date*. This enables the control clerk to match the correction page to the *original list of rejects*. She can keep the paired pages in a binder for reconciliation and reference purposes.

OUT-OF-BALANCE BATCHES

Out-of-balance batches pose a different problem, yet it ties into suspense accounting. The usual procedure is to test a batch total entry against the sum of all detail records with a common batch number; if the sum of the detail records does not agree with the batch total record, the batch is out of balance. Customary procedures call for printing the entire list of detail records for each and every batch that is out of balance.

The question is this: Should a rejected (invalid) record be counted as part of the batch total for balancing purposes—or should it not be considered as part of the valid batch total—thereby creating an out-of-balance condition?

Answer. Write your edit programs to cause a rejected record to create an out-of-balance condition. The reason for this suggestion is that any other approach complicates the control procedures for records in suspense, since it would be necessary to differentiate between input records correcting records originally rejected—as compared to records brought in to correct an out-of-balance batch condition!

Proof and Control Totals

Long before computers came on the scene, the need for extensive and carefully-developed proof and control totals was fully recognized wherever dollar amounts were involved in business operations. The use of a computer for processing records involving dollar amounts does not decrease the need for maintaining proof and accounting controls; it might even be said that controls become even more important because of the nature and speed of computer processing and file updating.

TWO TYPES OF CONTROLS

The systems analyst thinks in terms of controls of two types: internal and external.

Internal controls are the ones developed to prove the data processed through the computer from input to output. External controls are the independent sets of balancing figures maintained by proof and control clerks outside the computer room. Broad operating experience has shown that there is a very definite need for controlling computer files with external control figures. An actual case history discussed in the next paragraph shows the value of external controls to supplement the usual internal proving and checking.

To start an accounts receivable updating run late at night in a large firm that is a leader in its industry, the console operator mounted the receivables master file that had been routed to him for this purpose from the tape library. He proceeded to process the input transactions, and produced an updated receivables master file as a result of the processing run. The final proof and control totals developed by the program during the run and printed on the last page of the transactions register indicated that the new computer file was "in balance." That is, the debits and credits added to the file, plus the beginning balance figures extracted from the old master file used as today's input, produced a test trial balance figure that agreed with the actual total outstanding receivables (new trial balance) as recorded on the new, updated receivables file. Therefore, the new tape file was said to be "in balance."

Indeed it was—but the control clerk who maintained a separate set of external controls found the next day that the WRONG customer master file had been mounted as input for the run. (The librarian had pulled one of the backup magnetic tape files created during the prior week). The primary point is, that without external controls, this mistake might not have been detected for a period of time.

BUILD IN PROTECTION AGAINST MALFUNCTION

Certain built-in checks and controls should be aimed at detecting an occasional computer malfunction. For this purpose many systems analysts insist on building in record counts, sequence-checking of record-type codes, and other techniques that detect foreseeable types of malfunctions.

SERIES OF INTERLOCKING CONTROLS

Systems design specifications may well include a whole series of interlocking and related controls for ultimate protection against errors creeping into the system—and for cross-checking if a malfunction occurs in a computer sort run, a merge run, or a major processing run. As an example of how extensive such interlocking controls may be, consider the following steps or runs taken from an actual receivables installation.

1. Establish batch totals for each batch of sales, cash, or journal entry input transactions as part of normal operating procedures.
2. Edit run proves the detailed records in each batch to the batch total; if out of balance, com-

puter prints the difference amount and each record included in the batch for review and correction purposes.

3. During any sort or merge run, count all records in and out—and print control totals for all output files.
4. Print the details of records added to or deleted from the master file of open items—as an audit trial of what actually took place during the processing run. Such details are usually wanted anyway in the form of a Sales Register, a Cash Receipts Journal—or a General Journal that shows all journal entry adjustment items added to the customer file, and all records deleted by journal entry.

PRINT SPECIAL CONTROL PAGES

When a computer run that involves printing detailed records comes to an end in the middle of a page, the usual procedure is for the program to cause a spaceup of the paper, followed by printing one or many lines of transaction totals and grand totals. Now, the external control clerk requires access to these totals for posting to the control books.

A very effective solution is to program the computer to print all accumulated proof and control totals twice. Print the first group on the last page of the printed report, then space up to a completely new page—and print all the figures again on a specially-identified CONTROL PAGE. This page is then routinely routed to the proof and control clerk for entry into her control records.

Proof and Control Totals for the Customer Master File

The open item accounting records found on the customer master file (if the open item records are integrated into the master file) typically represent several million dollars in receivables. Security procedures must be developed to provide backup files at all times—and procedures must be developed to protect the integrity of the file during all processing runs.

The following internal tests and checking techniques are suggested.

- Set up a control record as the last physical record on the customer master file.
- Store in this control record the following counts and totals:

  Number of open debit records (plus amounts) and total value.

  Number of open credit records (minus amounts) and total value.

  Number of customer accounts and grand total of outstanding receivables.

PROVING THE UPDATED CUSTOMER FILE

During the updating run, which may involve adding new records and deleting certain records because of journal entries, sales or cash application, accumulate the number of records posted or deleted—and the dollar value of the above types of transactions.

At the end of the run, the counts and totals listed in the first paragraph above will be read into memory as the last record on the tape file. In effect, these totals represent the *trial balance before this run began.* Taking these figures as the beginning counts and balances—including the overall master trial balance figure—add the debit and credit amounts accumulated from this run—and CALCULATE the NEW TRIAL BALANCE TOTAL. Then, compare this calculated trial balance total with the ACTUAL TRIAL BALANCE TOTAL developed as the customer records were written out on the new, updated customer master file.

By proving the record counts in and out, and by proving the overall trial balance dollar totals, the integrity of each new customer file is assured.

CHAPTER 11

The Customer Master File: Contents, Structure, Maintenance, and Other Considerations

Because of the information requirements inherent in the credit checking function, plus statistical data required for credit interchange reports, a modern computer system for trade receivables should provide for the storage and fast retrieval of a considerable body of information about each customer. This information is kept on the ''master file,'' which may be stored on reels of magnetic tape, or on random access devices.

This phrase ''master file'' means different things and has different connotations in various types of computer applications. In connection with a receivables-oriented file it frequently is used to designate nothing more than a master file of customer names and addresses. Or, it may designate a file consisting of names and addresses, plus data bank information gathered and developed about each customer for the purposes of credit department reports, or for on-line credit inquiry—or for automatic credit checking through the use of a computer.

A file of open-item accounting records—invoices, credits, unadjusted deductions, on account credits, etc., grouped by customer number may be called the master file for accounting purposes. Finally, a much broader use of the phrase is found when an *integrated* customer receivables file has been structured to include the following data and records for each customer:

- Name and address
- Customer statistics, plus fixed and semi-fixed ratings and limits, and general-purpose data bank information
- Open item accounting records

The master file for receivables seldom includes customer ''ship to'' names and addresses, since this type of file more appropriately belongs in the order/invoicing system. Receivables take over when the order becomes an invoice.

Customer Data Bank

The file of statistical and other information accumulated and stored for each customer is frequently called the ''customer data bank.'' It usually is a physical subset of the name and address master file as distinguished from the *open-item file,* which refers to the collection of accounting records representing various types of charges and credits. In summary, two distinctly different sets of records are maintained for each customer. This may lead to the development and maintenance of two physically-separated files in a computerized system since the open-item records have little in common with the statistical and data bank records which constitute the data bank file. The remainder of this part of the discussion focuses on the data bank instead of on the open-item accounting records.

Some of the data in the data bank is semifixed and is provided by credit men from time to time. Other data, such as "pay habits" or net sales year to date, is quite variable and changes each time that cash is applied or sales are posted to the open-item file. Because of the updating requirements, it is necessary to access and rewrite the data bank contents during file updating runs in order to store the latest information developed as a by-product of processing transactions against the customer file.

CONTENTS OF MASTER FILE (NAME AND ADDRESS PLUS DATA BANK INFORMATION)

Laying out the master file records and determining data bank contents begins early in the systems development work phase and continues until all report contents have been defined and accepted by the report users. This open-end treatment is necessary in the early stages of systems development because, to a large extent, the availability of report data is based on information kept in the customer master file. The following is a typical list of information carried in such a file.

- Customer account number
- Name, address, and zip code
- D&B rating—and date of last rating
- Credit Limit—and date assigned
- Order limit—and date assigned
- Type of account—credit risk category
- State code
- Credit man number
- Date of last sale
- Date of last cash—and amount
- High credit; possibly for two or more time periods
- Pay habits history—possibly for two or more time periods
- Sales for last year and this year
- Credits for last year and this year
- Standard industry classification codes
- Dun & Bradstreet number for the customer (for cross-reference)
- Special indicative codes controlling the printing of monthly statements, past due statement, automatic dunning, etc.
- Account balance and date
- Latest past due status in aging format

LENGTH OF NAME AND ADDRESS DATA FIELD

When designing the master file, the systems analyst is immediately faced with a decision as to the number of characters required to properly print a customer's name and address. Without a precise knowledge of the requirements for trade names, this decision will be based on guesswork. The United States Steel Corporation systems specialists a few years ago analyzed the names of thousands of business firms and found the following facts:

- 25 characters are not sufficient for printing many firm names.
- 30 characters are close to ideal because 98% of all firm names can be printed without abbreviation.
- 34 characters are required to cover every conceivable firm name without abbreviations.

As for street number and name; leave 20 to 22 characters. For city and state, plus zip code, provide up to 27 characters.

The address for some customers must include a special line of information such as the name of a shopping center. This, in effect, is a four-line address. The arrangement for accessing and printing from a four-line address area should be flexible because most customers can be addressed with only three lines of information.

If the master file must cover customers in foreign countries, the structure of the name and address data blocks should provide the equivalent of five print lines. In one study we found customer *names* in Sweden, Germany, and South America that required up to 45 alphabetic characters. And, their method of designating the address of a firm or individual nearly always requires three complete lines just for the address.

Additional Information Stored in Master File

The master file, by design, may be a veritable storehouse of valuable information about customers. For example, in addition to storing all the data listed on a prior page, it may also include considerable financial data and hidden financial costs for each account.

HIDDEN FINANCIAL COSTS

Certain customers are constantly taking unearned or excess discount. Others may be labelled as chiselers in that their checks are always a few dollars short when audited. Some always pay late—will not pay late interest—and take all discounts anyway. The accumulated total of amounts involved in such payments may well be very substantial in a firm that receives 1000 checks or more per day. This adds up to 250,000 checks per year. Now consider the fact that our sample studies of checks received from trade customers indicate that up to 18% of all checks have an adverse affect on profits because of the financial losses mentioned above.

DEVELOP RECORDS FOR CUSTOMER PROFIT DILUTION ANALYSIS

The systems analysts and the credit manager working as a team in designing the customer data bank should consider building customer profitability data into the data bank. The financial leaks and losses resulting from cash application is one source of input to the data bank. Charge-offs of late interested billed, unearned discounts deemed uncollectible and charge-off of unadjusted discounts not allowed but uncollectible from the customer should be recorded in the data area set aside for accumulating such financial information.

The profit dilution report centers around three types of financial losses:

- The total unearned or excess discount taken—plus remittance differences absorbed.
- The interest value of all late payments.
- The unadjusted deductions and shortages charged off.

The credit manager may want to carry this data for the current year, and also keep the same information accumulated for last year. This makes it possible to show on any credit department report the financial losses that are associated with carrying a customer for all of last year and the accumulated current year-to-date figures.

VALUE OF PROFITABILITY DATA

This type of information is of value in several ways:

1. Reports the facts to the credit and sales departments.
2. Calls attention to accounts that are chiseling.
3. Enables a separation of profitable accounts from unprofitable or undesirable accounts.

Tom Edick, Assistant General Credit Manager of the huge Stanley Works in New Britain, Connecticut is an example of today's modern, progressive credit executive. He says this: "Under today's conditions it is of increasing importance for the credit manager to think more and more in terms of *account profitability.* This is essential in order to help increase his firm's profits by directing the attention of the sales department to developing *more profitable accounts*—and by controlling accounts which represent expense in various ways."

FINANCIAL DATA

Some firms are engaged in a highly volatile business environment that requires close credit control over customers at all times. An example of this is the textile manufacturing industry. In this trade it is customary for creditors to ask for and to receive financial statements at stated periods from practically all accounts on the books. When this is trade practice the customer data bank may be designed to carry the following financial information.

- Date of last statement
- Investment in merchandise inventory
- Working capital
- Total current liabilities
- Net Worth
- Net sales shown on profit and loss statement
- Gross profit percentage
- Indicators that personal guarantees have been obtained from corporation officers
- Type of business organization

The storing of financial information in the customer data bank where it is available for instant recall may be very useful in many ways. When an automatic order approval system is developed for computer implementation, this stored data may be one of the indices involved in automatic approval or referral of each order. Another use of the stored data is to print the financial data on specially designed credit department reports or on credit department copies of customer statements. This makes it possible to bring the latest financial report data to the credit man's desk; this has, in the past, proved to be one way of eliminating the call for the credit files to a large extent.

AUTOMATIC ORDER CODING

The Kawneer Corporation in Niles, Michigan has done an outstanding job of building a complete coding structure in the "customer profile" or data bank stored in their computer. They use the codes in the data bank for the automatic coding of customer orders.

All orders are routed into the home office for processing. Each order must include certain basic codes, such as the account number, the salesman's territory number, and the "ship to" location of the customer. In addition to these codes, the computer accesses the data bank and automatically adds other essential codes. For example:

- Sales report codes such as *warehouse number, region,* and *division numbers*—and *county* and *city codes* for tax and statistical reporting.

Chris Dresch is general credit manager of this progressive firm and is very enthusiastic about the computer system that he helped to develop.

TWO DATA BANKS

A special type of customer master file is required for the computer processing of orders and invoices. For example, a chain store organization may have several hundred ship-to names and addresses that must be accessed for heading up all shipping order forms, shipping documents, and for writing invoices. For accounts receivable record-keeping, this same firm may have only *one* paying office.

This brings up the question of whether a firm with computer processing of orders and invoices should maintain two separate data banks, or should attempt to use one central bank for order information and credit department reports and management information. This is a difficult question to resolve.

If the credit department customer information is kept on reels of magnetic tape, this probably would not be suitable for order processing, since the very nature of order processing requires random access to inventory records, and to *ship-to* customer names and addresses. Another consideration is the fact that information stored for order handling is quite different from that carried for credit department and management reports.

A nationally known cosmetics manufacturer has successfully developed a common data bank stored on a random access device that is utilized for both order processing and for receivables-oriented reports. However, it is important to note that the receivables open items are maintained on magnetic tape as a separate and independent file.

WHERE TO STORE MASTER FILE INFORMATION

The hardware configuration found in a computer installation determines to a large extent which type of storage device shall be used for the master file. For example, if the computer hardware configuration includes random access equipment, then both the name and address and the customer data bank information may be stored on disk packs or on any other type of similar storage devices.

Because of the relatively stable nature of most of the information usually stored in a customer data bank, it seems logical to use disk files for this purpose. This type of data storage also provides the capability of calling out information on a random basis for answering inquiries or for printed reports.

Concept of Integrated Customer Master File

Up to now we have discussed the customer master file as consisting of the name and address, and customer data bank information. If the open-item accounting records are added to these two data elements, then we have implemented the concept of an "integrated" customer master file. Such a file may be kept on disk packs or reels of magnetic tape.

This approach resembles in concept the sequence of information found on the accounting machine posted ledger sheets found in many receivables installations. For example, the name and address of the customer appear on the top of the ledger; open-item debits and credits are posted to the body of the ledger sheet, followed by the latest account balance.

This method of integrating the two files is very successful in practice and is especially recommended for those computer installations where the number of tape handler units is limited to four or five.

Refer to Figure 11.1; notice that the first two records are customer ''header'' records that contain the full name and address information, plus other account data which is semi-fixed. Then, all open-item records appear next, regardless of the number of records open on the account.

CONTROL RECORD

The last record in the integrated file representing a customer's account is always the Account Control Block, which serves more than one purpose. The machine-calculated *account balance and date* appear in this record. It also includes information that is dynamic; data changes resulting from processing transactions and updating the file, such as year-to-date sales and credits, pay habits history for current period, high credit amount, and the like.

DISK STORAGE VERSUS MAGNETIC TAPE FILES

An increasing number of today's computer installations include both tape and disk drives in the hardware configuration. Disk packs are an increasingly popular type of data storage device designed for direct retrieval of stored data. If both types of hardware units are available for use by the new receivables system, then the systems group should analyze and evaluate the advantages and disadvantages of both methods of record storage and file processing.

It seems logical to store the coded data that constitutes the data bank on random access files, because of its semi-fixed nature. The alternative approach, storing the data on reels of magnetic tape, requires reading and rewriting the entire customer data bank each time the customer file is involved in an updating run.

By contrast, the file of open-item accounting records logically indicate the use of magnetic tape files—because of the well-known ''accordion'' action represented by trade receivables, especially the ones subject to seasonal variations. Disk packs may be processed sequentially the same as magnetic tape files; this fact complicates the decision as to the use of tape versus disk storage to some extent.

DISK STORAGE IS COSTLY

The use of disk packs for backup storage of open-item files is an acceptable practice, but it is more costly than magnetic tape. Protection requirements for a file of open-item records may cause the fast buildup of a large number of disk packs maintained in the disk library. Magnetic tape reels, by direct contrast, cost only about one twentieth as much as disk packs—and normally store larger quantities of coded information.

POPULARITY OF MAGNETIC TAPE

Most trade receivables open-item records are kept on magnetic tape—even though the hardware configuration may include disk packs or equivalent random access storage devices.

This solves the protection and backup problem for the open items because of the low cost of storing several generations of open-item files in the tape library, plus keeping the monthend master file from which the detailed, aged trial balance is printed.

FINAL DECISION ON FILES

To recap, experience points to the use of magnetic tape for the open-item file—and random access devices for the customer headers and data bank information. However, even here the use of random access files for direct read/write functions may not save as much processing time as one would expect. It is possible that a completely integrated master file *including all open items* will prove to be a more efficient method of file processing and updating than the combined file concept and approach. To get the facts on which to base a decision, I suggest that your most experienced programmer be assigned the task of analyzing the comparative time factors, programming requirements, and data storage costs. His final report will indicate the best approach to take for your receivables system.

RT 1	Gen codes	Customer No.	TR No.	4-line Name and Address				STMT inst	Acct type	SIC code	State code	
				Name 1	2	3	City, state and zip					

Record 1—Name and Address Header

RT 2	Gen codes	Customer No.	TR No.	D & B		Credit Limit		D & B Acct No.	Date acct opened	etc. etc. etc.
				Date	Rating	Date	Amount			

Record 2—Name and Address Header continued

RT 3	Gen codes	Customer No.	TR No.	Batch		Item date	Item No.	PO No.	Store No.	Amount	Terms code	Extra days	As of Date
				Date	No.								

Record 3—Open Item record: invoice, credit or other

RT 3	Gen codes	Customer No.	TR No.	Batch		Item date	Item No.	PO No.	Store No.	Amount	Terms code	Extra days	As of date
				Date	No.								

Record 4—Open Item record

RT 4	Gen codes	Customer No.	TR No.	Account Balance		Last Cash		Accum. Sales		Pay Habits History		
				Date	Total	Date	Amount	Last yr.	This yr.	Period 1	Per. 2	Per. 3

Record 5—Account Control Block

Figure 11.1 Suggested grouping of records that constitute an integrated customer file.

SIGNIFICANCE OF RECORD TYPE CODE

Referring to the records shown in Figure 11.1 again, notice that the first character in each record is the record type. RT 1 identifies the first header record, for example. RT 2 identifies the second header record. All open item records carry an RT 3 identification. The control block is RT 4.

The presence of these codes enables the computer to constantly sequence-check all records brought into memory to assure that the structure of each account is valid. For example, if an RT 3 open-item record were the first record read into memory, after a change of account number has occurred during a file updating run, the computer would flash an alarm because the account structure is recognized as being invalid.

FIXED LENGTH RECORDS

Note that all records in the exhibit are of the same fixed length; and each record includes a common customer number. A few experienced programmers prefer to work with variable-length rather than fixed-length records. The objective behind the use of variable-length records is to save a few seconds or minutes of tape read/write time by reducing the total number of file characters to be read and rewritten on an output tape file. However, this advantage is usually offset by the difficulties encountered in initial programming and testing—plus the problems of program maintenance and changes during the life of the program. Also, some highly experienced computer technicians doubt that the use of variable-length records actually saves any processing time on balance.

By contrast the compensating advantages of using fixed-length records are many:

- Ease of initial programming and testing
- Ability to make full use of index registers
- Ease of programming changes and maintenance
- Eliminates necessity for file rewriting for sort runs
- Each and every record carries its own unique identification with a specific customer account

MERGED VERSUS UNMERGED CUSTOMER RECORDS

If your firm is a multidivision company or has a number of subsidiaries that sell products or services to customers, a basic decision must be made by the General Credit Manager in the early stages of systems design and development. The decision involves keeping the individual customer records on a "merged" or an unmerged basis.

If they are to be *merged,* this means that one account and one master file will be set up for each customer, regardless of the number of divisions or subsidiaries from which he buys goods or services. An unmerged file implies two things:

- A separate master file and account will be kept for each customer of each division or subsidiary.
- The individual customer account records will be maintained as a group for each division or subsidiary.

PROS AND CONS

Before computers were widely available for mechanizing trade receivables, there were many excellent reasons for maintaining unmerged receivables. This concept also fitted into the frequently encountered decentralization of receivables, credit, and collection functions where each division maintained its own credit department, plus its own accounts receivable section, and handled the entire cycle of transactions generated by its own sales department.

Computer techniques make it easily possible to bring all receivables, credit, and collection operations into a centralized department in the corporate Home Office—and maintain *merged receivables* without losing control of the individual sets of receivables represented by open items generated by the various divisions or subsidiaries.

From a credit and collection control standpoint, merged receivables represent the best file organization and operation. It offers the following benefits.

- Provides better credit control. The entire account status is available at a glance, regardless of the number of divisions from which the customer buys.
- Provides better collection control. The customer receives dunning documents or calls from one collector, rather than receiving numerous statements or dunning letters from several different divisional collectors.
- Reduces personnel costs, forms, and postage costs.
- The true value and profitability of the account can be evaluated, since it is no longer fragmented among the various divisions.

File Sequence and Grouping of Accounts

Once the major decision is made to carry all receivable records on a merged basis—one account for a customer entity, regardless of the number of divisions or subsidiaries selling the same account—the question as to how to structure the customer file can be resolved. Certain suggestions for your guidance are listed below:

- Organize the posting run (adding new records to the open item file) in such a way that all items for each division are grouped together. These divisional groups represent, in effect, subledgers within the customer's master ledger.
- Set up one data bank for the customer.
- Provide space in the customer master file for storing individual credit limit amounts for each division.
- Provide space for storing individual order limits for each division.
- Develop only one set of "pay habits" data for the customer entity, not for each division's items paid.

ACCOUNT GROUPS

The analysis of your overall customer list may indicate that your firm is actually engaged in selling to a variety of customers, such as:

- Manufacturers
- Wholesalers
- Retailers

Certain policies and dunning procedures may vary widely according to the customer group. This situation leads to the question as to whether all the customers should be carried on one common file in *A* to *Z* sequence, or would it be better to break them into three groups, each one including names from *A* through *Z*?

This is not an easy question to resolve without considerable thought. From the standpoint of account recognition and cash application, it is better to have one customer file rather than two or three. For flexibility in producing certain aging and special reports, and for dunning procedures, the segregated customer files offer some savings and benefits.

ACCOUNT CODING SYSTEM

The decision as to one file or multiple files most assuredly must be made well before coding the individual accounts with a customer number. If multiple files are going to be set up and maintained, the account coding structure must be developed and applied to each file so that the coded transactions will match only against the appropriate customer file. In effect, each customer's account number must indicate the customer file where his account is carried.

CHOICE OF THREE CODING SYSTEMS

One of the important work phases involved in a project designed to computerize receivables is the selection and application of an account coding system. There are basically three different plans in wide use today:

- Straight numeric system
- Alphanumeric "gap" system
- Alphanumeric modified gap system

STRAIGHT NUMERIC SYSTEM

Few commercial firms have adopted the straight numeric system simply because businessmen want working reports and management reports to appear with customer names in alphabetic sequence. If the customer file is maintained in straight numeric sequence, any trial balance, dunning documents, or any other type of report extracted from it will display names in random sequence. To get the benefits of an alphabetically organized report from such a file, it is necessary to first sort the records on the computer into alphabetic sequence.

ALPHANUMERIC "GAP" SYSTEM

This system attempts to keep all customer names in exact numeric sequence—and also in exact alphabetic sequence. The theory is fine, but broad experience reveals that there are many problems and operating difficulties with this numbering plan. However, it does produce reports with names in alphabetic sequence without presorting the records.

MODIFIED ALPHANUMERIC "GAP" SYSTEM

This plan combines the strengths of the straight numeric plan and the alphanumeric "gap" plan. Developed many years ago by the Lefebure Corporation of Cedar Rapids, Iowa, it has withstood the tests and rigors of time very well.

This very successful numbering plan is known as ARANS: *A*lphabetic *R*andom *A*ccess *N*umeric *S*equence. To explain how it works, here are the instructions for a clerical group working on a numbering project in preparation for a mechanized receivables system:

1. Arrange the names into exact alphabetic sequence based on the surname or last name.
2. Segregate the alphabetized names into small groups of approximately 20 names each to create alphabetic subdivisions. Each name in the group shares the same last name, or the same alphabetic characters such as the first three or four letters in the last name if the names are not identical.
3. Set up a preprinted Number Assignment Register for each of the alphabetic subdivisions. Type the last name identification letters and the *starting account number* on the top edge. Since each assignment register has 200 numbers printed on front and back, the effect of this step is to assign a block of *200 numbers* to each small group of about 20 names found on the original name list.

This provides an expansion factor of 10X for adding new names in future years.

Refer to Figure 11.2, which is the number assignment register for a group of names that shares the letters "JANS" in the last names.

Notice the check digit to the right of each 2-digit account number. This is a mathematically-calculated number based on one of three formulas that can be selected by the buyer of the account number registers. (The formula used on the page shown in Figure 11.2 is the double-add-double method.)

4. Assign numbers from the register to each name in the small group of names. Post the *date account was opened* to the face of the number assignment register so that the assigned number will not be used for the next new account.

ILLUSTRATION OF NUMBER BLOCKS

Here are the alphabetic subdivisions set up and the number blocks assigned to a Midwest name list:

Starting Account No.	*Last Name Identification*
13–000	JA
13–200	JACKSON
13–400	JACOBS
13–600	JACOBSE
13–800	JAE
14–000	JAMES
14–200	JAMESO
14–400	JANE
14–600	JANS
14–800	JAS

Notice that there were enough Jacksons and Jacobs on the name list to warrant setting up separate subdivisions for these surnames. More often the alphabetic grouping is identified by the first four or five letters of the last name common to the name group, such as JANE, JANS, JAS, etc.

FEATURES OF THE ARANS PLAN

Each block of numbers is in straight numeric sequence. To assign a number to a new account, the control clerk merely selects the next open number on the appropriate number register. The check digit has been precalculated and is part of the number assignment.

Note that a date is posted next to an assigned number. There is also space for entering the date the account is *closed.* The number can eventually be reused by entering the date of assignment in the space identified by the letter "R."

For a more detailed coverage of account numbering systems, review the chapter on account coding in either of the following two books published by Prentice-Hall:

Accounting Systems for the Small and Medium-Size Business (Whiteside)

Guide to Profitable Management Advisory Services for the Public Practitioner (Whiteside)

MASTER FILE SEQUENCE

In summary, any customer master file is usually organized and maintained in *account number sequence,* regardless of the account coding system selected and applied to customer accounts. Since numbers are the language of computers, the unique account number provides the basic and definite identification of each account. The name and address headers are merely corollary data banks that provide the name identification of each customer. Since the account number is the primary account identifier, it is obvious that the individual entrusted with the task of identifying new accounts, and with preparing the necessary documents for setting up the new records on the file, has a very responsible job assignment.

Determining Customer Identity

In the instance of certain types of accounts, determining the customer identity is not as easy

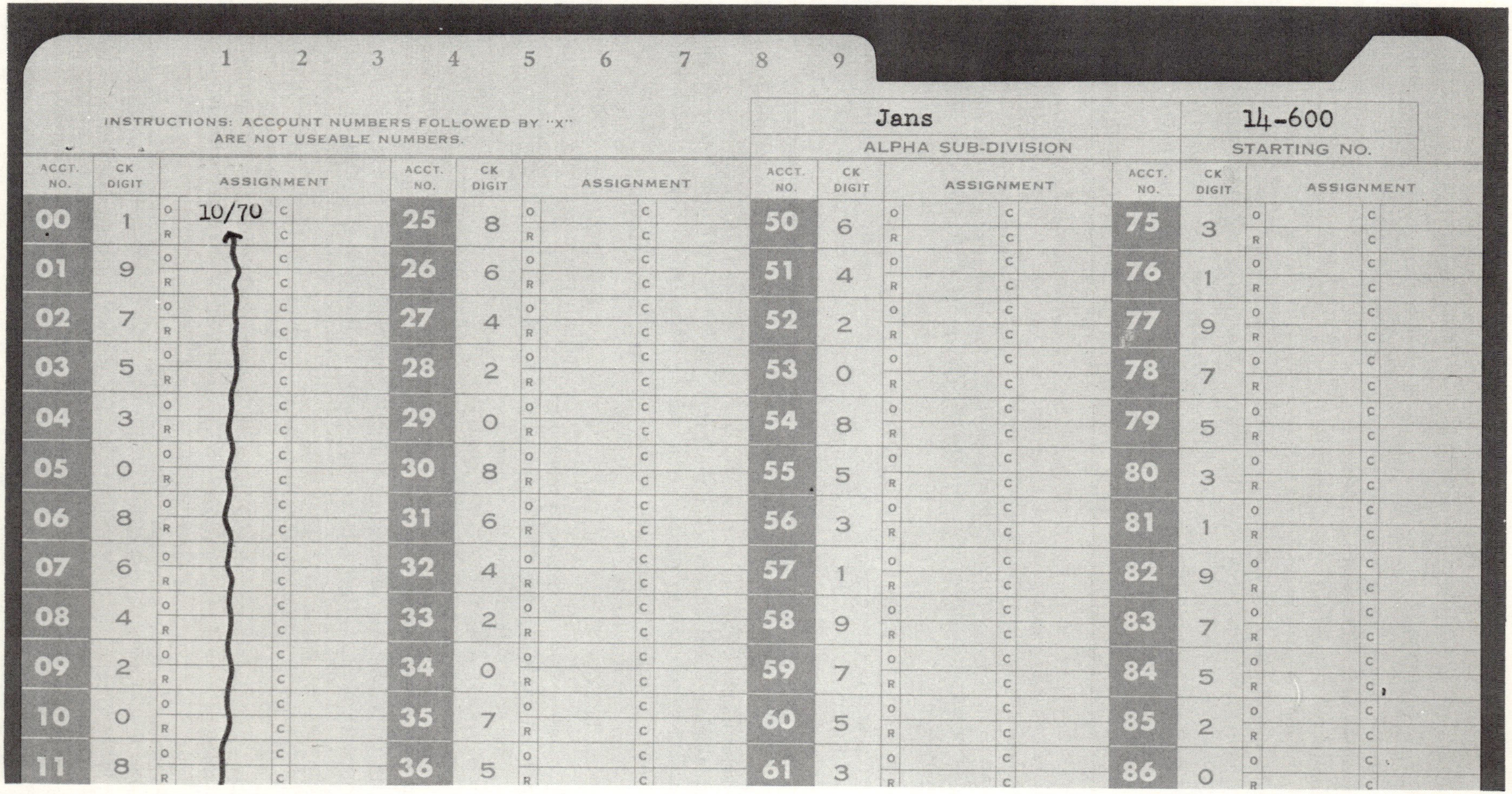

1 2 3 4 5 6 7 8 9

INSTRUCTIONS: ACCOUNT NUMBERS FOLLOWED BY "X" ARE NOT USEABLE NUMBERS.

Jans	14-600
ALPHA SUB-DIVISION	STARTING NO.

ACCT. NO.	CK DIGIT	ASSIGNMENT	ACCT. NO.	CK DIGIT	ASSIGNMENT	ACCT. NO.	CK DIGIT	ASSIGNMENT	ACCT. NO.	CK DIGIT	ASSIGNMENT
00	1	O 10/70 C R C	25	8	O C R C	50	6	O C R C	75	3	O C R C
01	9	O C R C	26	6	O C R C	51	4	O C R C	76	1	O C R C
02	7	O C R C	27	4	O C R C	52	2	O C R C	77	9	O C R C
03	5	O C R C	28	2	O C R C	53	0	O C R C	78	7	O C R C
04	3	O C R C	29	0	O C R C	54	8	O C R C	79	5	O C R C
05	0	O C R C	30	8	O C R C	55	5	O C R C	80	3	O C R C
06	8	O C R C	31	6	O C R C	56	3	O C R C	81	1	O C R C
07	6	O C R C	32	4	O C R C	57	1	O C R C	82	9	O C R C
08	4	O C R C	33	2	O C R C	58	9	O C R C	83	7	O C R C
09	2	O C R C	34	0	O C R C	59	7	O C R C	84	5	O C R C
10	0	O C R C	35	7	O C R C	60	5	O C R C	85	2	O C R C
11	8	O C R C	36	5	O C R C	61	3	O C R C	86	0	O C R C

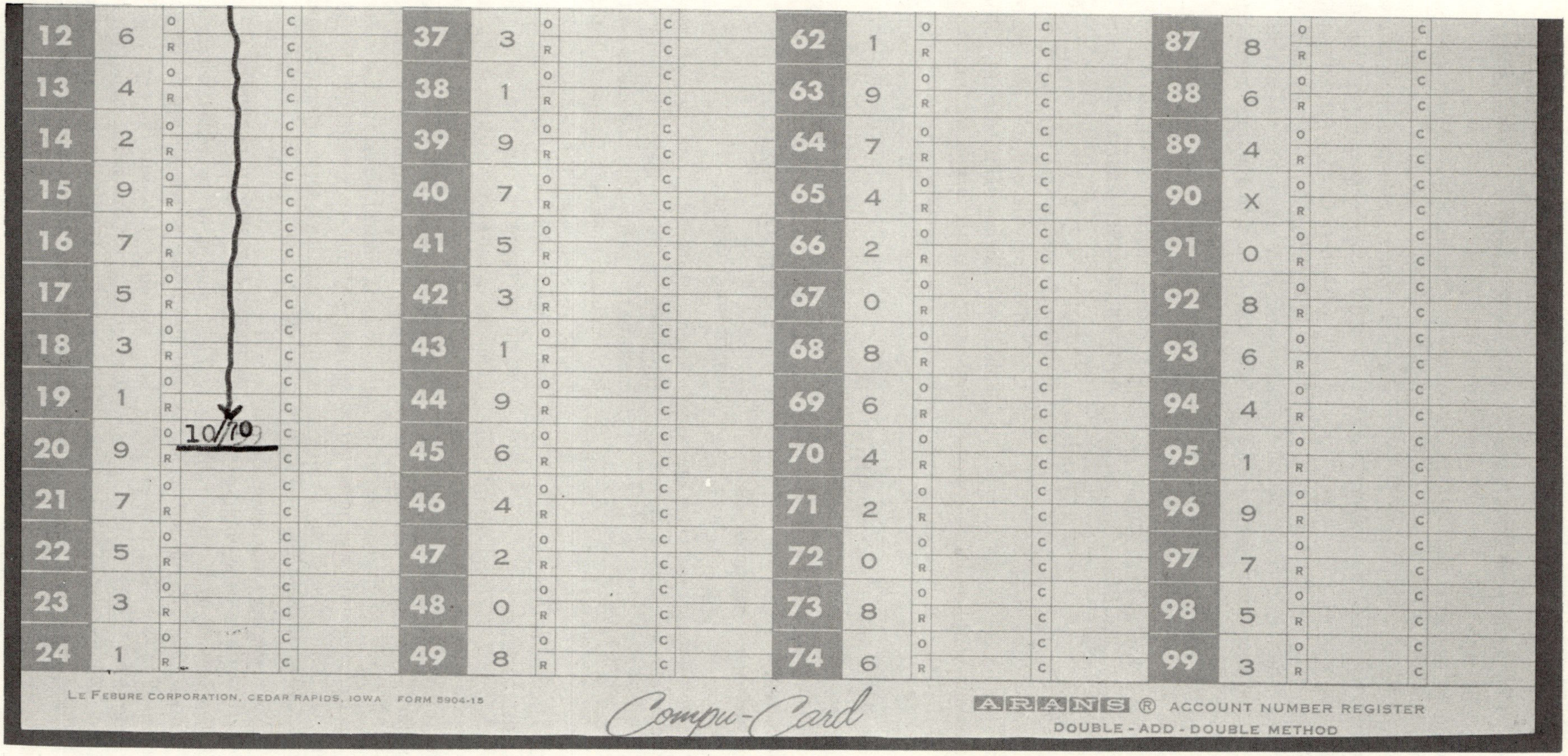

No.	Check	No.	Check	No.	Check	No.	Check
12	6	37	3	62	1	87	8
13	4	38	1	63	9	88	6
14	2	39	9	64	7	89	4
15	9	40	7	65	4	90	X
16	7	41	5	66	2	91	0
17	5	42	3	67	0	92	8
18	3	43	1	68	8	93	6
19	1	44	9	69	6	94	4
20	9	45	6	70	4	95	1
21	7	46	4	71	2	96	9
22	5	47	2	72	0	97	7
23	3	48	0	73	8	98	5
24	1	49	8	74	6	99	3

Figure 11.2 ARANS account number register.

as one might think. For example, a chain store operation involving 50 outlets at 50 different locations operates under five different subsidiary names. Researching the Dun & Bradstreet reference books indicates that the firm has a headquarters in a certain city—and your experience shows that all payments come from a *central accounts payable department* located in the firm's headquarters. The latter provides the prime clue about customer identification. An accounts receivable ledger record and assigned account number *should always reflect the account payable name and address of the payer.*

Accounts receivable ledger records seldom are tied to "Ship To" names or addresses. They usually reflect the "Sold To" name and address appearing on an invoice.

THIRD TYPE OF IDENTITY

A few firms further complicate the systems design problem in that they have a third type of identification:

1. "Ship To" name and address or addresses where merchandise is sent.
2. An accounts payable name and address for our ledger identification.
3. A *third* name and address where the customer specifies that all invoices and dunning documents are to be sent for processing clearance before they are routed to accounts payable for actual payment.

The Impact of Inactive Accounts on System Considerations

Experienced systems analysts are always aware of the cost of the computer processing time involved in any given computer run. A significant aspect of trade receivables is that the number of inactive accounts compared to accounts with one or more open items at any given moment frequently represent a ratio of more than 2 to 1. When an accounts receivable manager is asked to estimate the number of customer accounts represented by the receivables file, he usually thinks primarily of active accounts with balances. For example, if the manager states that he has 15,000 accounts, be prepared to set up and process a master file with 30,000 to 45,000 names on it. Only after they have carefully established the number of active and inactive accounts, can the systems analysts determine the correct approach to file processing with the objective being to save as much computer processing time as possible.

If a file has 15,000 names and addresses for active customers, and includes an additional 20,000 to 30,000 names and addresses for inactive accounts, a considerable amount of processing time will be lost in reading or reading/writing the characters represented by the additional names and addresses—each time the customer master file is involved in a computer run.

INACTIVE CUSTOMER MASTER FILE

One successful solution to the problem is to set up two customer master files; one is the "active" file and the other is designated as the "inactive" customer master file. The regular customer file (if organized on an integrated basis) would include all names and addresses and the data bank information, plus all open items for all accounts with one or more open items.

Accounts that temporarily are closed out appear on a separate magnetic tape file. This constitutes the *Inactive file.*

USE OF INACTIVE FILE

Unless transactions to be processed against the customer file are tested routinely against the inactive file, there would be a constant necessity to keypunch customer names and addresses to reactivate an account that was inactive for only a few weeks or months. To overcome this problem, set up a computer run that tests the account numbers in all current transactions against the account numbers found in the customer headers on the inactive file. When a match occurs, copy the full name and address header records and the related control block for the account to the transaction file. This routinely brings the full account data back to the active master file during the updating run.

MONTHEND TRANSFER OF ACCOUNTS

This concept of two files requires a special monthend run which is easy to program. Read both customer files into memory; test the last date of activity on each account on the *active* customer file. If an account has not been active for more than three months (as an example) and has NO open items, delete the account from the active master file and write it onto the *inactive file*. Likewise, when a match occurs between an account number on the inactive file and the active file, delete the records from the inactive file. *Reason.* The daily runs have already transferred the account name and address from the inactive to the active file!

DEAD ACCOUNTS

This special monthend run may also be programmed to eliminate "dead" accounts completely from the inactive file. The rule may be that if an account remains on the inactive file for 12 to 13 months, it is considered "dead." When it is eliminated possibly a special report should be printed to notify the sales department of the situation. This may call attention to accounts that have a great sales potential but have been allowed to remain dormant through oversight.

Conclusions

Designing the customer data bank is a highly creative function and a very important one. All data to be reported to management comes from either the data bank, or from the open-item file. If a report calls for certain data, the systems analysts must be certain that it has been provided for in the structure of the data bank, and in the processing runs.

AUDIT OF DATA BANK CONTENTS

Before concluding that the data bank is complete, it is suggested that you assemble every report to be produced by the new computer system. Take one report at a time and trace the source of all information which will appear on that report. This represents an audit of the data bank contents before the system has been developed and programmed; it assures that nothing is missing from the data bank.

CHAPTER 12

The Two Receivables Methods

There are two widely used, but opposing receivables methods commonly found in the business world: open-item receivables and balance-forward receivables. Manufacturing and wholesale firms embrace the open-item method; retail and department stores invariably feature the balance-forward method of receivables accounting.

Nearly everyone is familiar with retail receivables, exemplified by credit card billing, department stores, and retail establishments of all types. Considerable evidence has accumulated to indicate that many executives and systems specialists have a tendency to accept the retail method as standard, since its use is so widespread. This basic misunderstanding of the significant differences between open-item accounting and the balance-forward method has resulted quite often in the installation of the retail receivable methods in manufacturing firms—with disastrous consequences. The purpose of this chapter is to assist a systems group engaged in computerizing receivables to make the correct decision as to the basic method that should be incorporated into the new receivables project.

Characteristics of Balance-Forward Method

No invoice terms or conditions apply in the consumer-oriented retail or balance-forward method of receivables accounting. Purchases made this month are considered to be due and payable next month. Cash received next month is posted routinely to the account as a credit—and applies in total against purchases of the prior month.

It is not necessary to identify individual paid items because of the absence of invoice terms. This method may be viewed as a ''balance-control'' method, which is illustrated by the type of statement typically used.

ACCOUNT STATEMENT

The balance-forward method features a complete account statement that shows the following information:

Opening balance brought forward from last month
Payments credited this month
Sales and returns for current month
Final statement balance at end of current month

In Figure 12.1 note the accounting data shown on the statement for Month No. 1:

Balance Forward	\$10.00
Payment	\$10.00-
Current Month Transactions	25.00
BALANCE	\$25.00

Cash received was merely posted to the account, and it cancelled out the balance brought forward from the prior month.

SYSTEM CONCEPTS: RETAIL VS MANUFACTURING RECEIVABLES

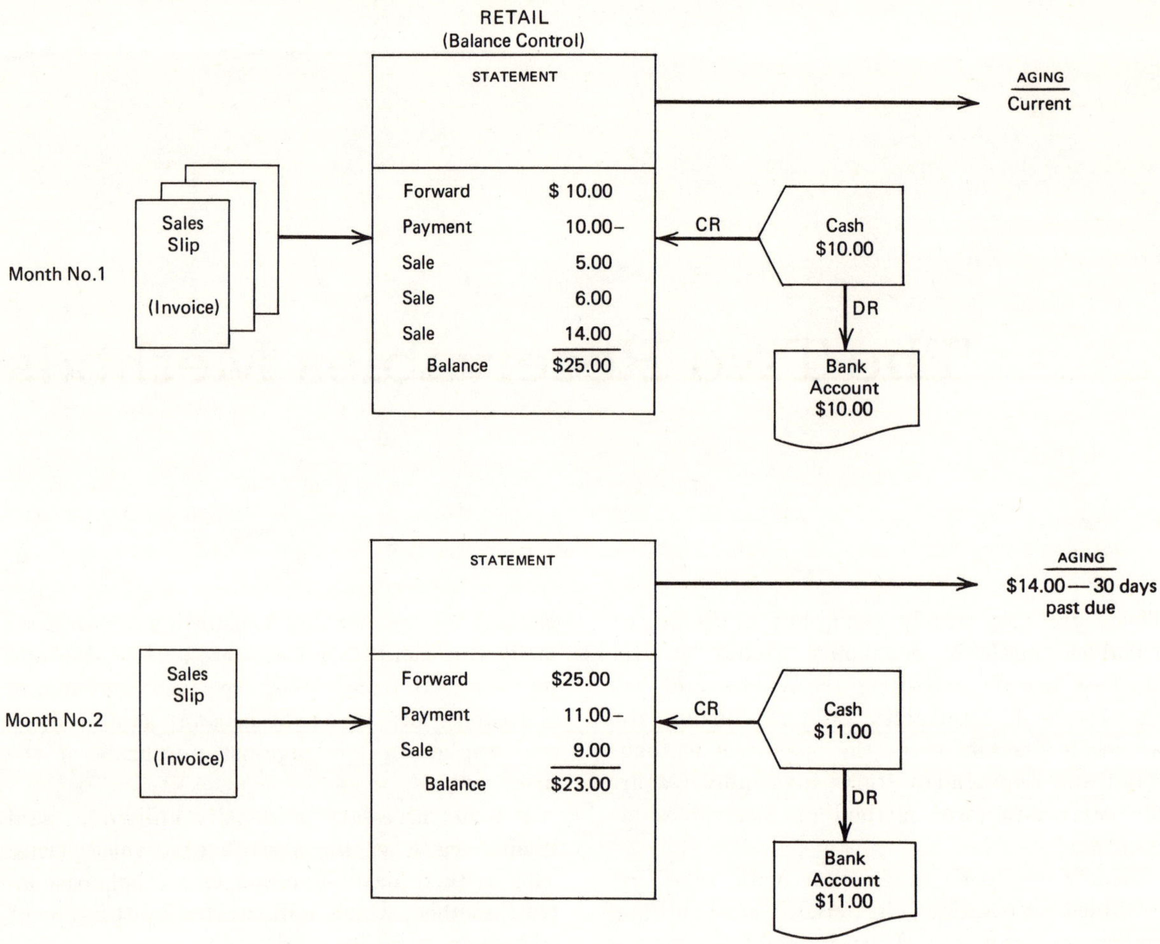

NOTE:

Terms: Balance net payable on one given date each month, usually the 10th. (No discounts or anticipation.)

Aging: Based on balance forward on each account.

Cash: Gross is posted to account without item analysis. Cash flows to the account.

Figure 12.1 Schematic of a retail-type account statement.

The statement for Month No. 2 shows the $25 balance brought forward from Month No. 1, then a payment received of only $11.00. One sale of $9 is reflected on the statement, resulting in a balance of $23.00 billed to a customer at month-end.

AGING POLICIES AND PROCEDURES

Since cash is not applied to specified open items, aging must be done on the basis of *monthly purchases* and *total cash received.* Therefore, cash received and posted to the account this month must be considered as applicable against purchases of last month.

Referring again to the statement schematic shown in Figure 12.1 as Month No. 1, the account balance of $25 is considered to be "current," since the payment received exactly offset the balance brought forward. However, the statement shown as Month No. 2 reveals that $14 is 30 days past due—because the cash payment of $11 does not cover the $25 balance brought forward from the prior month.

Characteristics of Trade Receivables

Trade receivables are neither retail nor consumer-oriented. They represent receivables from business firms and invariably feature invoice terms and conditions. When invoice terms are applied to an invoice, this creates one or more due dates. In effect, each invoice becomes a unique receivables item due and payable by the customer at a precisely calculated time.

Consider the following examples of how invoice terms create unique receivables:

	Date	*Terms*	*Discount Due Date*	*Final Due Date*	*Amount*
Invoice No. 1	9/03	2/10 N30	9/13	10/03	1000.00
Invoice No. 2	9/03	N60	—	11/02	1000.00

Each invoice bears the same date, but the second one is not due and payable until 30 days after the maturity of the first invoice because of the longer terms offered to the customer.

AS OF DATING

Another characteristic of trade receivables is the existence of "future dating" or "as of" dating. This may create a final due date extending several months into the future. For example, applying terms of 2/10 N30 *As Of 3/01* to an invoice dated 12/01 creates a final due date of 3/31.

CASH APPLICATION

When cash is received, the remittance must be carefully applied to specific open invoices. Cash is not posted to the account unless the customer specifies that he is making an on-account payment. The paid items are flagged, "keyed off" —or physically removed in the instance of a data processing system. When cash is taken on account, the customer must eventually designate the specific invoices to be covered by the on-account payment, plus additional cash paid, or credits used to settle indicated invoices.

Refer to Figure 12.2; this is a representation of a customer's open-item ledger record kept for trade receivables. A remittance received from the customer indicated that he was paying invoices No. 123 and No. 131. Invoice terms offered a cash discount of 2% on these items; the remitter properly deducted $2 from each $100 gross amount as discount earned. In addition, the remitter deducted 4 cents for "anticipation" or early interest.

After cash was applied and the paid items "keyed off," the gross credit of $200 was posted to the account, since the ledger shown here was maintained on accounting machines. (In a typical computerized receivables accounting system the paid items are simply *removed* from the account when cash is applied to them.)

In summary, trade receivables feature open-item control whereas the retail method features *balance* control.

CUSTOMER PAYABLES METHODS

A well-designed trade receivables system should be a mirror image of the prevailing payables methods and procedures found in customer payables offices. Moreover, accounts payable departments charged with processing and paying vendor invoices operate on the basis of paying each individual invoice when due, according to the vendor's terms and conditions. In other words, these departments function on the basis of processing individual invoices; they pay little attention to full account statements that are received from vendors which show current debits and credits and past due items also.

STATEMENT FORMAT AND DUNNING

Dunning is based on the final due date of an invoice. Since this is true, the use of past due statements is quite common in trade receivables. That is, the statement sent to a customer usually shows only those specific items that are past due at time of statement preparation. This serves the purpose of calling to the attention of the customer's accounts payable department the *specific invoices* that require processing and payment.

Experience has shown that a full account statement showing all open items, including current invoices, is an effective collection tool for small retail accounts that base their accounting and payment procedures on the vendor's statement. However, sending such a statement to a large department store or a manufacturing firm is a waste of time and postage.

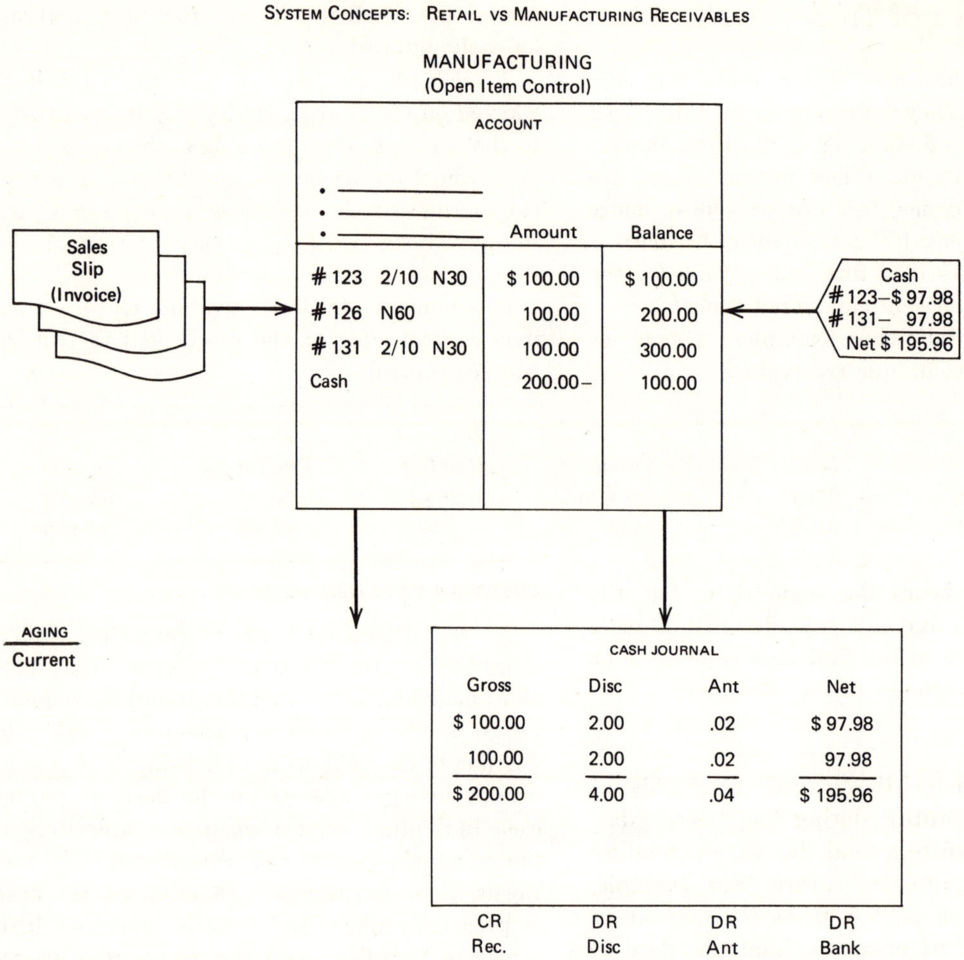

NOTE:

Terms: Terms are applicable to each invoice, not to account. Payment date and conditions are based on individual terms of sale.

Aging: Based on analysis of open unpaid invoices.

Cash: Gross is posted to account after item analysis. Cash flows through the account.

Figure 12.2 The representation of a customer's open-item ledger record.

AGING

Since each open invoice is due and payable on a specified final due date, aging must be done on the basis of each-open item. Any attempt to age on the basis of the total purchase for a month compared to cash received the following month would be meaningless.

As indicated, the basis for all aging is the *final due date* that was generated by the initial application of invoice terms to an invoice. This due date is the basis also for the preparation of past due statements or dunning letters. Because of the importance of the final due date, I suggest that it be included in each open invoice record when receivables are computerized and kept on magnetic tape or disk devices. This suggestion is explained more fully in a subsequent chapter dealing with mechanizing invoice terms.

AGING CREDITS

If invoice terms are applied to a credit, it may be aged on the basis of the final due date the same as an open invoice. However, remember that it is meaningless to use the date of the credit as the basis for applying invoice terms. If the credit can be referenced back to an invoice, the *invoice date* (considered to be the "as of" date) is the appropriate base date for application of terms.

Since experience indicates that more than 50% of all credits cannot, from a practical viewpoint, be identified as to the original invoice that started the chain of transactions—the aging of credits becomes a difficult problem. One solution for unidentified credits—applicable to credits for returned goods only—is to arbitrarily "back date" the credit by applying an "as of" date that is determined by subtracting the number of terms days usually granted to the customer from the date of the credit document.

An example of the back dating technique:

Date of Credit	*Usual Invoice Terms*	*As of Date to Apply*
6/25	N30	5/26

Now, by applying the invoice terms of N30 to the as of date of 5/26, we have created a final due date of 6/25—which coincides with the date of the credit document.

Some credit managers place open credits in the "current" column when aging receivables; others believe that it is appropriate to apply them against the oldest invoices on the account on an arbitrary basis. Actually, there seems to be considerable justification for offsetting credits against the oldest open invoices. For example, extensive studies indicate that credits for returned merchandise, when eventually issued, usually apply against invoices issued anywhere from a few days to several months prior to the preparation of the credit document.

MANY TYPES OF CREDITS

A major difficulty in determining appropriate policies for controlling the aging of credits is that they are issued for a wide variety of reasons. Consider the instance of credits issued for special purposes, such as cooperative advertising, merchandise displays, premiums, volume rebates, and the like. This type of credit cannot be associated with any invoice. Invoice terms do not apply. Therefore, credits of this type should be aged based on the date of issuance of the credit.

Summary

It is of paramount importance to the success of your receivables project to analyze the cash application and dunning requirements of your firm before making an empirical decision as to which receivables method should be selected as the basis for computerization. It is not unusual to find firms with both retail customers and trade customers. In this situation it may be necessary to install a system that features both approaches.

Credit managers and systems analysts should be aware of the dangers of applying balance-forward methods to trade receivables that feature invoice terms. When this is done, the collection function begins to collapse about four months after initiating the balance-forward system. This is true because of the sheer necessity of identifying to the customer those specific invoices that are now past due and payable. When collectors attempt to work from balance-forward amounts, the collection effort becomes increasingly futile and ineffective.

CHAPTER 13

How to Mechanize Invoice Terms

It is difficult to overemphasize the importance of accurately mechanizing invoice terms as the basis for maintaining trade receivables. This step is the foundation for many vital functions that are included in the overall computerized receivables system. For example, an aged trial balance cannot be accurately produced unless the final due date of each unpaid invoice is available. A past due statement may be very inaccurate if the determination of past due invoices is based on the invoice date plus standard or ''average'' terms days. For example, any invoice with an ''as of'' date in the terms may not be due for several months from the invoice date. Also, any invoice subject to terms that included extra days would not be due at the same time that invoices subject to normal terms come due.

DISCOUNT DUE DATE

A further consideration is that the process of applying cash discount terms to invoices generates a discount due date for each invoice. This becomes significant when an invoice is paid because of the necessity for determining whether the remitter earned the discount taken—or failed to meet the discount terms thus forfeiting the original discount amount available to him. To make this determination, the computer simply compares the effective date of payment with the discount due date. The discount due date is sometimes useful also for preparing follow-up letters which remind customers who usually pay on a discount basis that they apparently overlooked one or more items that have now gone past the discount due date.

PAY HABITS DATA

Another use for the two due dates created by invoice terms is the accumulation of *pay habits data* about each customer for use in credit-work and credit-granting functions. This requires the computer to determine whether each paid invoice was paid ''early—prompt—or late.'' These are the three categories generally used in building up pay habits information. (Early is synonymous with ''discount'' basis.)

The definitions of these three classifications are as follows:

Early. The customer pays in time to earn the discount—or pays an invoice subject to net terms well before the due date.

Prompt. The customer fails to earn the discount but pays in time to avoid the classification of paying late.

Late. The customer pays well beyond the final due date.

TRIGGERS COLLECTION LETTERS

Computers are increasingly being used for writing collection letters as well as for preparing past due statements. The basis for determining those accounts that require the preparation of a collection letter is a *comparison* of the date of last cash processed with the final due date in each open invoice—plus reference to a collection status code stored in the invoice record. The status code enables the computer to determine *which* collection letter (Nos. 1, 2, or 3) is applicable to each account—if one or more past due items are present at the time of reviewing all accounts.

TYPES OF TERMS

All trade terms may be classified as to two basic types: cash discount terms and trade discount terms. The difference between these two types becomes important in the computer audit of remittances, which involves determination of discount earned or unearned, and in calculating remittance differences.

CASH DISCOUNT TERMS

As all credit men know, cash discount terms are always multi-option terms; the last option is always "net," which precludes taking any discount. Several examples of these terms are:

1/10 N30
2/10 N30
5/10 4/70/ N71
2/10 EOM, N25th

The essence of cash discount terms is that the seller offers a cash discount to the buyer in return for payment before the final due date. If the buyer elects to pay on the basis of the final, long terms he is not supposed to qualify for any cash discount.

TRADE DISCOUNT TERMS

Trade terms also offer discounts; the difference is that the available discount is considered to be a *reduction* of the selling price—and is always available to the customer regardless of the lateness of payment. Examples of trade discount terms are:

2/10 Prox
2/10 EOM
2/30, 1/31
2/10
3/30

Notice that it is possible for trade terms to include more than one option. However, these terms never include the code letter "N" (for net) in any option.

TERMS MUST BE CONVERTED TO MATHEMATICS

For the purpose of programming and mechanizing invoice terms, they must be viewed as representing a definite number of days to add to a base date—to calculate the discount due date and a final due date. Terms of 2/10 N30 offer two time periods to the customer: payment in 10 days or in 30 days. By using an invoice date of 6/12 as the base, you add 10 days to 6/12 to calculate the discount due date of 6/22. Likewise, we find the final due date by adding 30 days to the base date of 6/12.

BASE DATES

Invoice terms are nearly always added to one of two base dates:

- Invoice Date
- As of date (future dating)

The "as of" date takes precedence over the invoice date *whenever it appears as part of the invoice terms.*

FUTURE DATING

Future dating is employed as a sales tool by manufacturers of seasonal merchandise. By offering long terms through future dating, the manufacturer can induce the distributor or retailer to buy now, accept the merchandise—and pay during the season when the merchandise will be turned over for cash.

APPLY TERMS TO EACH INVOICE

When mechanizing invoice terms, beware of applying terms to invoices based on a terms code that is part of the customer header information or found in the data bank. By assigning a terms code to the customer, the seller becomes locked into a situation where only one line of products or one division can sell to the customer—assuming typical situations where various products or those sold by various divisions are subject to variable terms. Application of terms from the overall terms code may produce inaccurate due dates because of invoices introduced into the customer's account from time to time that have terms at variance with the standard terms code included in the customer header record.

For these and other reasons the invoice terms should always be applied to each individual invoice. Furthermore, the results of the application of terms should be stored in the unit invoice record for permanent use and reference. That is, each invoice record found on the customer's open-item file should contain the *discount due date* and the *final due date.* (Figure 6.1, in Chapter 6, shows a typical open-item invoice record including these two due dates.)

The discount amount or amounts may also be stored as part of the invoice record for convenience during the remittance audit function. The actual terms may also be stored—or a code indicating the terms may be utilized in lieu of recording the actual discrete terms.

MULTIPLE DISCOUNT DUE DATES

As a basis for mechanizing invoice terms, prepare a master list of all invoice terms found in the firm. These terms then must be analyzed and reviewed very carefully by all concerned. Audit requirements as they relate to invoice terms should receive special attention at this time. For example, a decision must be made as to the advisability of storing more than one set of discount terms and due dates in each invoice record: Consider these terms:

5/10 4/70 3/130 N131

You may decide to ignore the middle options and store only the discount due date developed from the first option, plus the final due date.

SPECIAL PROBLEM TERMS

Suppose that the sales department uses special terms as part of an overall sales program which offers the following terms:

5% April 10, 2% August 10th, N25th

Notice that the discount rate drops from 5% to 2%—and that the period of time between the two due dates covers several months. For audit purposes it would be advisable to store both discount due dates and the final due date in the invoice record.

USE OF TERMS CODE FOR AUDIT

In addition to considering the mathematics involved in mechanizing invoice terms, there is also, quite often, a need to identify each set of terms by a *type* code. The reason for this is that the programming routines written for a high-speed computer audit of remittances may necessarily have to be variable—based on the terms type. For instance, consider the difference between auditing an invoice subject to cash discount terms as compared to an invoice subject to trade discount terms. In the case of the latter, the computer should credit the available discount amount to the customer regardless of the lateness of payment.

Cash discount terms are usually identifiable by the presence of the code letter "N" in the final option. When the computer recognizes that the applicable terms are "cash," it will apply a special set of tests to the invoice to determine if the available discount was earned by early payment, or if the customer lost the discount by going past the discount due date plus a prefigured grace period.

In actual practice, the presence of the code letter "N" may not be the final determinant as to allowing the discount. You may find, for example, that the credit department treats certain "cash" discount terms as *trade terms* as a matter of policy. Consider terms such as 8% 10 EOM, N25th. The discount rate of 8% is obviously too great to be considered as an incentive to pay early; it is a reduction of the selling price. Therefore, even though the last option indicates "net," these terms would normally be handled as trade terms. By including a terms type code when mechanizing this set of terms, the computer can be programmed to base its discount calculations on the indicative code instead of on the basis of the code letter "N."

USE OF TERMS TABLE

When order/invoice preparation is handled by a computer, terms are usually applied to each invoice by use of a terms table. The table contains a list of all the possible terms plus a key number of two or three digits known as the terms code. Under this arrangement it is necessary to store only the terms code in each invoice *along with the due dates.* The full meaning of the terms code can be found by referencing back to the terms table wherever necessary.

EOM AND PROX TERMS

EOM and Prox terms are different from other terms in many respects that affect the mechanization process. These terms typically appear as follows:

1% 10 EOM
2% 10 Prox
2% 10 Prox, N 25th

There is *always an implied "as of" date* included in EOM or Prox terms. That is, if 10 days are added to an invoice date of 6/10, the due date calculated mathematically is 6/20. Yet the terms promise the buyer that he can take a discount if he pays by the *10th of next month.* If the program recognizes the special situation inherent in EOM or Prox terms, it will automatically bring in an as of date that is the *last day* of the current month. Now, by adding 10 days to *6/30* the computer calculates and stores the correct discount due date of 7/10.

Another unusual aspect of these terms is that the customer (by trade practice) gains an extra month if the invoice is dated the *25th or later.* (In some trades the cutoff date is as early as the 20th). Therefore, the computer must scan the invoice date, then determine the appropriate "as of" date. For example, the *as of date* for an invoice dated 6/27, and subject to terms of 2% 10 Prox is 7/31, not 6/30. One way to handle this is merely to add the digit 1 to the month number when terms are EOM or Prox, and the invoice date is equal to or greater than the stated cutoff date (20th or 25th).

It is worth noting that mechanizing single option EOM terms produces a discount due date and a final due date that are identical.

EFFECTS OF EXTRA DAYS FOUND IN TERMS

Many terms grant extra days to the buyer. Typical terms are:

2% 10 N 30 plus 30 extra
1% 60 plus 60 X
2% 30 N 31 plus 60 extra

Extra days without interest (free to the customer) should have the effect of increasing *both due dates.* This is done by adding the number of extra days to both sides of the equation.

Example. 2/*10* N*30* plus 30 extra; invoice is dated 9/12/71.

	Discount Days	*Long-Term Days*
Regular terms days	10	30
Plus extra days	30	30
Totals	40	60

Therefore, to calculate the two due dates for the invoice dated 7/12, add 40 days and 60 days to this base date.

EXTRA DAYS AT INTEREST

Where the seller grants the buyer extra days *at interest,* the entire situation changes. Extra days that are to be paid for as interest by the customer have *no effect* on calculating the discount due date—but are part of the equation for figuring the final due date. See the example below for terms such as 1% 10, N 30 plus 30 × @ 8%. The invoice date is 4/10.

	Discount Days	*Long-Term Days*
Regular terms days	10	30
Plus extra days	—	30
Totals	10	60

The two correct due dates are 4/20—and 6/09. Notice that the extra 30 days are not reflected in the discount due date.

OTHER ASPECTS OF "EXTRA DAYS"

It may be unwise to add the extra days into the due date calculations, and then lose sight of the fact that the original terms included this element of extra days. One reason for stating this is that audit requirements frequently include the calculation of anticipation, or early interest. And, the anticipation may not be allowable beyond the final due date as calculated *without considering the number of days.* (The rules governing the taking of anticipation vary from one line of business to another.) This aspect of the cash audit function should be studied carefully before a final decision is made regarding the necessary terms data to store in each invoice record.

APPLICATION OF TERMS TO INVOICE CREDITS

There are two types of credits in a trade receivables environment: invoice credits representing returned merchandise, and all others. Credits issued as a promotional allowance, for a price adjustment, for a concealed shortage, or other adjustments usually are issued with no terms applied. The customer is entitled to the full face amount of the credit document. Therefore, this represents "net" terms.

Invoice credits representing returned merchandise should have the same terms applied as those found on the original invoice. This requires identifying the source of the returned shipment as to invoice number, then applying the appropriate terms to the credit. The application of discount terms to a credit has the effect of reducing the face value of the credit. A credit for $1000 subject to terms of 2% is worth only $980 cash to the customer.

Failure to consistently apply invoice terms to merchandise credits may be considered as a profit leak of substantial proportions. If a firm sells $100 million per year on terms of 2% 10, N 30 and writes credit memo for returned goods totalling $5 million, there is a potential profit loss of 2% × $5 million or $100,000.

DUE DATES

Since a credit invoice is the reverse of a regular invoice, the record should include terms and the resulting due dates. However, the question arises: Should terms be applied to the date of the credit document the same as is done with an invoice? Actually, terms should be applied to the *original invoice date,* if known. This means that each merchandise credit automatically has an "as of" date—the date of the invoice to which the credit is related.

Unfortunately, it is not possible to pinpoint the invoice date involved in more than 50% of all credits issued by a typical, large industrial firm. Therefore, some arbitrary method of establishing the base date must be found. One method is to estimate the average length of time that elapses between the original transaction and the subsequent issuance of a credit of any type. Let us assume that a special study shows that this time period is 60 days. Once this is established, set up a policy of *back-dating any credit 60 days* from the date of the credit document for the application of terms.

CHANGES OF TERMS

After terms have been applied to each invoice as part of a special computer run and the invoice is on the customer master file, it may be necessary subsequently to change the terms in the invoice record, and also to change the due dates. This is accomplished by a special input entry described in the chapter dealing with journal entries.

Methods for Calculating Due Dates

Having studied the meaning of terms and the mathematics involved in multi-option terms, let us now examine ways and means of calculating the various due dates that result from applying a set of terms to a base date. Programmers utilize, at least, three different methods of accomplishing this.

INTERNAL CALENDAR REQUIRED

For calculating the invoice due dates, the computer program must include a subroutine that is the equivalent of an internal calendar to enable the machine to convert calendar-oriented numeric dates to internal mathematical values. Then, through the addition or subtraction of the number of days from the calendar or table, the computer can determine the due dates as absolute mathematical values, and then reconvert the result to an understandable calendar date for the benefit of users of the forms and reports that include printed dates.

As mentioned before, this may be accomplished in various ways, several of which are explained on subsequent pages.

Table 13.1
Table of Calendar Differences

Month Number	Number of Days' Adjustment
01	−1
02	−1 (Adjust table for Leap Year)
03	0
04	0
05	+1
06	+1
07	+2
08	+3
09	+3
10	+4
11	+4
12	+5

This table is based on the assumption that each of the 12 months include 30 calendar days. The number of days in the adjustment column represents the *cumulative adjustment* for any month during the year.

The programmer may prefer to use the simple table shown below:

FOCAL DATE METHOD OF CALCULATING A TIME INTERVAL

Suppose that the computer is required to calculate the number of days from 9/29/69 to

Table 13.2
Calendar Months With Actual Number of Days

01	31
02	28 (29)
03	31
04	30
05	31
06	30
07	31
08	31
09	30
10	31
11	30
12	31

3/5/70, using a focal date as a starting point and the values in Table 13.1. The equation, using 1/1/68 as the focal date, looks like this:

1/1/68 $\quad I_1 = 1Y + 8M + 29D$ $\quad$ 9/29/69

X____________________________X

$I_2 + 2Y + 2M + 5D$ $\quad$ 3/5/70

X____________________________________X

$$\text{Interval} + I_2 - I_1$$
$$= (730 + 60 - 1 + 0 + 5) - (365 + 240 + 3 + 0 + 29)$$
$$= 157 \text{ days}$$

JULIAN CALENDAR METHOD

Many manufacturing firms convert each day of the year to a manufacturing day number. January first on the calendar becomes day No. 001, January second is No. 002, etc. December thirty-first is either day No. 365 or No. 366. If a large table of day numbers is included in a computer program, the computer can utilize these days numbers for calculating the due dates. Let us examine how it would figure the time interval from 9/29/69 to 3/5/70:

1. Convert 3/5/70 to the Julian equivalent: 70*064* (70 is the year)
2. Convert 9/29/69 to the Julian number: 69*272*
3. Subtract the lesser value from the greater value: 70064 − 69272
4. The result mathematically is 157 (number of days)

CALCULATING DUE DATES

The reverse procedure is, of course, utilized for determining due dates when the number of days is applied to a base date.

Invoice Date	*Terms*
3/12	2/60 N61

The Julian equivalent for 3/12 is 071. Add 60 to this; the result is 131. By converting back to the calendar equivalent of this Julian number, we find that 131 is 5/11—which is the discount due date.

TIME PERIOD TO BE COVERED BY CALENDAR

The method selected for calculating the due dates and time intervals should make it possible to set up due dates for extended terms, which create maturities far into the future. Also, the method should make it possible to "back-date" a credit from one to two years in the past—since the *date* of the original merchandise invoice is the "as of" date for a credit.

Summary

The proper mechanizing of invoice terms is of the utmost importance when computerizing trade receivables. The due dates produced by the program written for this purpose are the bases for all aging and dunning—and for the determination of earned versus unearned discount when an invoice is eventually paid and is audited by the computer.

CHAPTER 14

Application and Control of Cash

This is the first of two chapters that cover cash application, computer auditing of remittances, and control over differences which result from the audit. Several different methods of cash application will be explained and illustrated. In order to establish the appropriate foundation for such an extensive subject, let us first review the fundamental nature of trade receivables and then examine the cash application methods generally used before the advent of computers.

TRADE RECEIVABLES ARE SIMILAR TO AN INVENTORY FILE

In a prior chapter we established the fact that trade receivables are quite different from retail receivables. Whereas cash is posted *to* the account in a retail system, cash must be applied to specific open items when invoice terms and conditions create invoice records that are potentially or actually unique records insofar as the due dates are concerned.

The unpaid invoices and other items that constitute one customer's account may be looked at as an inventory of open items which, together, represent his total liability to the seller. Likewise, the open items that make up the entire customer receivables file may be considered to be the same as a finished goods inventory account —an asset that is about to be converted to cash.

Under these conditions, cash cannot be merely posted to the account; it represents the authority to identify and to remove those ''inventory'' items that are ''settled'' by the remittance. We see, then, that the application of cash reduces our inventory of open customer items. The typical data processing approach follows this theory in that each paid item is *physically removed* at once from the customer file as a result of cash application. Invoices remaining on the file at any given time are those that are still open and unpaid.

Cash Application Methods Before Computers

Before computers became generally available for application to trade receivables, business firms used three primary methods of maintaining detailed receivable records:

- Machine or hand-posted unit ledger sheets
- Invoice copies filed in trays or special housing units
- Punched cards for processing by tabulating machines

UNIT LEDGER SHEETS

For many years the receivables record most commonly found in the business community was customer ledgers. Every invoice or credit was posted to a sheet that bore the customer's name and address at the top. When cash was received, it was first applied to specific items by ''keying'' the paid items to tie them into the cash amount that was posted later as a credit. For example, if the first check received paid three invoices, all three debit amounts would be identified with key code 1. In turn, this code was entered next to the gross cash credit *posted to the account.*

If the customer records were posted by a bookkeeping machine, it was customary to subtract the gross cash credit from the account balance and to extend a new balance. If the key-off were done properly, the sum of all open items would always equal the account balance. However, it is important to note that there was no proof of accuracy of keying off paid items manually (see Figure 14.1). Notice that the key-off method shown on the sample customer ledger utilizes the *cash payment date* as the paid item identifier.

UNIT INVOICE METHOD

Over the years many firms selected an accounting plan that eliminated the necessity for posting debits or credits to a customer record. Under the "simplified unit invoice accounting plan"—often referred to by the trade name of SUIAP (Remington-Rand)—one copy of the original invoice was placed in a file folder or in a specially designed document pocket within a fire-resistant desk. The accumulation of documents represented the receivables records for each account.

When cash was received, the bookkeeper reviewed all the accumulated documents and removed the ones that were paid. If cash was taken on account, the bookkeeper prepared a special form that was inserted into the file or pocket. When the cash was eventually applied to specific invoices, the bookkeeper pulled the received-on-account cash form from the file.

This method worked reasonably well for firms with short due dates and with a minimum of unadjusted deductions. However, there were several major disadvantages of the unit invoice plan:

- No customer pay habit history.
- No convenient, chronological history of debits and credits for reference or back-tracking. Paid items were physically filed in a special paid file; this was the source for references of all types.
- Trial balance difficulties were common. Unless the document paper flow into and out of the file was carefully audited and controlled, it was very difficult to trace the reason for an out-of-balance situation at monthend.

THE PUNCHED CARD METHOD

As tabulating equipment came into wide use in the decade of the 1950s, an increasing number of firms mechanized their trade receivables by installing receivables accounting systems featuring the use of a punched card for each invoice —and for every other type of open item which makes up a typical receivables file of accounting records. These cards were interpreted (printed) across the top; the coded information punched in the cards was visible to the bookkeeper because of the printed data across the top edge of the card.

Each punched card representing an invoice typically contained the following information (see Figure 14.2):

Account number
Invoice date
Invoice number
Terms or terms code number
Discount amount
Discount due date
Final due date
Invoice amount

The unit punched cards were usually kept in metal trays under the control of a seated bookkeeper. To apply cash, the bookkeeper located the file of interpreted cards, studied the paid item information supplied by the customer's remittance voucher—then removed the punched cards representing each invoice being paid or credit being used by the customer. If an unadjusted deduction appeared as part of the remittance, the bookkeeper prepared the necessary papers and routed one copy to a keypunch department. Here, the deduction information was punched into a card with a distinctive color band across the top which was later placed in the bookkeeper's file of punched cards. Cash received and identified as on account was handled in a similar manner.

FUNCTIONS PERFORMED BY A CASH APPLICATION BOOKKEEPER

A review of the typical functions of a cash application bookkeeper working with unit ledger records, invoice copies, or punched card files pro-

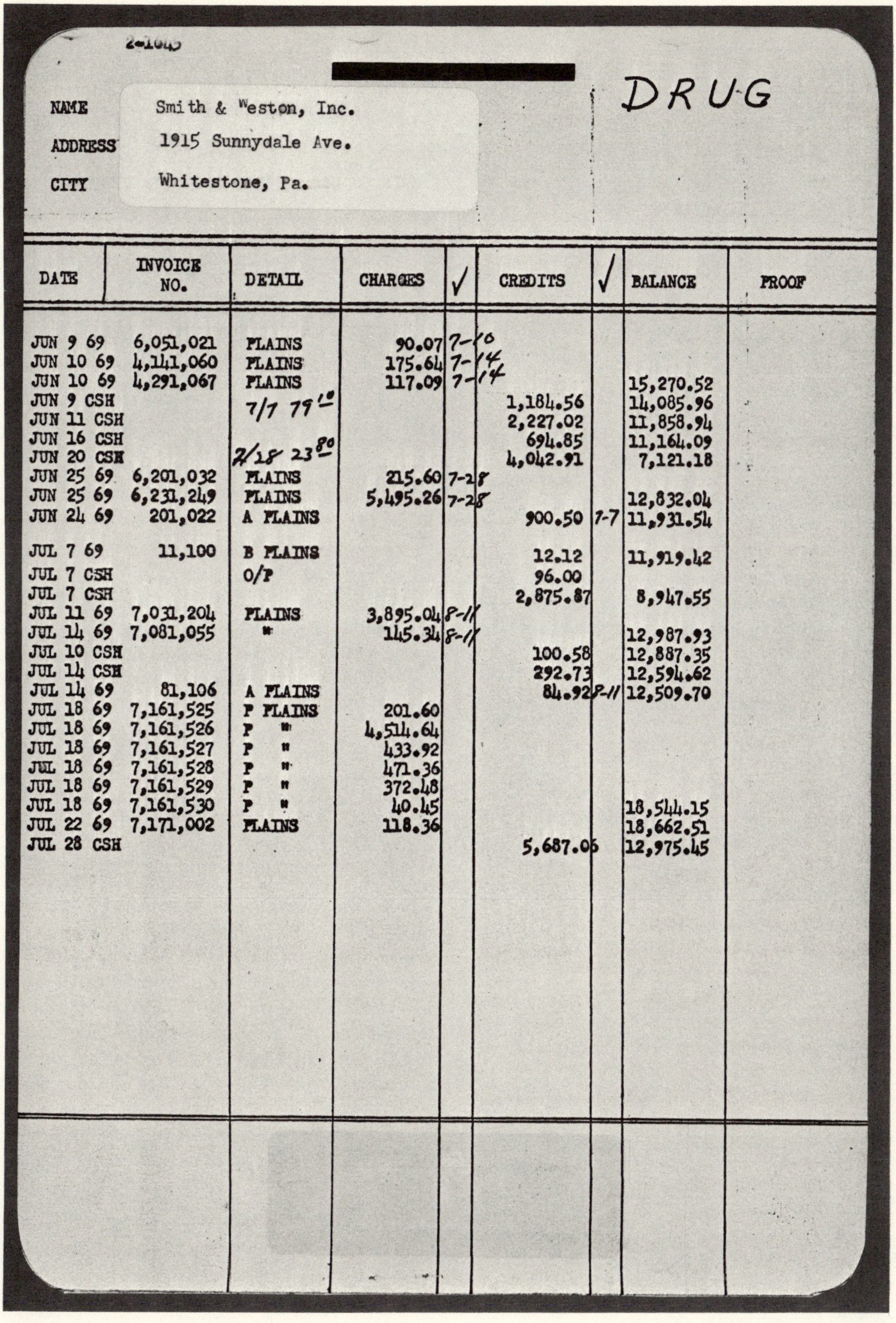

2-1645

DRUG

NAME Smith & Weston, Inc.
ADDRESS 1915 Sunnydale Ave.
CITY Whitestone, Pa.

DATE	INVOICE NO.	DETAIL	CHARGES	√	CREDITS	√	BALANCE	PROOF
JUN 9 69	6,051,021	PLAINS	90.07	7-10				
JUN 10 69	4,141,060	PLAINS	175.64	7-14				
JUN 10 69	4,291,067	PLAINS	117.09	7-14			15,270.52	
JUN 9 CSH		7/7 79.10			1,184.56		14,085.96	
JUN 11 CSH					2,227.02		11,858.94	
JUN 16 CSH					694.85		11,164.09	
JUN 20 CSH		7/28 23.80			4,042.91		7,121.18	
JUN 25 69	6,201,032	PLAINS	215.60	7-28				
JUN 25 69	6,231,249	PLAINS	5,495.26	7-28			12,832.04	
JUN 24 69	201,022	A PLAINS			900.50	7-7	11,931.54	
JUL 7 69	11,100	B PLAINS			12.12		11,919.42	
JUL 7 CSH		O/P			96.00			
JUL 7 CSH					2,875.87		8,947.55	
JUL 11 69	7,031,204	PLAINS	3,895.04	8-11				
JUL 14 69	7,081,055	"	145.34	8-11			12,987.93	
JUL 10 CSH					100.58		12,887.35	
JUL 14 CSH					292.73		12,594.62	
JUL 14 69	81,106	A PLAINS			84.92	8-11	12,509.70	
JUL 18 69	7,161,525	P PLAINS	201.60					
JUL 18 69	7,161,526	P "	4,514.64					
JUL 18 69	7,161,527	P "	433.92					
JUL 18 69	7,161,528	P "	471.36					
JUL 18 69	7,161,529	P "	372.48					
JUL 18 69	7,161,530	P "	40.45				18,544.15	
JUL 22 69	7,171,002	PLAINS	118.36				18,662.51	
JUL 28 CSH					5,687.06		12,975.45	

Figure 14.1 Typical machine-posted ledger card.

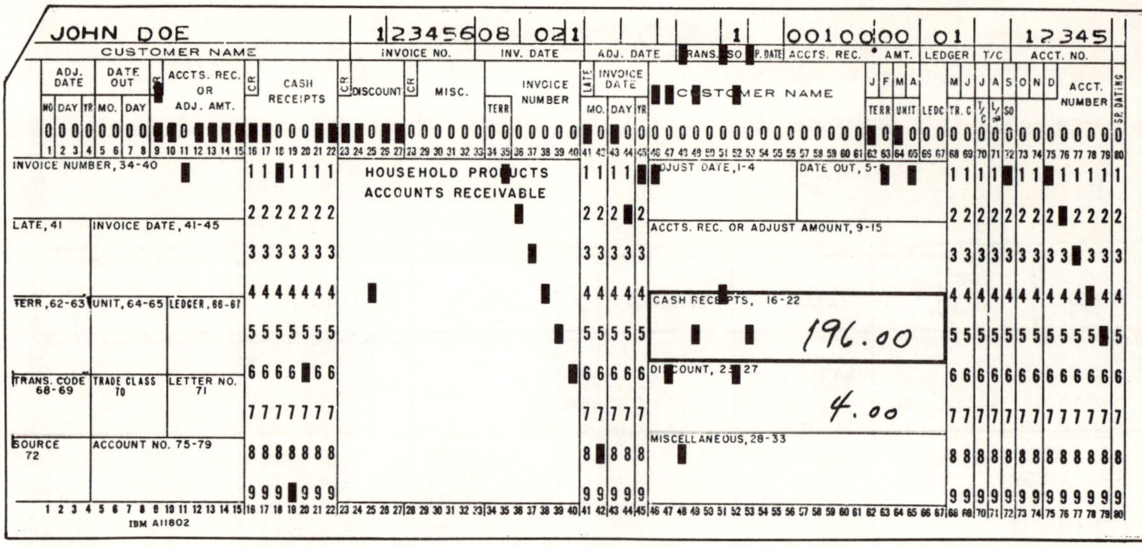

Figure 14.2 Sample tab card representing an invoice.

vides evidence that cash appliers perform many very important functions—including an audit of each remittance plus the creation of the necessary documents representing unadjusted deductions, unearned discount taken, and miscellaneous shortages and overages (see Figure 14.3).

Figure 14.3

Typical Functions of a Cash Application Bookkeeper

1. Studies remittance—determines the specific invoices being paid, or credits applied.
2. Keys off paid items—or PULLS paid items from file.
3. Audits the remittance to detect:
   a. Correct amount of earned discount, if any.
   b. Unearned discount taken.
   c. Excess discount taken.
   d. Error difference.
4. Writes some type of record for later posting of cash credits.
5. Creates paper work for special problems encountered, such as:
   a. Unadjusted deduction found on remittance (freight allowance taken, damaged goods, wrong price, wrong quantity, etc.—customer claims)
   b. Excess or unearned discount taken.
   c. Remittance shortage.
6. Balances the batch of cash processed.

CHECK PRODUCTION USUALLY FOUND

1. For receivables other than trade accounts selling to retail businesses, each check pays, on the average, 2.5 invoices.
2. If accounting machine ledger sheets represent the receivable records, even an experienced cash application bookkeeper will seldom handle more than 80 checks per day.
3. If open items are represented by punched cards filed in indexed tubs, a well-trained cash application bookkeeper—who also performs the same steps listed above—should process from 80 to 100 checks per day.

AVERAGE BOOKKEEPER PRODUCTIVITY

It is well known that clerical productivity varies greatly from one firm to another, even when the personnel are performing precisely the same duties. The volume of productive work done by clerical workers hinges on the three key elements of training, motivation, and supervision, and will vary accordingly. The production figures quoted here are taken from many actual installations found in many different types of business firms and may be used as a guideline for evaluating the work done in your own office:

- *Applying cash to open items on machine-posted ledger sheets.* If each check pays an average of 2½ to 3 items, the work standard for an experienced cash applier is about 80 checks per day. If the average number of items paid by each check is 5 (typical of customers who are retailers), the number of checks handled will drop to about 60 per day.

- *Punched card system.* Given the same statistics as those in the prior paragraph, the cash applier will process about the same number of checks under the punched card system as under the ledger card method.

Cash Application Methods with Computerized Receivables

Several large firms first computerized their trade receivables in the 1959 to 1960 era when computers for business uses were still in their infancy. The availability of the small, low-priced IBM 1401 computer in large numbers, beginning in late 1961, opened the door to hundreds of computer installations handling receivables. This trend toward mechanization has intensified in recent years because of the increasing paper work volume and high interest rates, which made it imperative to control the receivables asset at all times.

FIVE METHODS OF CASH APPLICATION

During the past ten years hundreds of firms have computerized their receivables, credit, and collection functions. As a result of broad experience and recent technical developments, there are now five different methods of cash application to consider when planning the computerization of trade receivables.

1. Apply cash by referring to a computer-printed list of open items.
2. Use the original deck of interpreted, punched invoice cards as a means of informing the computer of specific paid items.
3. Apply cash by studying a list of open items displayed on a view screen resembling a TV screen. This device is a cathode ray tube—known in the trade as a CRT unit—and is cable-connected directly to the computer. The cash applier signals to the computer which items are being paid; the computer flags the paid records and performs an audit instantly.
4. Apply cash by studying a list of open items displayed on a microfilm reader screen. The items making up each account are extracted from a magnetic tape written during a file updating run and provided in print-format for the conversion process known as "Micromation."

   Under this method the cash applier may use various methods of recording or reporting paid items to the computer; one method involves obtaining a ledger copy instantly from the microfilm reader by depressing a print button.
5. Program the computer for "automatic cash" processing. There are two versions of automatic cash:
   (1) Keypunch only the customer's account number and the net check amount. The computer brings into working memory the entire file of open items and proceeds to perform a series of algorithms to determine which invoice, or combination of invoices, equals the check amount. When a "hit" is made, the computer flags or deletes the items as "paid."
   (2) Keypunch specific paid item data for each invoice as supplied by the customer's remittance advice or voucher. If the remitter has provided a list of invoice numbers, then keypunch the numbers for input to the computer, along with the check information.

The computer is programmed to search out the indicated invoices on the open item file, and to flag or delete the paid item or items.

As explained in the next chapter, the computer usually is required to print a detailed list of open items for an account if the cash application steps fail to find the indicated items—or the mathematical audit of the remittance indicates a major difference. This "exception report" is routed to bookkeepers who make a manual application of the check, and manually audit the remittance before entering the data into another computer run.

TWO PRIMARY METHODS

Analysis of the five methods reveals that basically there are only two different approaches—and each of these includes certain characteristics of the other basic method:

- The pre-identification method
- The "post identification" method, otherwise known as "automatic cash"

The pre-identification method involves matching the check or remittance advice to a list or a display of all open items on the remitter's account. The cash applier is required simply to identify each item indicated as being paid, and to set up unadjusted deductions for input and for posting back to the customer's account.

The "automatic cash" method may entail a certain amount of *pre-identification of paid item data* as provided by the remitter for input to the computer test runs. And, it will be necessary to provide a backup staff of cash appliers to handle and to dispose of the accounts where the computer was unable to handle properly the respective remittances. This is strictly a manual process of applying cash, auditing each remittance, and of preparing input for a secondary set of computer runs. This step is the "post identification" process referred to above.

Pre-identification Methods of Cash Application

Before providing the details of procedures under a pre-identification method, it should be clearly recognized that the step of identifying specific paid items is only the *first* of many steps involved in processing cash against customer accounts.

The complete cash application and processing steps involve all of the following functions:

- Identify every paid item or credit used as part settlement.
- Set up all unadjusted deductions taken by the remitter.
- Set up cash identified by remitter as "on account."
- Set up cash as *on account* that cannot be applied at this time.
- Keypunch cash input data for the open item file updating run.
- Mechanically audit each remittance, print differences.
- Review and dispose of major difference amounts resulting from the audit.
- Prepare necessary paper work for deductions, shortages, overpayments, late interest charges, etc., resulting from review.
- Print Final Cash Received Journal, which reflects the final adjustments resulting from the review of differences.

DEFINITION

The pre-identification method of cash application in connection with a computerized system is defined as any method that requires a clerical *matching* of paid-item reference data provided by the remitter with comparable information found on a printed list of open and unpaid items—or displayed on view screens of various types—or found in the form of interpreted punched cards placed in trays for quick visual location and handling.

BASIC PURPOSE

The basic purpose of the matching process is to positively identify for the computer each invoice paid or credits used in lieu of cash to settle one or more invoices. As indicated above, the pre-identification method covers a variety of ways of *displaying* the list of open items. The most commonly used method to date features customer ledger records printed by the computer on a scheduled or request basis.

Some firms use a copy of a printed statement prepared at monthend—or a copy of a detailed, aged trial balance.

PUNCHED CARD METHOD

Still another preidentification method features the filing of the punched invoice cards in indexed card trays. A certain number of trays, consisting of several thousand accounts, are assigned to each cash application bookkeeper. When applying a check, the bookkeeper studies the paid-item data provided by the customer's check or voucher, and then pulls the interpreted, matching item cards.

The cards pulled from the deck represent paid items; they are later fed into the computer for matching with corresponding open item records kept on reels of magnetic tape, or on direct access disk files. When the punched cards are used in conjunction with a receivables master file kept on disk or tape, the cards themselves do not constitute the file of open items; they merely represent a convenient device for feeding paid-item information back to the computer for cash applied.

DISPLAYING ACCOUNT RECORDS ON A SCREEN

The use of CRT units is practical only when a firm has the required computer hardware configuration. The user of such a system, when sitting in front of the screen, is able to see only the terminal device itself where the items are displayed on the screen. To effect this result, the computer configuration must include some type of data storage that is accessible on a random basis, plus a working memory large enough to store the complex software programs necessary for on-line inquiry and for processing batch-type jobs on stream at the same time.

The overall cost of an on-line system is apt to be very substantial. In a recent situation where the management of a credit department with eight men was thinking about installing on-line credit inquiry, the following facts and costs were developed and documented:

- Number of active accounts: 15,000.
- Total number of names and addresses on file: 35,000.
- Total number of open items on customer file: 100,000.
- Operating cost for eight CRT devices and related computer hardware: $64,800 per year. (Cost of *additional equipment* required to implement the on-line concept. This firm already had a couple of medium-scale computers installed and servicing other departments.)

In addition to the annual operating cost, a heavy one-time investment would first be necessary to develop and to design the system, followed by the extensive programming, testing, and debugging of programs. The budget for such a project typically exceeds $100,000.

MICROFILM SYSTEM AS AN ALTERNATIVE

The recent, little-known advances in the field of computer-output-to-microfilm make it possible now to design and install, in a few weeks' time, a suitable alternative to an on-line credit inquiry system. This is done through the use of Micromation techniques that convert data from magnetic tape—prepared by the computer—at tremendous speed to report format or ledger format on microtapes. Copies of the film file are made for distribution to each credit man; merely by inserting the film cartridge in a microfilm reader, he is able to locate and scan the open records on any desired account.

An important point is that the status of the account under this approach may be equally as current as the information that would appear on call on the screen of an on-line system utilizing the CRT units! (see Figure 14.4).

The costs of this approach are extremely reasonable. Initial costs are small, and operating costs are also greatly reduced.

USE OF PRINTED CUSTOMER LEDGER

The computer can produce a printed customer ledger on a scheduled basis, or each time a check is received. This provides an open item list, including data such as the invoice date, number, and amount. The bookkeeper who is applying the check studies the paid item data, finds the item that is being paid on the list, and proceeds to *identify* in some way the particular item to be later removed from the customer file. This identification is done by circling or marking the invoice amount or some special "finder" number used for item identification.

After the items have been marked and check data entered for keypunching, route the ledger or a stub detached from the ledger, to the keypunching department for the input of remittance data. The stub device has worked very well in actual practice. It is possible to design the form to provide two or more stubs to handle multiple checks received from the customer before new ledgers are printed. (Or, provide a supply of blank stubs to the bookkeepers). Notice that the *account number* is preprinted on the stub in the illustration that follows (Figure 14.5). This *eliminates the necessity for precoding checks.*

FINDER NUMBER DEVICE

At first thought the invoice number should be the primary device for identifying paid items when a computer file updating run is made. However, many types of records appear on the customer file other than invoices. To name a few, there are credit memos, received-on-account amounts, late interest debits, remittance shortage debits, overpayment credits, unadjusted deduction debits, unearned or excess discount debits, and the like.

CHARACTERISTICS OF PRE-IDENTIFICATION METHOD

The preidentification of paid items requires matching the actual remittance (or a photostatic copy of same) or a remittance voucher to a

Figure 14.4 Microfilm reader-printer for displaying customer ledger items for cash application (courtesy of 3M Company).

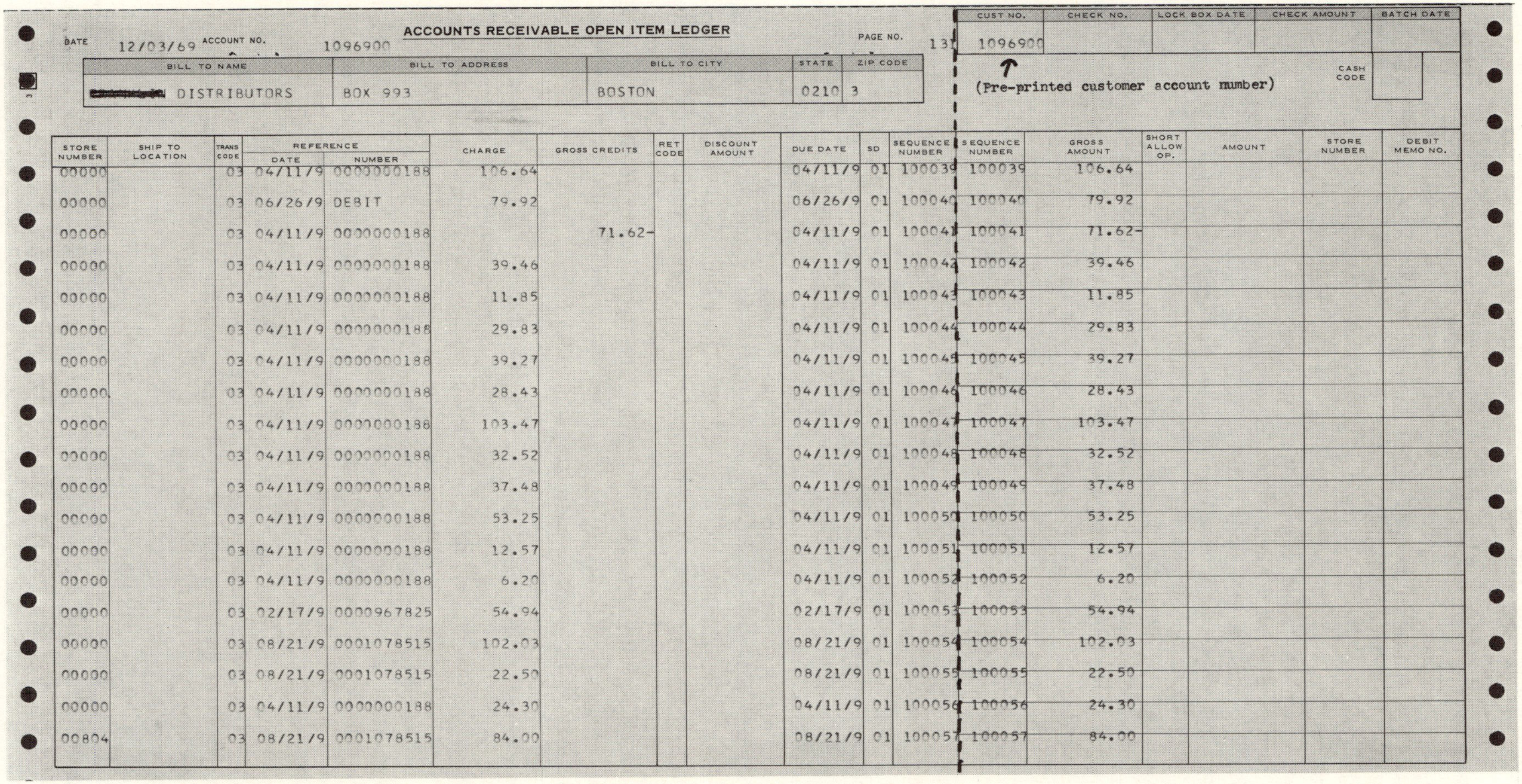

DATE 12/03/69 ACCOUNT NO. 1096900

ACCOUNTS RECEIVABLE OPEN ITEM LEDGER

PAGE NO. 13

BILL TO NAME	BILL TO ADDRESS	BILL TO CITY	STATE	ZIP CODE
DISTRIBUTORS	BOX 993	BOSTON	0210	3

CUST NO.	CHECK NO.	LOCK BOX DATE	CHECK AMOUNT	BATCH DATE
1096900				

(Pre-printed customer account number)

CASH CODE

STORE NUMBER	SHIP TO LOCATION	TRANS CODE	REFERENCE DATE	REFERENCE NUMBER	CHARGE	GROSS CREDITS	RET CODE	DISCOUNT AMOUNT	DUE DATE	SD	SEQUENCE NUMBER	SEQUENCE NUMBER	GROSS AMOUNT	SHORT ALLOW OP.	AMOUNT	STORE NUMBER	DEBIT MEMO NO.
00000		03	04/11/9	0000000188	106.64				04/11/9	01	100039	100039	106.64				
00000		03	06/26/9	DEBIT	79.92				06/26/9	01	100040	100040	79.92				
00000		03	04/11/9	0000000188		71.62-			04/11/9	01	100041	100041	71.62-				
00000		03	04/11/9	0000000188	39.46				04/11/9	01	100042	100042	39.46				
00000		03	04/11/9	0000000188	11.85				04/11/9	01	100043	100043	11.85				
00000		03	04/11/9	0000000188	29.83				04/11/9	01	100044	100044	29.83				
00000		03	04/11/9	0000000188	39.27				04/11/9	01	100045	100045	39.27				
00000		03	04/11/9	0000000188	28.43				04/11/9	01	100046	100046	28.43				
00000		03	04/11/9	0000000188	103.47				04/11/9	01	100047	100047	103.47				
00000		03	04/11/9	0000000188	32.52				04/11/9	01	100048	100048	32.52				
00000		03	04/11/9	0000000188	37.48				04/11/9	01	100049	100049	37.48				
00000		03	04/11/9	0000000188	53.25				04/11/9	01	100050	100050	53.25				
00000		03	04/11/9	0000000188	12.57				04/11/9	01	100051	100051	12.57				
00000		03	04/11/9	0000000188	6.20				04/11/9	01	100052	100052	6.20				
00000		03	02/17/9	0000967825	54.94				02/17/9	01	100053	100053	54.94				
00000		03	08/21/9	0001078515	102.03				08/21/9	01	100054	100054	102.03				
00000		03	08/21/9	0001078515	22.50				08/21/9	01	100055	100055	22.50				
00000		03	04/11/9	0000000188	24.30				04/11/9	01	100056	100056	24.30				
00804		03	08/21/9	0001078515	84.00				08/21/9	01	100057	100057	84.00				

Figure 14.5 Computer-printed customer ledger with cash application stub (courtesy of Clairol, Inc.).

printed open-item list—or to items displayed on a view screen. The bookkeeper is thereby able to study all items that are currently open—and to make a determination as to the specific invoices paid, the credits used—and the deductions taken without the authority of an *open credit* being on the customer's file. (This is the situation that permits the cash applier to identify an unadjusted deduction arbitrarily taken by the remitter and which must be properly handled as an add-back by the cash applier).

For the purposes of reviewing and discussing typical steps followed by a cash application bookkeeper, the procedures followed when a *customer ledger record* is provided to the bookkeepers are outlined, since this is the one most popular version of the preidentification method.

The typical procedures are as follows.

- The bookkeeper compares the remitter's name and address as it appears on the check or the remittance envelope with the comparable name and address appearing on the printed ledger.
- The bookkeeper studies the paid-item data as supplied by the remitter and marks or circles the identifying sequence or "finder" number on the body of the ledger *and* on the detachable cash stub.
- If the customer has taken a deduction other than discount, bookkeeper enters the required information on the cash stub for later keypunching.
- If the customer clearly indicates that the check is an on-account payment, the bookkeeper enters the check data on a blank cash stub with a special code or symbol identifying the cash as "on account."

If the bookkeeper cannot find all of the paid items on the open account list, the check is applied anyway as completely as possible. Even though the bookkeeper knows that a certain amount of cash thereby *remains unapplied,* she does not enter a partial on-account amount. *Reason.* The subsequent cash audit function will calculate the unused cash and will show it as a credit difference. Then, during the review of differences (explained in the latter part of this chapter), the reviewer will handle the disposition of the unused cash credit.

One important point—the bookkeeper should *not* be permitted to perform *a manual audit* of remittances applied. This slows down the work considerably, and the computer can perform a much more accurate audit following the rules included in the audit subroutine most consistently.

CASH STUB CARRIES INPUT DATA

After the bookkeeper has identified and marked all paid items, she then enters the basic check information on the stub, either at the top or at the bottom. The information required for printing all subsequent cash journals and for the computer audit is:

- Effective cash date (the postmark date or bank deposit date)
- Check number
- Check amount

The bookkeeper then detaches the cash stub from the body of the ledger for subsequent routing to a control clerk who, in turn, sends the stubs to a keypunch department for punching remittance and paid-item information in cards (see Figure 14.6).

Now, if the invoice number is the means for identifying an invoice or credit invoice, a comparable identifier must be assigned to each of the other types of records that go on an open-item file. This requires assigning an arbitrary number or check number that can be referenced when the item is paid—or cleared by journal entry.

The "sequence or finder number" device is a very practical solution to the problem of identifying a record on a customer's file. At the time an invoice, a credit, or any other type of record is posted to an account, the computer examines the last open sequence or finder number found on the account—then it increases this number by one and assigns that number to the posted item. For example, if the finder number for the last item on the account is No. 0035, the new record now being posted in assigned No. 0036.

This technique overcomes many problems encountered when the invoice number is used as a prime identifier. For example, it is not unusual to find many duplicate invoice numbers in large, diversified firms with decentralized billing. Also, some firms routinely assign the original invoice number to a credit when the credit relates directly to a specific invoice.

It would seem to be a good procedure to use the check number as the basic identifying number for records that originate from cash audit.

CUST NO.	CHECK NO.	LOCK BOX DATE	CHECK AMOUNT	BATCH DATE
1096900	12678	12-15-71	1933.45	12-17-71

CASH CODE: 1

SEQUENCE NUMBER	GROSS AMOUNT	SHORT ALLOW OP.	AMOUNT	STORE NUMBER	DEBIT MEMO NO.
100058	28.26				
100059	11.30				
100060	369.70				
100061	1,234.62				
100062	101.16				
100063	25.86				
100064	21.78				
100065	25.60				
100066	51.90				
100067	24.86				
100068	294.51				
100069	19.47				
100070	24.41				
100071	25.14				
100072	1,625.00				
100073	149.87				
100074	25.77				
100075	151.20				
100076	25.04				

Figure 14.6 Typical cash application stub (courtesy of Clairol, Inc.).

However, this would generate a problem in that more than one record may be set up as a result of applying one check. If each new record carried the *same check number,* you would be unable to instruct the computer at a subsequent time as to which records to remove—unless the input for cash includes the amount.

Caution. Even if you select a 4-digit sequence or finder number for automatic assignment to each open-item posted to one account, the day will inevitably arrive when the numbers assigned to open-items approach the limit of 9999. For this reason one of the monthend computer runs, such as the Aged Trial Balance Report, should include instructions that can be activated to RE-NUMBER ALL OPEN ITEMS IN SELECTED ACCOUNTS when then open-item file is being rewritten on a new tape or disk file.

Unless this is done, an account may show items with numbers 9997, 9998, 9999—then followed by numbers 0001, 0002, etc. This presents cash application problems when a check pays items with both the high and low finder numbers.

HANDLING UNADJUSTED DEDUCTIONS

Unadjusted deductions are those amounts, other than discount, subtracted from a remittance without advance authorization. The customer arbitrarily makes these deductions for any number of reasons he considers reasonable and valid. The usual accounting practice is to post a deduction back to the account as a debit entry, where it remains until the appropriate internal research work has been done to ascertain the validity of the customer's claim. In a data processing system the best practice is to flag or to delete the paid item or items from the open-item file, then post the unadjusted deduction amount or amounts back to the receivables file as an open debit items.

SET UP DEDUCTIONS INDEPENDENTLY OF PAID INVOICES

At first thought it seems logical to attempt to link an unadjusted deduction to a paid invoice. This approach usually will not work for several reasons. First, a detailed study of the deductions situation frequently reveals that more than 50% of all deductions simply *cannot be related to a specific invoice.* The analysis of reasons for deductions indicates this. For example, if a deduction is made for a promotional allowance, this obviously does not relate to any invoice being paid.

Even deductions made for returned merchandise may not relate to one invoice—because the customer accumulated merchandise from several invoices and then returned the goods as one shipment. Another point is that deductions may be taken long after the applicable invoice has been paid.

In summary, the best practice is to set up and charge back one or more deductions appearing on a remittance in "free form." That is, handle the add-back of deductions independently of the removal of paid items.

INPUT OF DATA FOR UNADJUSTED DEDUCTIONS

The essential data for keypunching deductions found on a remittance may be entered on a separate coding voucher or entered on the cash application stub. The information is sometimes entered on the back of the stub or on the front. Observe the sample ledger stub shown below; it provides special boxes for entering all necessary data on the face of the stub (Figure 14.7).

The deduction entries shown on the stub have no connection with the invoices that happen to appear on the left side of the preprinted cash application stub.

MANUAL AUDIT OF REMITTANCES

Many computer receivables installations provide for a manual audit of remittances. This provides a satisfactory installation, but it adds considerable work to the cash application procedures—and requires additional training of the cash application clerks.

The mechanizing of the remittance audit function offers many benefits and should help reduce the number of cash appliers required to handle the volume of checks to be applied daily, weekly, or monthly.

Another aspect of the cash application input is that it is not necessary to bring in the gross amount being paid as input—if the audit function is shifted from the bookkeeper to the computer. The cash input requires only the customer number, the effective cash date and check number, the check amount—and the *sequence or finder numbers* which identify each item paid or credit used.

CUST. NO.	CHECK NO.	LOCK BOX DATE	CHECK AMOUNT	BATCH DATE
1096900	13600	2-14-71	209.60	2-16-71

CASH CODE

SEQUENCE NUMBER	GROSS AMOUNT	SHORT ALLOW OP.	AMOUNT	STORE NUMBER	DEBIT MEMO NO.
100077	225.00	01	35.40		1278
100078	54.12	05	60.00		1279
100079	25.85				
100080	35.32				
100081	31.57				
100082	13.88				
100083	43.67				
100084	20.72				
100085	32.96				
100086	25.73				
100087	12.26				
100088	77.86				
100089	107.05				
100090	20.20				
100091	21.17-				
100092	25.69				
100093	89.47				
100094	83.84				
100095	33.57				

Figure 14.7 Cash application stub which provides for deduction entries.

CHECK INFORMATION REQUIRED

As indicated above, it is essential to input certain check data. The check date and check amount are required for determining whether available discount is earned or unearned and for auditing the remittance. Furthermore, the computer is usually required to print one or more cash journals, which must show all indicative remittance information as well as paid items and deductions set up.

CHECK DATE

The actual check date found on the customer's check is frequently not a satisfactory date to use when auditing remittances. One reason is that certain customers will predate checks and then hold them for several weeks before mailing. A better practice is to use the postmark date on the remitter's envelope.

If bank lockboxes are used for remittances, then the lockbox deposit date represents the date of constructive receipt of funds; for this reason it is a very satisfactory date to use for the audit of remittances.

IMPORTANCE OF ACCURATE "CHECK DATE"

The check date is the basis for determining whether the remitter earned the discount available through discount terms. It is also used for classifying each invoice for the purposes of building up pay-habits data on the customer. This requires establishing appropriate definitions to determine whether an invoice was paid:

- Early (discounted)
- Prompt
- Late

For example, consider an invoice subject to two-option terms such as 2% 10, N30. If the remitter pays within five days of the discount due date, he paid on a discounted basis (early). If he exercises the second option and pays within five days of the final due date, he paid on a *prompt* basis. However, if he did not pay until six or more days after the final due date, the computer will tag the paid item as paid *late*.

Another example of the importance of selecting an accurate cash date is that this is the basis for calculating early or late interest where such calculations are built into the computer audit. Some firms calculate interest on each remittance (early or late) for the purposes of developing statistical cost data for customer profit and loss reporting, even though they will not charge late interest to the customer.

CHECK NUMBER IS VITAL

The check number should always be a component of data entered as cash input. It is important for several reasons. First, it is the basis for auditing individual remittances where more than one check is received from a customer and entered together in the same batch for processing. Without the check number as part of the input data, the computer will lump all paid items for one customer together and audit the entire group. Also, if there are two checks present for the same amount, the computer will not be able to recognize that two different check amounts must be added to the grand total of cash processed.

PROVING CASH INPUT

If the audit function is assigned to the computer, the only proof of dollar amounts required of the cash application bookkeepers is to prove that the check amounts have been accurately copied to the ledger stubs. This is usually done by requiring each bookkeeper to prepare an adding machine tape of all check amounts in a batch. Then she adds the pencil check amounts written on the individual ledger stubs. The two totals should agree before routing the stubs, along with a Cash Batch Voucher, to a cash control clerk. The control clerk enters the batch number and cash amount on a cash control log, then routes the ledger stubs with the batch ticket attached to the keypunching department.

"CASH-EQUALS"

A well-designed computerized receivables system must handle many types of situations that are encountered in the application of cash. One of them is the "cash-equals" problem.

The origin of a cash-equals situation is a check that arrives for application *before* the paid invoices appear on the customer ledger. This occurs for several reasons:

- The invoice terms are 1% 10 days and the customer pays promptly.

- The terms are 10 days and the customer pays early, deducts anticipation.
- The customer pays early and the customer ledger is printed only once each week. The invoices may be on the file when the check arrives, but the cash application bookkeeper has no way of knowing this—unless the daily runs provide a progressively updated transaction list to her, beginning with the second or third day of the week. This list is intended to supplement the regular customer ledger provided to bookkeepers, perhaps, each Monday morning.

When the check is being applied, and the bookkeeper cannot find the items being paid on the ledger or on a supplementary list, she necessarily takes the cash on account. However, a *special transaction code* should be used to clearly identify this early cash for later disposition. Also, the bookkeeper should make a photocopy of the check and its attachments and should place the documents in a special follow-up file.

When new customer ledgers are received, bookkeepers should be instructed to pull all items from the special file, match them to the new ledgers—to determine if the invoices paid by the early check are now visible on the ledger record. If so, the bookkeeper applies the cash by circling the paid items—*and* the cash credit item. She can create a dummy remittance input record by filling in the check date and check number on the ledger stub—but no check amount (or use all zeros) plus a special transaction code which identifies the input record as a cash-equals.

Ledger stubs representing the application of this prior cash should be handled and batched separately from regular, current checks being applied. However, the keypunched cash input can be handled along with regular checks as far as the updating, remittance audit and other computer runs are concerned.

AUTOMATIC CASH APPLICATION

Cash application methods covered in this chapter may be classified as preidentification methods. The next chapter covers the unique alternative approach usually referred to as ''automatic cash'' application.

CHAPTER 15

Automatic Cash Application

Because of the known capabilities of today's electronic, digital computer, it is only logical to conclude that it is feasible to program a medium or large-scale computer to apply all cash to specific items to the customer file automatically. Furthermore, many statistical studies show that up to 85% of all checks received provide the necessary ''keys'' to identifying items being paid. This inevitably leads one to the conclusion that an automatic cash approach would result in major savings in time and overall personnel costs in a trade receivables installation.

These conclusions are correct when applied to the conditions found in life or casualty insurance accounting and public utility receivables. However, the ''automatic cash'' approach should be selected with caution because optimum results are frequently obtainable only when the conditions in the receivables environment are favorable to this approach:

- Majority of invoice terms are EOM.
- Customers pay by statement.
- Customers take few unadjusted deductions.

DEFINITION

''Automatic cash'' is that approach or cash application method that accepts all paid-item data provided by the remitter at face value. The keys to identifying items to be flagged or removed as paid are:

- Invoice date
- Invoice number
- Store number
- Purchase order number
- Invoice amount

The majority of remitters will identify items that they are paying by listing the invoice number, date, and amount on the voucher apron—or the date and amount—or just the amount may be shown. Retail stores may also list the store number, which is quite helpful in cash application.

CHARACTERISTICS OF AUTOMATIC CASH APPROACH

The usual approach to automatic cash requires that the paid-item information provided by the remitter be keypunched directly from the remittance and fed into the computer. By definition, no visual reference is made to account open-item lists, nor to data displayed on screens—procedures typically found in a pre-identification method. In fact, *no verification* of paid-item data is attempted by the check reviewers at the time of coding the checks.

DETERMINE PAID ITEM IDENTIFICATION MODE

Depending on the concept employed by the systems group that determines how automatic cash application is supposed to work, one of the key preliminary manual steps may be to require the bookkeeper to review the paid-item data carefully—to determine how the paid items are being identified. For example, is the remitter providing invoice numbers as identification? Or, does the remittance voucher show only invoice dates and amounts? Or amounts only?

Does the payment reflect a "split" situation in that invoice numbers are provided for some items and not for others being paid? Is the remittance apparently using one or more credits as partial settlement—or do these deductions represent unadjusted deductions that must be charged back?

Because of these variables, an automatic cash approach may require the check reviewers to analyze the paid-item information supplied by the customer—and then assign a payment code to each check for subsequent keypunching. This payment code assists the computer's subsequent cash application testing and application processes, since it indicates the type of search that should be accomplished:

- Search on invoice number
- Search on invoice date and amount
- Search for open credit being used as part of the payment
- Post the cash as "on-account"

If the computer is unable to match the paid-item data to a record on the customer's file during the initial search stage, it may be programmed to begin a series of calculations and tests based on invoice amount to determine if the remittance amount matches any *combination* of open items after taking into consideration all applicable discount. It then may make the same tests ignoring the discount aspects to see if the remittance "fits" this situation.

KEY DECISION

Developing an automatic cash application system requires that many vital decisions be made by the systems analysts and other interested parties. These decisions are then incorporated into the detailed instructions that become part of the cash audit programs. Here are some of the problems that must be resolved:

1. Suppose that the computer is able to find and identify two out of three items paid by a check; should it be programmed to remove the two records that it found, then post the remaining cash "on account?" Or, would it be better to keep the computer from removing any record as paid, and pass the entire check to a trained bookkeeper to handle later?
2. Suppose that the computer finds all indicated paid items with no difficulty—but the audit of the remittance reveals that a major difference (over or short) exists for reasons unknown? Should the program permit the machine to apply the check anyway and post the major difference amount to the account? Or, would it be a better practice to stop the application of this check and let a trained bookkeeper do the necessary review and research on it?

NO PARTIAL APPLICATION

There are a few installations on trade receivables where cash is applied automatically—successfully. Lessons learned from experience indicate that the computer should not be permitted to apply a check *partially;* if it cannot apply the entire check, it should be programmed to do the following:

- Post the *full check amount* to the account as a temporary on-account amount.
- Print a customer ledger showing all open items for review by a trained bookkeeper.

AUDIT DEVELOPS MAJOR DIFFERENCE

In those instances where the computer finds and properly identifies *all records* being paid by a remittance, but the audit produces a large difference amount (over or short), two opposing methods may be adopted. One, the computer may apply the cash by removing the paid items—but *post back to the account* at once the major difference amount.

An alternative method is to block the application of any part of the cash when a major difference results from the tentative application—then post the check amount to the account and print a customer ledger for the clerical review and manual application of the check.

The reasoning behind the alternative method is that any unexplained major difference amount must be examined by a trained person anyway. Now, if the computer is programmed to post the differences to the account after removing the paid items, the reviewer is faced with handling the problem in two steps:

1. Create paper work and instructions to be keypunched—the net result of which is to *remove* the difference amount from the customer file.
2. Create paper work to put one or more records back on the file that were erroneously removed by the computer's application of cash or that provide the appropriate transaction code to identify the major difference amount on the file. Sometimes it is necessary for the reviewer to first remove the difference amount, and then provide information for setting up two or three different records that account for the difference.

A key point to bear in mind is that it is far easier and simpler for a bookkeeper to apply a check manually to an account than it is to first correct the computer's application and then dispose of the difference amount on the file.

MANUAL CASH APPLICATION

A successful automatic cash system inevitably includes procedures for *manually applying* a certain percentage of the total checks fed into the system for application. As indicated above, the program under certain conditions requires the computer to print a complete customer ledger showing all open items. These are routed to trained bookkeepers for manual application of all checks put on the file as "on account." (Checks identified *by the customer* as on-account do not cause the printout of a ledger.)

What is the volume of ledger sheets typically printed? This will vary from 15% to 50% in a typical situation. That is, if 1000 checks are fed into the system, the computer will be unable to handle properly from 150 to 500 checks, which then cause the printing of 150 to 500 customer ledgers (see Figure 15.1).

MANUAL APPLICATION PROCEDURES

The trained bookkeepers, who initially coded the checks with the customer account number and established the mode of payment, now take the printed ledgers records and apply the matching checks manually. The bookkeeper studies the paid-item data provided by the remitter, finds the item on the printed record, and marks the invoice number for each paid item.

HANDLING UNADJUSTED DEDUCTIONS

As part of the manual cash application procedures, the bookkeeper enters all necessary data (See the chargeback section shown on the customer ledger in Figure 15.1) for unadjusted deduction amounts taken by the remitter.

The handling of unadjusted deductions is one of the major problems inherent in an automatic cash approach. When the check reviewers look at a check during the coding process, it frequently is impossible for the reviewer to determine the difference between a deduction amount representing an open credit now being "used" as part of the remittance—or a deduction amount that is an unadjusted deduction. The reason is that the remitter will provide a reference number with the amount deducted—but this number may represent an open credit memo—or it may be his own debit memo reference number!

PREPARES PAPERWORK

If the bookkeeper finds that the amount or amounts deducted are unadjusted deductions, she will write up an internal Notice of Deductions. These documents are routed to a customer service or adjustment group who follow up with the appropriate department from time to time to obtain a credit memo that will serve to clear the unadjusted deduction debit from the customer file.

MANUAL AUDIT REQUIRED

One important step in the manual application of cash is the audit performed by the bookkeeper. If this audit develops a major difference amount, the bookkeeper is then required to prepare a Notice or Statement for transmittal to the customer notifying him of a shortage or overage. A shortage might be due to unearned or excess discount taken, for example.

PROVES APPLICATION OF CASH

After a bookkeeper applies a check to the printed ledger, she proves the application by adding all the gross amounts to be removed from the file. The total of items paid, less discounts allowed, less unadjusted deductions set up, should equal the check amount.

KEYPUNCH CASH INPUT FOR SECOND PASS

The printed ledger sheets and other documents are routed to the keypunch department where the paid-item information and deductions are keypunched. All of the input records are

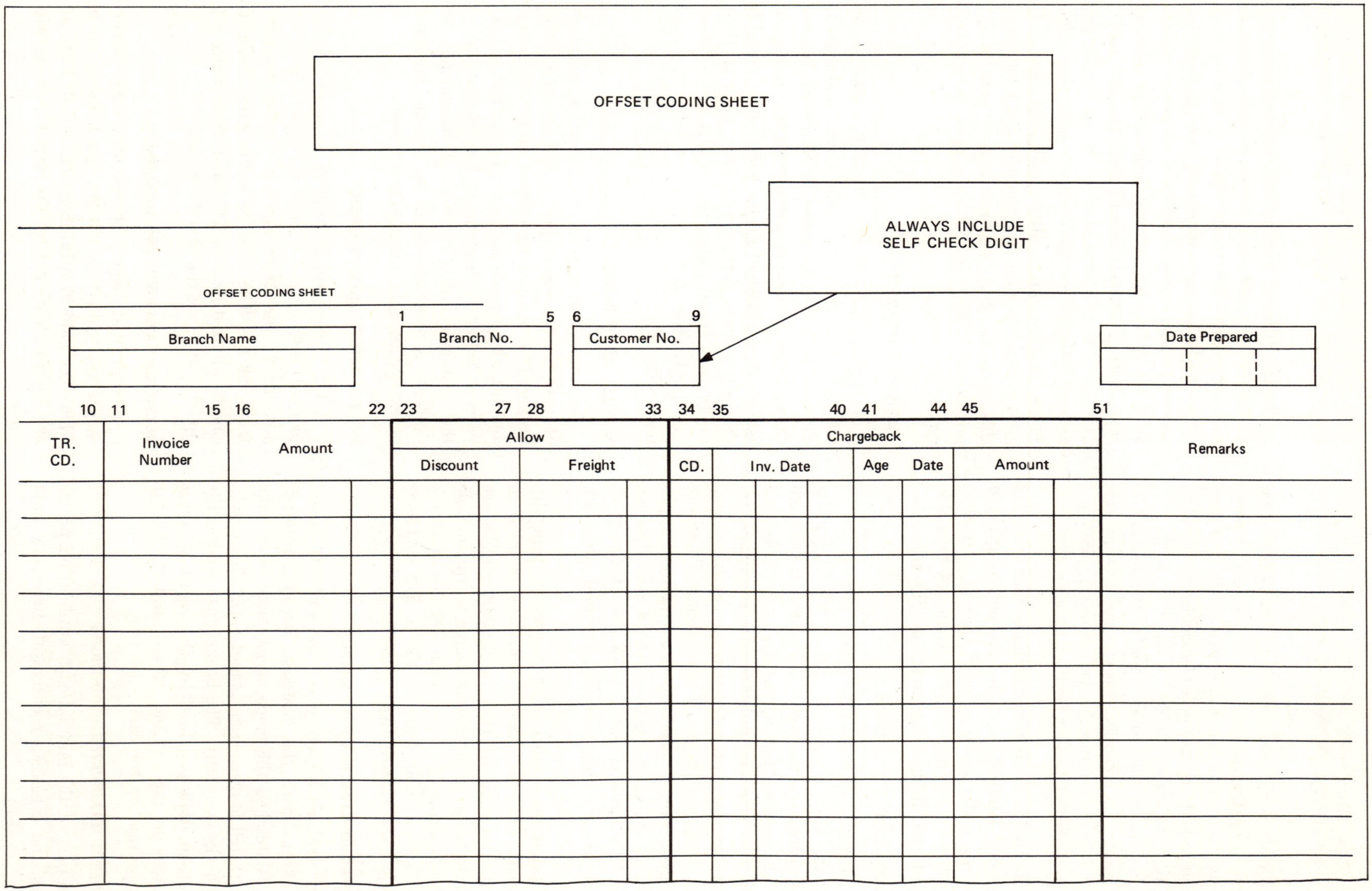

Figure 15.1 Customer ledger for manual application of cash.

later fed into the computer, which now makes a second pass against the customer master file in order to apply the cash that the computer could not apply.

CASH JOURNAL PRINTED

After the computer has processed the cash applied manually by the bookkeepers to the customer file, it should then print a complete Cash Journal, showing each check applied and the details of each paid item, plus charge-backs, and the disposition of differences. This is an accounting journal; debit and credit totals printed on the last page are entered into the General Ledger.

Special Considerations and Requirements for a Successful Approach to Automatic Cash Application

If the automatic cash approach is to be successful, there must be a very careful correlation of manual procedures with the mechanized system functions. This approach requires considerable clerical handling of the checks both before and after the computer run or runs. And, the customer file of open items must be organized in a specific way for matching the paid-item information fed into the computer to a specific record on the customer file. The problems that will result from feeding in erroneous indicative data and items which provided insufficient information must be fully explored in advance, and rules must be written to handle each type of situation.

REVIEW OF PRELIMINARY PROCEDURES

Manual procedures performed by the bookkeepers before the paid item data can be keypunched and fed into the computer are as follows.

1. Rough-sort checks alphabetically.
2. Look up the customer account number for each check, then write the account number on the face of the remittance or on the voucher apron for keypunching.
3. Assemble checks in batches, number each batch, then prepare a batch control ticket after adding all check amounts in the batch.
4. Analyze paid-item data on the remittance and circle the key data for subsequent keypunching. (Key data are the invoice number, invoice date, store number, invoice amount, etc).
5. Determine the payment mode code; write the code number on the remittance.
6. If documents are attached to the remittance for a freight damage claim, the bookkeeper prepares an input document for keypunching the unadjusted deduction amount and reference data.

LIST OF PAYMENT CODES

The use of preestablished payment codes to assist the computer in its matching and searching functions has considerable merit in that it simplifies, to some extent, the computer function of automatic cash application. The following list of codes, which are frequently used, provide clues as to what is involved in analyzing the mode of payment:

No. 01. Customer is paying by invoice number.
No. 02. Cannot determine what the customer is paying.
No. 03. Post remittance to the account as an on-account payment.
No. 04. Customer appears to be using a credit.
No. 05. Customer is paying by statement.
No. 06. Customer is paying by invoice date and amount.
No. 07. Application of cash has already been made by bookkeeper.
No. 09. Request complete printout of customer record for subsequent manual cash application.

CUSTOMER PAYS BY STATEMENT

In retail-oriented lines of business it is common practice for the creditor to prepare and mail a complete account statement to all customers at monthend. Quite often the customer who receives this statement will pay the statement balance. Where this practice prevails the automatic cash system should include a code that tells the computer to remove all open items which appeared on the statement.

The use of this technique requires careful planning, however, because the records to be removed must be *only those which appeared on the statement*—not all open records which may, at the time of receiving the check, be on the account.

COMPUTER RUNS REQUIRED FOR CASH PROCESSING

The overall programming approach and computer runs involved in processing cash against the customer open-item file automatically will vary significantly in each installation—because of the variable hardware parameters and other considerations. Factors that must be taken into account during the systems design phase are the size of the working memory; the structure and organization of the open item file; the type of storage device used for open-item file (magnetic tape or some type of direct access storage), the number of tape drives available—and the overall concept behind the automatic application of cash.

MEMORY LIMITATIONS

The determination as to how to use working memory is of paramount importance. The essence of automatic cash application requires the testing of *each paid item* brought into the processing run potentially against *every* open item on the customer receivables file. This is necessary because of the matching process—to identify and flag open items that are paid by a remittance being processed to the file.

TABLE CONCEPT

Consider the problem involved in applying a remittance that paid 30 items, used four credits—and included five deductions. Suppose that the customer file consists of 150 open items. The 34 input records identifying the 30 paid invoices and four credits must be matched, one by one, against the customer file records.

The realization of the requirements of the basic approach leads into programming based on a table concept where the input records are brought into memory as a group for the testing process.

Next consider the requirement of bringing in 150 open items from the customer file—testing each input record against each of these open items—determining matched records—then rewriting the customer file.

LIMITATIONS ON PAID ITEMS

One solution to this very difficult problem is to limit the number of paid items (one remittance) that can be applied automatically. The United States Plywood Corporation has developed a successful automatic cash approach based on limiting the paid items within a remittance to 30. Any check that pays more than 30 items is handled by the bookkeeper-reviewers.

AVOID LIMITATIONS ON CUSTOMER FILE

It is satisfactory to limit the number of paid transactions that can be processed—but systems analysts should avoid any approach that requires limiting the number of open items on a customer's file to a specific number. The customer file should remain as an ''open end'' file to accommodate any number of records. In a recent conversion of trade receivables, we found that one chain store had 4000 open items on the account at time of conversion from ledger records to the new computer system.

HOW TO ORGANIZE CUSTOMER FILE

The adoption of the automatic cash application approach requires organizing the open-item file in invoice number sequence. This is logical, since the majority of remitters provide the invoice number as the primary method of identifying paid items.

Maintaining a file in invoice number sequence is not as simple as it sounds. One vexing problem that may arise is the existence of duplicate invoice numbers. Also, some firms make it a practice to assign an original invoice number to a credit. Both records may appear on the customer file at the same time—with identical reference numbers.

Another aspect of the problem which must be faced is that many types of debit and credit records appear on the customer file, *other than invoices:*

- Received on account cash credit
- Unearned discount debit
- Late interest debit
- Unadjusted deduction debit
- Overpayment credit, etc.

Each of these miscellaneous records must be assigned a unique number for positive control and removal at some future date. This requires systems analysts to develop a formula or a method for the computer to assign a unique number (called the invoice number) when these records are posted to the customer file.

PROVIDE ADEQUATE CLERICAL SUPPORT FOR THE COMPUTER

Many firms that selected the automatic cash approach as the method for applying and controlling cash report that they initially underestimated the problems encountered in such a system, and also that they failed to anticipate the number of trained bookkeepers required to support the system. The first section of this chapter listed the many steps that must precede the input of cash information into the computer—and the post-audit procedures that are required after the computer has made the first pass of cash against the customer file.

One aspect of the post-audit procedures is worth stressing because of its extreme importance. That is, be sure to provide a bookkeeper staff large enough to keep all unapplied cash cleaned up insofar as possible. Management sometimes does not recognize in time that a buildup of cash *on account* has a debilitating effect in many ways in a receivables and credit department.

Several factors in a trade receivables installation may lead to taking a considerable amount of cash into the records as on-account instead of applying it to specific invoices. First, the volume of cash may reach the point where the bookkeepers are simply unable to cope with it—especially between the twelfth and twentieth of the month wherein checks are received to cover invoices that reflect EOM or PROX terms due on the tenth. Putting the unprocessed cash *on account* may appear to be a good expedient from an accounting and control viewpoint.

Second, the automatic cash approach sometimes requires the computer to post any unapplied cash to the account on a ''temporary'' basis. That is, the post-audit bookkeepers are supposed to review the accounts to which any amount of unapplied cash was posted and to make a disposition of the remaining cash through a manual application procedure.

AVOID BUILDUP OF UNAPPLIED CASH

Unfortunately, we sometimes find a major discrepancy between theory and practice. If the support group is too small, there is a tendency for the unapplied cash to remain on the accounts for longer and longer periods of time. Once the post-audit bookkeepers fall behind one or two days, the situation usually gets progressively worse. As a specific example of why this is more serious than it may appear to be, consider the situation where a firm puts in 1000 checks per day. Let us assume that the computer properly applies up to 85% of all checks but posts 15% of the checks to the account as ''on-account'' cash. Let us also assume that each check, on the average, pays three invoices.

- In a calendar month the computer has handled 22,000 checks.
- If 15% of all checks are posted as on-account, then about 3300 checks have been added to the accounts. These checks actually paid roughly 13,200 invoices—which remain on the file, since the checks have not been applied. If the same situation continues for two months, the open-item file now includes about 26,000 items that are actually paid —but that appear increasingly on past due statements, on collection letters, and on the aged trial balance.

In a short time the entire collection function begins to disintegrate because past due statements are misleading and inaccurate. Customers resent being dunned for items that they have paid. The aged trial balance reports current and past due status figures that are distorted and erroneous. When credit men or collectors analyze an individual account, they see the cash on account—but cannot determine the true status of the past due items.

When the collection function begins to deteriorate, many customers will realize that they are not being followed properly on past due invoices. Some will take full advantage of this fact. If dunned, they will blandly state that they will pay—when the creditor firm submits an itemized list of the unpaid and past due invoices.

The situation mentioned above accentuates the importance of selecting and installing a cash application and control system and procedures that will enable the bookkeepers and the computer to apply all cash properly, accurately, and consistently at all times. One principle to be observed in a well-organized receivables department is that any cash taken on account should be reported and controlled very carefully.

Summary

Management has a tendency to expect too much from an automatic cash application approach. And, the use of the word "automatic" is actually a misnomer because of the many manual steps and procedures required to feed paid data into the computer—and to support the computer functions in general. The net savings in personnel (if any) and the other benefits realized are often quite disappointing to management.

Before deciding to adopt this method of handling cash in a trade receivables environment, study the situation long and carefully. It is entirely possible that one of the four pre-identification methods outlined in the preceding chapter will be safer, much easier to program and install—and will possibly do the job as efficiently *overall* as the "post identification" approach anyway.

CHAPTER 16

Updating Customer File and Related Functions

Chapter 11 covers the structure and maintenance of the customer master file; this chapter explains how the customer open-item file is updated and it reviews all of the related functional runs connected with the audit of cash applied, review of differences, printing necessary statement and notice forms, and the like.

The open-item file is constantly changing; records are added, deleted, and changed in accordance with the necessity for posting new sales, applying cash, and handling journal entries.

CASH APPLICATION

The application of cash is the major source of deleting open-item accounting records from the open-item file—if the ''direct'' approach is adopted. Under the direct approach, cash is not posted to the account; it is used as the *authority for removing* specified invoice and other records from the file. Only received-on-account cash is actually posted to the account for subsequent application when additional cash or credits are utilized to settle and clear one or more invoices.

The antithesis of the direct approach is a method whereby the computer finds each paid invoice record, calculates the amount of cash required—and constructs and posts a satellite record that is identified as a ''cash offset'' record to the original open invoice record. At a specified time the computer eventually removes all the offsetting records which, in effect, represent paid invoices.

MULTIPLE COMPUTER RUNS REQUIRED

The application of cash and the identification of paid items by cash appliers is only the first step in a chain of computer runs and related clerical functions. Assuming that the preidentification method of cash application is in use, the application of cash, processing, and reporting covers all the following functions and clerical procedures.

- Identify all paid items and prepare basic remittance data for input.
- Keypunch all cash input, including deductions to be charged back (posted) to the account.
- Prove cash batch totals as part of input edit.
- Update the customer open-item file by adding sales and deduction records—and by deleting paid items.
- Audit each remittance, calculate and print audit differences.
- Print Cash Received Journal.
- Review all major differences developed by audit.
- Provide disposition instructions for each major difference amount reviewed.

- Merge paid records and records deleted by journal entries into a paid transactions file.

COMBINING RUNS

Depending on the size of the computer's working memory, it is feasible to combine the functions of finding and deleting paid records with the audit of each remittance. However, this approach requires some complex programming. One reason for this is that each remittance should be individually audited in the event that several checks from the same customer are being processed against the open-item file at the same time. This requires bringing all paid items resulting from the application of one check together in memory for the determination of the difference amount resulting from the audit. This may require limiting the number of checks that may be put through at one time.

MAJOR DIFFERENCE AMOUNT

If the audit develops a major difference, the question then arises as to what to do with it. The usual approach, when the audit function is combined with the file updating function, is to create an open-item record and post the difference amount to the file at once as an *unidentified transaction.*

The details of each check would be subsequently printed and major difference amounts would be reviewed. The reviewers then would be required to submit coded instructions that would delete the original, unidentified major difference amounts and would substitute coded transactions as input to be put on the file or charged to discount.

COMBINING RUNS REQUIRES CAREFUL EVALUATION

The concept of combining several related functions in one run has considerable appeal. However, the systems analyst should analyze the problems and end results of this approach very carefully before making a final decision. For example, the approach described above results in unadjusted deductions set up by the cash applier being posted to the account before the entire remittance has been audited. Errors in deduction amounts result in a major audit difference. This, in turn, requires the reviewer to do all of the following.

- Delete the deduction record in error.
- Delete the major difference record.
- Prepare input for the correct deduction amount.
- Prepare new paper work for the deduction set up.

ALTERNATE APPROACH

An alternative approach is to separate the audit function completely from the file updating run. This greatly simplifies the programming, and it requires a much smaller working memory. The paid-item work tape can then be sorted on check number within customer number for the cash audit run. The audit reveals major differences, errors in deduction records, and can include a calculation of early or late interest; none of these amounts have been added to the customer open-item file as yet.

REVIEW AND DISPOSITION OF DIFFERENCES

The cash audit run results in printing a detailed Cash Journal; major differences print on the right-hand side of this journal.

Trained reviewers concentrate on remittances that have developed major differences and submit coded instructions for the disposition of each difference amount. It is important to note that each difference amount must be accounted for to the penny.

The review function and disposition instructions are simplified by the fact that it is not necessary to delete any unidentified records on the customer file.

WRITE PAID ITEMS FILE

The file updating run should include writing all paid items (and the ones deleted by journal entry) on a special output work file, regardless of whether the audit is part of the updating run or is performed subsequently. This file has many valuable uses:

- The basis for the computer audit of each remittance if the audit function is separated from the updating function.
- The source for printing cash journals. (The basic cash remittance record is always included on the paid item file.)
- The source for printing all documents and notices connected with cash application differences and unadjusted deductions.
- The source for developing a complete Paid History File—printed weekly and monthly by customer number for the benefit of cash appliers and accounts receivable reference and backtracking functions.

CHECK NUMBER IS VALUABLE

Many computerized trade receivables systems have omitted the check number as part of the data input. The check number is invaluable for the individual audit of each remittance and provides the basis for communicating with customers or for reconstructing a customer's account when this becomes necessary.

To obtain the check number as part of the paid history file, move the check number from the cash finder record *into each paid record* written out on the special work file of paid items. New deductions set up as part of the remittance should also be included on the paid-items file for reference. It is now obvious that the paid-items file includes all records necessary for cash audit, for printing the Cash Journal—and for subsequent printing of all necessary paperwork connected with cash application and deductions.

CASH RECEIVED JOURNAL

The cash journal is a printed report showing each check and all items paid by that check, plus the deductions set up or charged off against internal expense. The program must develop all necessary control totals and print them on the last page because this journal is the source of entries for the General Ledger (see Figure 16.1).

The Audit Function

The cash journal reflects not only the results of applying cash, but the end result of the audit of each remittance. A properly designed computer audit is implemented by a fairly complex set of program instructions necessary to perform all the interest and shortage calculations. Some of the special problems to be considered are explained in the following paragraphs.

IMPORTANCE OF ALGEBRAIC SIGNS

The programmer should be instructed to develop the calculated *audit difference* amount bearing the appropriate sign. For the benefit of the trained reviewers, shortages should develop and print as a PLUS AMOUNT; overages should develop and print as a negative amount. To accomplish this result the following method of crossfooting remittance totals is suggested:

Discount (Percent)	*Gross Amounts*	*Discount Allowed*	*Unadjusted Deductions*	*Cash Required*	*Check Amount*	*Difference Amount*
1	1000.00	10.00	100.00			
2	470.00	(9.40)				
2	300.00	6.00				
2	50.00-	1.00-				
	1720.00 + T	15.00 + T	100.00 + T	1605.00	1600.00	5.00 + T
Algebraic sign	Plus	Minus	Minus	Subtotal	Subtract	Plus or minus

By following the sign pattern shown above a short amount will develop as a plus, and if the check amount exceeds the cash required, a minus amount will develop. This is easier for reviewers to understand and work with than reversing the sign situation.

DO NOT REVERSE AMOUNT SIGNS

Print gross invoice amounts as normal plus amounts, even though these paid items amounts are—from an accounting viewpoint—credits to accounts receivable. Credits removed from the customer file by a remittance print with the minus sign.

DISCOUNTS: EARNED AND UNEARNED

Discount amounts allowed according to terms are credited to the account when calculating the amount of cash required to settle the paid items involved in a remittance. If the computer determines that an invoice which originally had available discount was not paid in time to earn the discount, print the discount amount *in parenthesis.* This helps the reviewer determine the reason for a major difference developed by the audit.

DEDUCTIONS AND DISCOUNT TERMS

For a receivables system to be precisely correct, terms should be applied to unadjusted deductions set up by a cash applier. When a customer deducts the full available discount

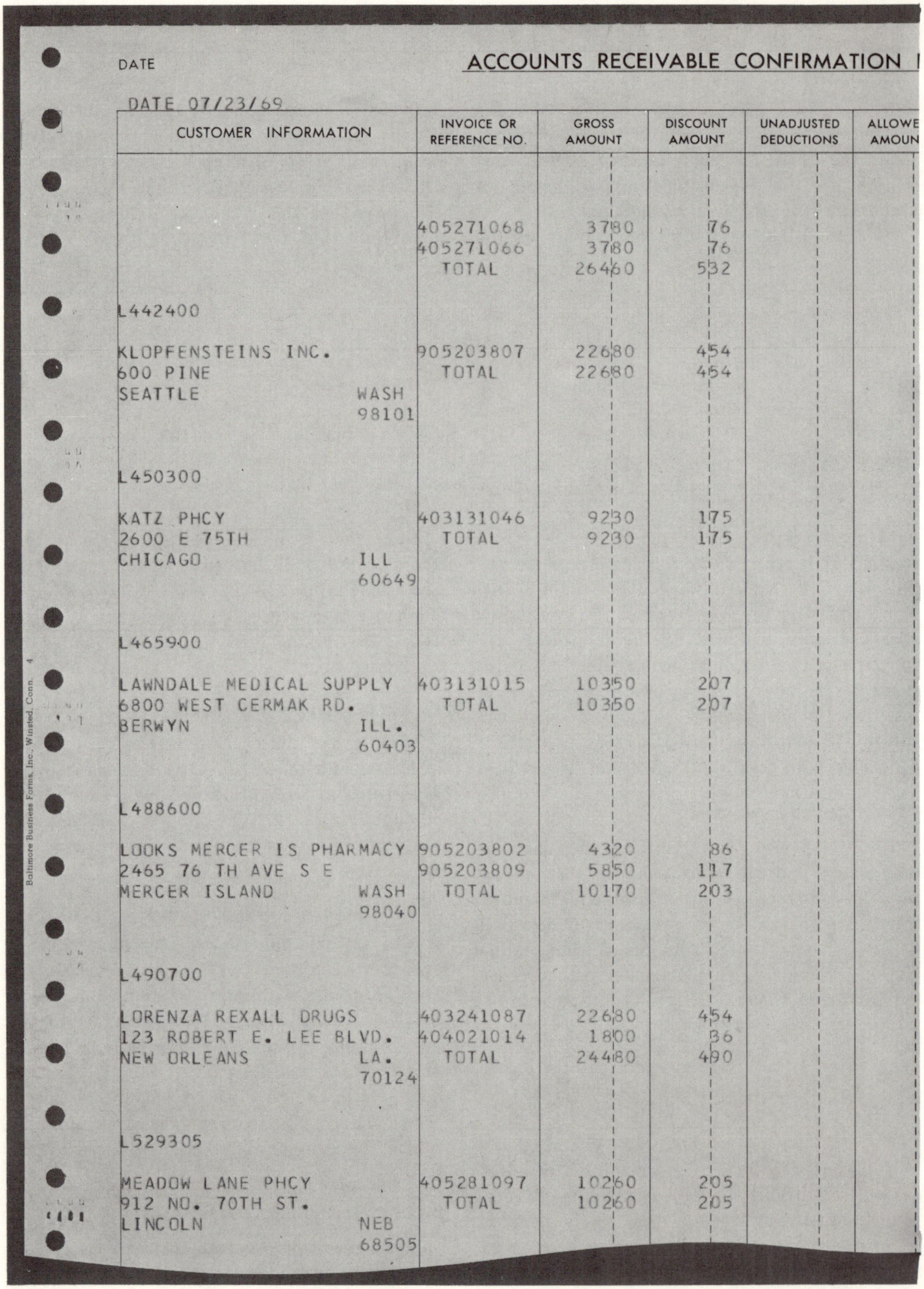

DATE

ACCOUNTS RECEIVABLE CONFIRMATION

DATE 07/23/69

CUSTOMER INFORMATION	INVOICE OR REFERENCE NO.	GROSS AMOUNT	DISCOUNT AMOUNT	UNADJUSTED DEDUCTIONS	ALLOWE AMOUN
	405271068	37 80	76		
	405271066	37 80	76		
	TOTAL	264 60	5 32		
L442400					
KLOPFENSTEINS INC.	905203807	226 80	4 54		
600 PINE	TOTAL	226 80	4 54		
SEATTLE WASH 98101					
L450300					
KATZ PHCY	403131046	92 30	1 75		
2600 E 75TH	TOTAL	92 30	1 75		
CHICAGO ILL 60649					
L465900					
LAWNDALE MEDICAL SUPPLY	403131015	103 50	2 07		
6800 WEST CERMAK RD.	TOTAL	103 50	2 07		
BERWYN ILL. 60403					
L488600					
LOOKS MERCER IS PHARMACY	905203802	43 20	86		
2465 76 TH AVE S E	905203809	58 50	1 17		
MERCER ISLAND WASH 98040	TOTAL	101 70	2 03		
L490700					
LORENZA REXALL DRUGS	403241087	226 80	4 54		
123 ROBERT E. LEE BLVD.	404021014	18 00	36		
NEW ORLEANS LA. 70124	TOTAL	244 80	4 90		
L529305					
MEADOW LANE PHCY	405281097	102 60	2 05		
912 NO. 70TH ST.	TOTAL	102 60	2 05		
LINCOLN NEB 68505					

Baltimore Business Forms, Inc., Winsted, Conn. 4

Figure 16.1 Typical computer-printed cash journal.

REPORT

PAGE

PAGE 4

CASH REQUIRED	CHECK AMOUNT	TR CD	DIFFERENCE AMOUNT	DISCOUNT DATE	PAYMENT DATE	CUSTOMER & CHECK NO.	SEQ. NO.	LATE INDICATOR
				06/28/69	06/30/69	2491	500043	
				06/28/69	06/30/69	2491	500045	
25928	25928					2491		
						L442400		
				06/28/69	06/30/69	10494	500004	
22226	22226					10494		
						L450300		
				06/30/69	06/30/69	1023	500001	
9055	9055					1023		
						L465900		
				06/30/69	06/30/69	17880	500001	
10143	10143					17880		
						L488600		
				06/27/69	06/30/69	13073	500001	
				06/28/69	06/30/69	13073	500002	
9967	9967					13073		
						L490700		
				06/30/69	06/30/69	6877	500001	
				06/30/69	06/30/69	6877	500002	
23990	23990					6877		
						L529305		
				06/30/69	06/30/69	3996	500001	
10055	10055					3996		

from an invoice, even though a deduction for a substantial amount was taken by the customer, the question arises as to the application of terms to the deduction for profit control purposes. Consider this situation:

Discount (Percent)	Gross Amount	Discount Taken	Unadjusted Deduction	Check Amount
2	800.00			
2	700.00			
	1500.00	30.00	300.00	1170.00

Noticé that the remitter took the full available discount of $30.00. He did not deduct the unadjusted deduction amount of 300.00 before figuring the earned discount. In this instance the deduction entry should be coded as "net," meaning that the customer has already taken the full discount amount; therefore, the credit that may be subsequently issued to cover the deduction must bear net terms. If the credit is issued subject to 2% terms, it will not fully cover the deduction amount set up as a debit —and indicates that the remitter took too much discount at time of payment.

The general rule is that invoice credits are subject to the same terms as the original invoice where the credit represents a return of merchandise from a specific shipment covered by an invoice. Now, if the customer takes the full discount amount when paying the invoice or invoices, yet claims a deduction of $300 for returned merchandise, then he has deducted 2% on $300 improperly; this is a direct loss of $6 to the seller.

Now consider the fact that a credit subject to discount terms is not worth the face value of the credit document; its cash value is the discounted amount.

Discount Terms	Unadjusted Deduction	Discount Terms	Invoice Credit Amount	Cash Value of Invoice Credit
Net	300.00	2%	300.00	294.00

If the credit of $300.00, subject to terms of 2%, is used to clear off the open deduction (net terms) of $300.00, a shortage of $6 is indicated.

BENEFITS OF COMPUTER AUDIT FUNCTION

There are many benefits gained from a properly programmed computer audit of remittances:

- Reduces number of cash appliers that otherwise would be required for a manual audit and application of checks.
- Accurately determines whether discount is earned or unearned.
- Consistently brings out amount of early or late interest, without fail.
- Accurately calculates audit difference amounts—and prints them on the Cash Journal for review.
- Captures all remittance data for management reports.

The Review Function

On completion of the audit run and printing of the Cash Journal, the reviewers then begin their work of reviewing major differences. This review work and related coding may be done by the cash appliers, or by a separate, specially-trained group. There are advantages and disadvantages to both approaches.

The reviewers inherit the remittance advices and other paper work left over from the initial cash application steps. Their primary purpose at this point is to determine the reason or reasons for each major difference amount revealed by the audit and to resolve the differences.

CODING WORK

In essence the reviewers are required to prepare certain transactions for input and to code each transaction properly for keypunching. There are several methods for preparing the coded transactions for routing to the keypunch section.

1. *Use punched cards.* The cash audit run may provide punched cards as a by-product; one card for each check that developed a major difference. By

writing code numbers and amounts on the face of the punched work card, the reviewer communicates the disposition instructions to the keypunch section. (See Figure 16.2)

2. *Use Printed Work Sheets.* Suppose that the computer prints a separate work sheet showing all major difference amounts after printing the Cash Journal. The reviewers write their codes and amounts on this work sheet and prove that their breakdown amounts equal the original difference amount, then turn in the work sheets to keypunch.

TYPES OF DISPOSITION INSTRUCTIONS

There are several types of disposition instructions:

1. Those that create unit records which will be posted back to the customer receivables file:
   - Unearned Discount DR
   - Excess Discount DR
   - Unadjusted Deduction DR
   - Late Interest DR
   - Remittance Shortage
   - Overpayment Credit
   - Received-on-Account Credit, etc.
2. Those that create unit records that will be charged to a division or a subsidiary of the parent firm:
   - Deduction
   - Late Interest
   - Anticipation Amount (early interest taken)
3. Those that add amounts into an internal expense account or adjustment account:
   - Bank charges
   - Collection fees
   - Discount Allowed
   - Interest Adjustment
4. *Special-Function Instructions:*
   - Repost a deleted record
   - Change cash amount in remittance record
   - Reverse an unadjusted deduction amount set up
   - Delete a record now on master file

DISPOSITION REPORT

The disposition report is prepared only after a careful audit is made of all grouped disposition instructions brought into the system. A key point is that the reviewer's coded instructions should dispose of the original difference amount to a penny; if the amounts keypunched for one check do not take care of (dispose of) the original amount exactly, all of the transactions bearing the common check number should be rejected.

After the disposition instructions have been edited, proved, and accepted into the system, the next step is to print the Disposition Report for management. This report shows the customer's name and address, the check number, and the original difference amount. Then, the remaining columns show the various amounts and transaction numbers that indicate the disposition of the difference.

NEW RECORDS CONSTRUCTED

Many new records are created by this run in accordance with the reviewers' instructions to charge back certain major differences to customer accounts. If the instruction code represents an internal absorption charge, a record is created anyway for internal reporting purposes. If a code indicates that some internal department or division is to be charged, a special record is created for monthend reporting of charges and charge-backs.

This run creates a new, adjusted paid-items file and a special accounts receivable charges and charge-back file, including all records to enter into a subsequent posting run for posting to the indicated accounts.

THE REPOST PROBLEM

Occasionally, a cash applier will mark or circle the wrong item record when identifying paid items. Since the amount of the record incorrectly deleted during the updating run is apt to be quite different from the correct record, the audit run will develop a major difference, over or short. This situation presents a major problem to the reviewer.

Primarily, the reviewer must take steps to restore to the receivables file the record incorrectly removed. There are two methods for doing this. First, find the original record on the paid-items work file and copy all the details to a new ''add-back'' file of accounts receivable charges and charge-backs that are generated by the review of differences function. Second, the reviewer writes all the invoice data with pencil on an input form for keypunching.

The first method is the better of the two for many reasons. It precludes introducing an error into the record to be restored. It also eliminates

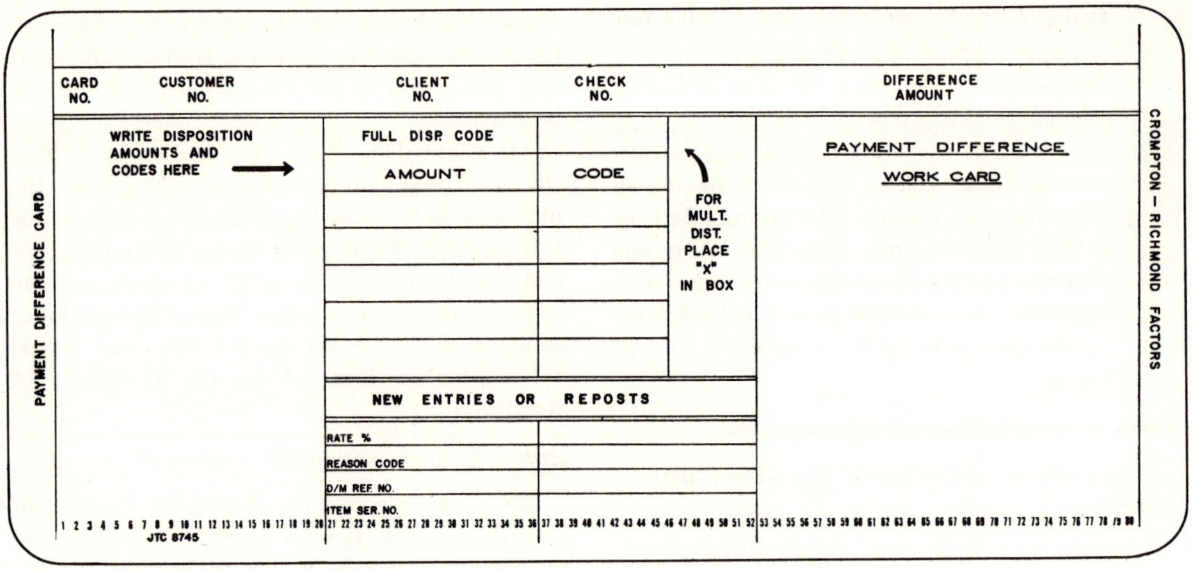

Figure 16.2 Cash difference work card (courtesy of Crompton-Richmond Factors Company, Inc.).

the difficulty of finding all the necessary invoice record data that may not appear, in its entirety, on printouts readily available to the reviewer.

When the reviewer provides the input information for a repost situation, it consists of customer number and the *sequence or finder number,* as well as the check number. By including the paid-items file as input to the disposition of differences run, this procedure can match the input record with the special "repost code" in it to the original invoice record—and cause the program to *copy the original record* to the new work file of items to be subsequently posted to the customer file.

The reviewer is not relieved of the repost problem yet, however. When you put a record back on the file, there is *unapplied cash* remaining. And, the invoice that *should have been removed* is still on the open-item file. If the open items are kept on magnetic tape there is no opportunity to get at and to remove the invoice that was actually paid but is still on the open file—until the next updating or delete run. Therefore, the reviewer can handle the situation as follows:

- Sets up a received-on-account entry for the amount of unused cash. This will put the unapplied cash on the account temporarily.
- Handle the on-account cash as an offset against the open invoice through the "cash-equals" cash application process described in Chapter 14. (As a reminder to do this, it is suggested that the reviewer keep a copy of the remittance paper work until the on-account cash is actually applied to clear the invoice or invoices from the customer file.)

Print Final Cash Journal

The disposition of major audit differences represents changes to the various control totals originally printed on the Cash Received Journal. One popular approach to cash reporting is to bring the disposition instructions back into the computer system and to adjust the original cash remittance totals as to discount allowed, deductions set up, early or late interest amounts, and the like. After the adjustments have been made, then print a Final Cash Journal. This is usually a simple, one-line summary for each check showing the actual cash amount, the adjusted discount amount, the final total for deductions set up, the amounts charged back to receivables, internal amounts, etc.

Another concept eliminates the Final Cash Journal; adjustment totals are taken directly from the Disposition of Differences Report. In other words this report is considered to be a supplement to the Cash Received Journal.

Preparing the Paper Work

The final step is the preparation of all necessary papers for internal and external routing. Unadjusted deductions and internal charges require the writing of certain information to be routed internally; errors in remittances, unearned or excess discount taken, or unknown shortages require the preparation of notices or statements to be sent direct to the customers.

Many computerized receivables systems have never automated the preparation of the above-specified paper work. However, all of the details about the remittance and the paid items have been captured on a work file for other reasons anyway, so it is only logical to program the computer to quickly print both types of forms after all differences revealed by the audit run have been taken care of. A typical notice form produced by a computer is illustrated in Chapter 17.

CHAPTER 17

Unadjusted Deductions and Other Financial Costs

Nearly all business firms with trade receivables share a problem of increasing magnitude: the number and total amount of unadjusted deductions taken by customers from remittances. Deductions represent both an operating problem requiring trained personnel and a source of profit leaks.

Possibly, because of the present high cost of capital, the total amount of funds involved in unadjusted deductions is increasing constantly. Recent computer analyses of the receivables investment in scores of firms indicate that open deductions found on receivables files frequently amount to as much as four or five percent of the total investment in receivables. This fact provides a clue as to the sheer necessity for top management to focus its attention on this aspect of trade receivables administration. One purpose of this chapter is to acquaint management personnel and systems analysts with the nature and scope of the deductions problem.

CHARACTERISTICS

Consider these facts about each open, unresolved deduction found among the receivables records:

- It is a potential charge against profits—if it is allowed and charged to internal expense or to sales returns.
- It may represent a dispute with the customer and is, therefore, a threat to customer goodwill.
- The internal paperwork and research necessary to make a decision to allow or disallow the deduction adds materially to the overhead expense in the office.

DEFINITION

An "unadjusted" deduction is any deduction from a remittance, other than discount or anticipation, that is not covered by an open credit on the receivables records at the time of cash application. The cash applier is responsible for noting such amounts arbitrarily deducted from a remittance; and for preparing input information as well as the necessary paperwork that a deduction creates. Quite often the customer will attach debit memo documents to his check explaining the reason for and the details behind his calculation of the deduction amount.

REASONS FOR DEDUCTIONS

The reasons for deductions vary from one industry to another, but some are common to nearly any type of business trading with other business firms:

- Freight allowance claimed (freight was prepaid and added to invoice).

- Freight damage claimed by customer. There are two types of damage claims:

  The claim is supported by bill of lading signed by carrier's driver.

  The claim is unsupported except by customer's own debit memo.

Other deductions may be made because the customer claims the following:

- Wrong selling price
- Concealed shortage in shipment
- Wrong sizes, colors shipped
- Wrong product picked and shipped
- Merchandise returned
- Advertising allowance
- Promotional allowance
- Spoiled merchandise, etc.

PAPERWORK AND CONTROL

The detection of an unadjusted deduction by a cash applier is the start of a chain of paper work and related clerical and follow-up procedures that may involve several departments and areas within a firm before the deduction is resolved and properly disposed of.

The follow-up work and control over open deductions is usually vested in a group of people working in the accounts receivable operations area referred to as "customer correspondents" or "adjusters."

Follow-up work involves a firm's own internal departments exclusively unless the customer failed to provide a reason or details supporting his deduction. In this case it is necessary to call or write the customer's accounts payable department requesting additional information about the deduction.

DUTIES OF ADJUSTERS

The adjusters may assist with some of the necessary research involved in disposing of a deduction. For example, one of their duties may be to search through credit memos on hand to see if the deduction has already been covered by a credit. (The credit was not on the books at the time the check was received and applied.) If the deduction is the type that involves reference to the original invoice (such as a claimed pricing error), the adjusters may be charged with finding the invoice to obtain a working copy.

Primarily, however, their main function is to set up a control file of deduction papers and to follow up on the departments that are supposed to take over the problem for research and eventual disposition. Then, when a reply is received from the department the adjuster may be required to prepare the working papers necessary to request the preparation of a credit memo.

MANY DIFFERENT DEPARTMENTS INVOLVED

As indicated, deduction follow-up work potentially covers many different operations sections and functions within a firm. The reason for the deduction—if known—provides the clue as to which department should do the research:

Reason	*Department Typically Involved in Researching Deduction*
1. Wrong selling price claimed	1. Order department
2. Concealed shortage	2. Shipping department
3. Wrong merchandise shipped	3. Order/shipping departments
4. Soiled goods shipped	4. Shipping department
5. Wrong sizes, colors shipped	5. Order/shipping departments
6. Freight allowance claimed	6. Sales department
7. Freight damage claimed	7. Traffic department
8. Promotional allowance taken	8. Sales or advertising department
9. Advertising allowance taken	9. Advertising department
10. Merchandise returned	10. Receiving department or inventory control

FREIGHT CLAIMS

If claimed freight damage is documented by the attachment of a bill of lading signed by the carrier's driver or representative, the traffic department will file a claim against the carrier for the amount of the damage. This step creates a receivables situation in the traffic department. For this reason, some firms do NOT set up this type of deduction as an accounts receivable charge-back; they charge the deduction to the traffic department as an internal charge. The amount is returned to the customer's file only if the traffic department is unable to collect from the carrier and makes a decision that the customer should pay the additional amount represented by the deduction.

DETERMINE SOURCE OF DEDUCTIONS

Before management can institute effective control methods and procedures designed to reduce the overall profit leaks through deductions, it is necessary to determine the sources of most of the deductions—and the reasons for them.

Here are two examples of the information resulting from an analysis of deductions over a period of time:

1. A cosmetics manufacturer found that 300 accounts out of 15,000 accounts generated most of the deductions, both in number and in total dollars. The 300 accounts were large department and chain stores.
2. A manufacturer of wearing apparel analyzed all deductions set up for a month and found that 77 accounts out of a list of 14,000 originated 67% of all open deduction dollar amounts. The list of 77 accounts was exclusively made up of department stores, discount houses, and chain stores.

VALUE OF REASON CODE

The use of a reason code has a great deal of merit potentially. This makes it possible to accumulate the data about deductions and to prepare meaningful reports to management. After discussing how to use a reason code, we shall examine the tremendous benefits to be gained from the reports.

Prepare a master list of reasons for deductions in your firm. Then assign a 2-digit code to each reason description, starting with "01," which may be the designation for "Reason unknown." Assign code 02 to "Wrong selling price," 03 to Freight Allowance Claimed, etc.

SPECIAL REPORTS BASED ON REASON CODE

The value of the reason code is that special management reports can be prepared which provide clues as to what is happening that generates expensive deductions. In a data processing system it is easy to capture each deduction set up during a calendar month and store it on a work tape. At monthend, sort the deduction records by major sales division, then by region or district—then by the *reason code*. Print a list of the deductions, or add the amounts and report totals for each reason code.

REPORT FORMAT

Sales Division Number	*Region Number*	*Reason Code*	*Number of Deducts*	*Total Amount*
No. 1	No. 1	01	126	$ 6,777.45
		02	205	20,444.33
		03	166	10,289.50
	No. 1 TOTALS		899*	52,775.35*
	No. 2	01	144	7,209.88
		02	58	4,555.42
		03	66	5,042.74
		04	89	7,524.65
	No. 2 TOTALS		512*	31,914.33*

As shown above, print the grand total of deductions—number and amount—for Region No. 1, then continue the report for Region No. 2, etc.

VALUE OF REPORT

Firms that utilize this type of report as a management tool gain great value from it, since it serves as a monthly problem indicator. For example, suppose that a sudden sharp rise in the number of deductions taken for "wrong price" is noted in a certain region. Management may find that several new order clerks were recently hired in the order department—and obviously need more training.

The management of one firm, after receiving this type of special report for a period of time, concluded that their product containers were not substantial enough to withstand the rough handling that is received during shipment by common carriers. *Reason.* The report consistently showed a large number of *substantiated* freight damage claims, which caused an investigation of the containers. The conclusion was that heavier containers had to be adopted. This was done and the number of freight damage claims dropped sharply.

If the report shows an abnormal number of freight *allowances* claimed in a certain region, it is very possible that the sales department is overpromising in order to get orders.

Similar valuable results can be gained from analyzing the reasons for the issuance of credits. However, since deductions precede most credits, a report of the type shown above has more value in that management can move faster to solve the problems revealed by the analytical report.

I once analyzed manually 1700 credit memos issued by an apparel manufacturer and tabulated the major reasons found on the face of each credit memo. Without going near the manufacturer's factory or shipping warehouse it was obvious—based on the tabulated results—that the firm had no quality control or that the shipping department was incredibly careless. This conclusion was reached because several hundred of the credit memos bore the same comments, such as "soiled goods," "oil spots," "streaked," "torn," and the like.

DEDUCTION HANDLING COSTS

Few firms have calculated the internal cost of processing and disposing of deduction debits. The overall cost in a large firm is obviously of considerable magnitude because of the number of people involved in various ways, and because of the extensive paper work and follow-up work required. Consider the following steps typically required to set up a deduction and eventually to clear it from the files:

1. The cash application bookkeeper sets up deduction as a debit to accounts receivable. Clears paid items from the account.
2. The bookkeeper prepares deduction notice forms for subsequent use internally for investigation and processing of the claim.
3. The bookkeeper routes the deduction papers to a group of adjusters.
4. The adjuster files one copy of the forms for later follow-up and may handle initial steps such as finding a copy of the applicable invoice (where the deduction requires reference to a specific invoice) and sends the remaining copies to the department indicated by the reason code for action.
5. The department involved in the problem performs further research to determine the validity of the claim and eventually produces a decision to:
   (1) Allow the claim in full
   (2) Allow part of it
   (3) Disallow the entire amount
6. If allowed, the customer service section authorizes the issuance of a credit invoice to the customer.
7. When the credit is received in the accounts receivable section, a bookkeeper posts the credit to the customer's account.
8. When the adjuster receives a copy of the credit, he pulls the matching deduction papers from the suspense files and matches them for further filing.
9. The adjuster prepares a journal entry to instruct the receivables bookkeeper to clear the offsetting debit and credit entries from the customer's account.
10. The receivables bookkeeper receives the journal entry document and keys off the offsetting items on the account.

The overall time period required for clearing a deduction ranges from a few days to many weeks, depending on the type and extent of research required.

ADJUSTERS VERSUS COLLECTORS

Usually the deduction follow-up and control function is kept separate from the collection of past due accounts. The usual organizational structure provides for a special group of adjusters, as mentioned previously, who work with the internal departments and who occasionally contact a customer for more information about an unknown deduction. Also, if the eventual decision on a deduction is that it will not be allowed, then it becomes necessary to notify the customer of this fact and to attempt to collect the deduction amount from the customer. In this instance, a deduction problem becomes a collection problem.

SEGREGATE CREDIT MEMOS

Credit memos issued to cover deductions should be kept separate from regular credits and should be clearly stamped: "DO NOT MAIL —return to Adjusters." The reason for this is that the customer has already deducted the amount and should not receive the credit document. If a mistake is made and a copy of a credit memo covering a deduction is mailed to the customer, he is very likely to use the credit as part payment of other items at a future date.

AUTOMATIC CHARGE OFF OF DEDUCTIONS

Many firms have experimented with the policy of charging small deductions to internal expense immediately, instead of charging them back to the account and doing expensive research on each one. The theory is that if the paper work costs are higher than the amount charged off directly, or that the eventual disposition of such items is to allow them anyway, then the direct route may provide a lower cost and a cleaner way of handling the problem of small deductions.

Some firms charge off all deductions up to \$10. Occasionally the credit manager sets the amount as high as \$15. Experience has shown that this approach has merit. However, there is one important point to consider here. First, observe the large number of varying reasons for deductions listed on a prior page. Then ponder over the many different departments involved and the variable procedures followed in accordance with the *reason* for the deduction. Now, expensing \$5 may be quite appropriate for one particular type of deduction, but it may not be enough to cover a deduction taken for a different reason. But, if the amount is raised to \$15 to cover one of the more expensive types of deductions, this may be excessive for other types of deductions.

The point is that a considerable amount of money is involved in deductions in a firm receiving several hundred checks per day. (On the average 10% of all checks paying trade receivables include one or more deductions). To set one amount as policy for absorbing deductions of all types and for many variable reasons should be examined carefully. It may well prove to be a very expensive policy overall. Consider dividing the deductions into groups, calculate or estimate the costs involved in processing those in each group—then establish *different policy amounts for each group.*

ARE AUTOMATIC CHARGEOFFS PRACTICAL?

Suppose that the credit manager decides to absorb automatically all deductions for amounts up to \$10. Let us consider certain aspects and possible repercussions resulting from this policy. For example, automatic absorption of small deductions implies that no credit memo documents will be issued. However, this affects several different types of accounting records, such as sales reports, sales commissions payable, tax reports, and the like. Usually, all of these reports reflect sales reversal entries (credits). Therefore, deductions have the effect of reducing sales (where goods are returned and a deduction is made). In turn, sales reports and sales commissions are affected. All of these problems should be taken into consideration before it is decided to absorb small deductions automatically.

One method of handling the charge-off of small deductions is for the cash application bookkeepers to prepare a set of credit memo documents as part of applying checks. That is, they write a short-form credit memo manually in lieu of preparing deduction notice documents.

AUTOMATIC PRINTING OF DEDUCTION PAPERS

A by-product of cash application is the writing of customer notices re unearned discounts taken, overpayment credits, or major differences detected by the cash audit. Unadjusted deductions also require the preparation of notices for review by various internal departments. Historically, these notices are prepared manually by the cash application bookkeepers as part of the process of applying cash. This paper work takes time and inevitably increases the number of bookkeepers required to handle a given volume of checks.

Several years ago those of us specializing in the computerization of trade receivables decided that this paper work should be handled by the computer. We knew that the necessary details for printing the paper work, such as check data and paid-item information were available on various work tapes written as a by-product of updating the open-item file and resulting from the cash audit run. Therefore, the project involved primarily forms design and then programming to implement the concept that the computer could produce all necessary notices, both for the customer and for internal use. This approach has been very successful and has been installed in many well-known firms (see Figure 17.1).

SET UP SPECIAL RECEIVABLES

The usual way of handling deductions is to charge them back to the remitter's account until such time as a credit memo has been issued. If the amount of the credit is approximately the same as the debit, then both are removed from the account through a journal entry. Until this happens, however, the open deduction is a part of the regular receivables account.

A few firms have adopted the policy of passing all deductions along to the department within the company that is responsible for investigating and disposing of the deduction. Under this approach the deductions are not set up on the remitter's account; they are charged to the department directly. This means, in effect, that each department such as sales, traffic, order processing, shipping, and others must maintain their own receivables section. The evaluation of the pros and cons of this method leads one to wonder about the economic and practical feasibility of it.

Each department now requires the equivalent of one or more adjusters to follow the paper work and, possibly, to contact the customer for more information. Central management has now lost control over the problem, since it is fragmented. And we know that the total amount of money involved at any one time in open deductions is apt to be very large in a firm doing a sizeable sales volume on credit.

In connection with this approach it should be mentioned that the traffic department is one department that legitimately handles its own type of receivables—those with the common carriers. For example, when a customer deducts an amount for freight damage and attaches a signed delivery receipt, the traffic department files a claim against the carrier. This sets up a receivable that is cleared when the carrier finally pays the claim.

Controlling the Deductions Paper work

Following up on deductions and eventually removing the ones that have been processed properly is a function of the adjusters or customer correspondents. This should be systematized so that the issuance of appropriate credits will enable the adjuster to match the credit to the open deduction papers and thereby to clear the in-process file. Unless routine procedures are established, the file of open deduction papers will continually grow.

SPECIAL REPORTS FOR FOLLOWUP

A basic procedure requires that credit memos which refer to a deduction will be routed to adjusters for the matching process described above. However, we know through experience that these credits are not always routed to the adjusters. Other follow-up methods are required to assist the adjusters to keep updated. One method is to accumulate all credit records processed through the computer room when posting sales to accounts receivable files for one week. Print a *list of all credits processed* for the week in customer number sequence and route to the adjusters.

The adjusters refer to the customer numbers and/or names on the list and check to determine if they have documents for a corresponding open deduction. If so, they pull the deduction papers and place them to one side.

CLEARING "EQUALS" FROM RECEIVABLES FILE

Clearing papers from follow-up files is only one of two essential steps in the deduction processing cycle. The two offsetting amounts, debit and credit, must be removed from the receivable account of the customer. Some firms prefer that the cash application bookkeepers handle this function; others insist that the adjusters should initiate this important procedure.

If the adjusters are required to handle this clearing process, they will identify both the credit and the deduction to be removed from the account and will send the necessary notated documents or special list to the bookkeepers for this action.

REPORT OF OPEN DEDUCTIONS AND CREDITS

One of the most valuable and useful reports that can easily be printed monthly when re-

NOTICE OF CUSTOMER DEDUCTION

SUPPLIER:

YOUR CUSTOMER:

DATE	CUSTOMER NO.	NOTICE NO.

REASON CODES:

01 - UNKNOWN	05 - SAMPLES	09 - ADVER. ALLOW.
02 - PRICE DIFF.	06 - P.P.	10 - MDSE. NOT REC.
03 - FREIGHT ALLOW.	07 - MDSE. RTD.	11 - TERMS DIFF.
04 - MDSE. SHORT	08 - CREDIT	12 - LATE INT.

CHECK DATE	CHECK NO.	CUSTOMER REMITTANCE AMOUNT

WE HAVE RECEIVED YOUR CUSTOMER'S CHECK AS DETAILED ABOVE

LIST OF PAID INVOICES							DEDUCTIONS					
INVOICE		INVOICE AMOUNT	ALLOWANCE DISCOUNT AMOUNT	FINAL DUE DATE	NO. DAYS LATE		DATE	D/M REF. NO.	CODE	TERMS		DEDUCTION AMOUNT
DATE	NO.									%	DYS	
	TOTAL										TOTAL	

AS TO CUSTOMER DEDUCTIONS LISTED ABOVE, PLEASE ADVISE US BY CHECKING ONE OF THE BOXES BELOW AND RETURNING TO US ONE SIGNED COPY OF THIS NOTICE. THE ABOVE DEDUCTIONS WILL BE CHARGED TO YOUR ACCOUNT UNLESS OTHERWISE ADJUSTED.

CLIENT: YOUR CREDIT SHOULD BEAR SAME DISCOUNT TERMS AS THE DEDUCTION ABOVE

WE WILL ISSUE CREDIT FOR THE DEDUCTION. . . . . ☐

WE WILL CORRESPOND WITH THE CUSTOMER AND NOTIFY YOU WITHIN 30 DAYS. . . . . ☐

CHARGE OUR ACCOUNT FOR THE AMOUNT DEDUCTED (WE WILL NOT ISSUE A CREDIT) . . . . ☐

PLEASE RETURN IMMEDIATELY X SIGN ______________________

Figure 17.1 Notice of customer deduction (printed by computer).

ceivables are on the computer is the "Report of Aged Open Deductions" (see Figure 17.2 below).

This report should be designed so that the adjusters can first review it, account by account, and then can indicate on the *face of the report itself* those offsetting entries to be removed by journal entry. If this concept is followed, the item finder number should be shown on the right side of the report for ease of keypunching the required data from the report.

A MANAGEMENT REPORT

The original purpose of this report was for use as a working report. However, the actual installation of the report in many different firms produced a surprise in that management at different levels was quite interested in it. *Reason.* It is an *aged trial balance* of open deductions! For this prime reason, field sales managers are frequently eager to receive a copy.

Sources of Profit Dilution Through Receivables

Surveys of limited scope and duration over the years indicate that up to 17% of all checks received have an adverse impact on the profits of the creditor firm one way or another. This fact becomes very clear when one studies a detailed remittance audit after this function has been computerized and put into daily operation. The reason is that the computer does a very accurate, precise job of determining whether the discount was earned or unearned, calculates early or late interest involved in each remittance, and mathematically determines the amount of cash required to "settle" the paid items removed from the account by virtue of receiving and applying a check. It then compares the cash required with the actual cash received —and prints the *difference* in a special column. Recognizable deductions are set up by the bookkeeper initially; this means that many checks will reflect a .00 difference as a result of the audit because the unadjusted deduction was properly set up as part of the application of the check. Yet, it should not be overlooked that the deduction itself probably will be charged to expense eventually as a result of the necessary internal investigation.

CHECK LIST FOR SYSTEMS ANALYSTS

The following discussion of the many elements involved in cash application which represent potential sources of loss is intended to serve as a checklist for the systems analysts to use for developing and building control and reporting devices into the new computerized system to cover these sources of loss.

1. *Earned Discounts Taken.* This is a financial expense that is a legitimate deduction by the remitter if he pays within invoice terms. Since the annual expense reflected here is a direct reflection of the discount percentages included in sales terms, the financial officers of any firm should periodically review all terms and conditions offered. It seems that this is seldom done in many firms, yet the terms frequently have been changed in meaning so that they no longer accomplish the original objectives . . . and are accepted without question by all concerned.
2. *Unearned Discounts Taken.* This is not a new problem. This is controlled by the credit department in that it is either allowed or disallowed. Frequently we find no uniform, firm policy in connection with administering this problem. If most unearned discounts taken are absorbed as a matter of practice, one suggestion is to build a customer *profit and loss data field* into the customer master file kept on the computer. Then, for each unearned discount amount absorbed and added to discount expense, *post the amount* into the customer's data bank for subsequent reporting to credit management. This does not solve the problem, but it reports the amounts involved for each customer for possible policy review and better control over this expense.
3. *Errors and Differences Absorbed.* An audit of remittances will reveal a surprising number of checks where the amount required is different from the actual cash amount. The difference may be a plus or minus amount. Differences result from errors on the part of the customer's accounts payable personnel; occasionally a major difference may be an unadjusted deduction *not so identified* by the remitter.

Omitting this factor from the overall situation for a moment, systems analysts should not confuse an audit difference with a true, unadjusted deduction. If the difference is a short amount, it is the same as a deduction from a

MONTHLY REPORT OF AGED OPEN DEDUCTIONS

DIVISION : NO. 05 MONTH OF: JUNE 1972

CUSTOMER NAME	Account No.	Item Date	Check or Ref. No.	Debit Memo No.	RSN Code	DEDUCTION AMOUNT — and Open Credits	No. Days Outst.	DEDUCTION AGING				FINDER NO.
								1–30	31–60	61–90	91 and Over	
CHARLES ALBERSON & CO.	001–214–6	03–14–72	63,140	15,123	04	89.40	108				89.40	14–0076
1234 MAIN ST.		04–21–72	299,078			88.35–						14–095
NEWARK, N.J.												
KARL ATTEBURY MAN'S SHOP	001–417–9	04–10–72	12,456		06	112.90	81			112.90		01–0234
1616 MARLBORO		04–15 72	12,600		08	50.00	76			50.00		01–0235
DALLAS, TEXAS												
ROBERT BROWN & SON	002–016–3	03–25–72	33,980	1,478	04	215.00	97			215.00		03–0044
5500 DUNWAY ROAD		04–20–72	35,016	1,735	02	94.75	71			94.75		04–0076
HICKSVILLE, N.Y.		05–31–72	36,777	1,914	02	104.20	30	104.20				04–0143
BURLE & SMITH	002–815–7	05–11–72	7,724	36,999	06	66.90	50		66.90			05–0166
1622 OAK ST.		06–04–72	8,215	37,333	12	75.00	26	75.00				05–0219
ATLANTA, GA.												

Figure 17.2 Monthly report of aged open deductions.

mathematical viewpoint, but the two items should be handled quite differently. For example, an unadjusted deduction so identified by the remitter calls for creating paper work processed internally until the case is disposed of. However, a major difference resulting from an audit that is unexplained or seems to be the result of an error requires that a notice be sent directly to the customer requesting an explanation or payment.

Considerable thought should be given to the shortage amount to be absorbed without creating paper work and without charging or crediting the customer's account. The amount to be absorbed varies by policy from $1 in a few firms to as much as $15 in other firms. The use of $5 as a policy amount is quite commonly found in commercial firms.

A suggestion. Whatever the policy amount is today, do not assume it is inviolable. Since the total amount of money charged to expense through this procedure is apt to be very substantial on an annual basis, management should obtain facts and figures on what is happening in this area of operations—and should review the policy amount periodically.

4. *Excess Discounts Taken and Allowed.* Apply the same rules to excess discounts as discussed above for unearned discounts.
5. *Changes of Terms.* An old adage says, "Time is money." To prove the point, when the sales department casually grants a customer's request for an extra 60 days on an invoice of $5000, the creditor firm has just incurred an expense of $83.34 because that is the cost of money for 60 days on $5000 at 10%.

This indicates the necessity for control over changes of terms. Frequently, this control is vested in the credit manager. He should approve all changes of terms that require the requester to prepare a special document. This approved form is then used to create a journal entry to introduce the new terms into the computerized receivables system.

6. *Excess Anticipation.* Firms in the apparel industry permit their customers to deduct interest if they pay before the invoice is due. Amounts so deducted should be audited and carefully controlled. It is basically the same problem as excess discounts.
7. *Late Payments.* Most remittance audits, outside of the commercial factoring firms, ignore the element of late interest. Yet, when a customer pays one or more invoices late, he has used the creditor firm's capital without authority and without penalty. It is recommended that your new system be designed to calculate and *print* the early or late interest applicable to each individual remittance. This provides internal financial cost data that may be valuable, even though management may not consider billing late interest to customers.
8. *Failure to Apply Terms Discounts to Credits.* Quite often we find large firms issuing credits for returned goods that are "net." That is, no invoice terms are applied to credits as a matter of policy. Yet, the invoice that billed the merchandise to the account may have granted terms of 2% or 3% to the buyer, either as a cash discount or as a trade discount. To present an extreme but not an unusual situation to dramatize the dollar costs of this policy, let us consider the following steps in a sale.

- The customer is shipped $1000 in merchandise; the invoice is sent to him for $1000 showing sales terms of 3% 10 N 30.
- The customer remits promptly, paying $970 on discount basis.
- The customer receives and examines merchandise and returns all of it.
- The selling firm prepares and issues a credit memo (with no sales terms applied) for $1000.
- The customer requests a check to cover the open credit now on his account. The check is prepared for $1000, which is the net credit amount.

This points up the interesting fact that the seller incurred all the expense of selling, shipping, billing, receiving the merchandise back into stock, issuing a credit memo—and lost $30 cash on the original transaction!

9. *Bad Debts.* This loss has no connection with the routine application of cash but is included, since the topic on these pages is the sources of profit dilution through receivables.

Even suspense accounts (accounts turned over to collection agencies or attorneys) can be systematized with good results. This indicates the scope and magnitude of the systems analysts' responsibilities when they undertake the job of successfully computerizing trade receivables.

CHAPTER 18

Journal Entries and Special Transactions

When designing a receivables system, there is a tendency on the part of the systems designers to devote considerable time and attention to cash application and to other facets of the system developed for the application of cash, for controlling audit differences and for the preparation of paper work and reports. However, everyone concerned with a systems development project must recognize that journal entry processing is equally important. Journal entries cover a wide range of functions and require considerable time to plan and develop the necessary forms and procedures—and accounting controls.

THREE TYPES

From a functional viewpoint, journal entry transactions fall into three categories:

- Those that add debit or credit records to the customer file.
- Those that cause existing open-item records to be flagged—or *deleted entirely* from the open item file.
- Those that accomplish changes in the open-item records.

In addition to accounting-type journal entries, the list of transaction codes must include special transactions that handle file updating, changes, and maintenance.

Examples of special transactions are:

- The transfer of a single record from one account to another.
- The transfer of an entire account from one file location to another.
- The change of terms in an invoice record.
- Introducing indicative codes into invoice records.
- Name/Address header transactions.
- Those that update or change information carried in the customer data bank, etc.

ADDITIONS TO THE CUSTOMER FILE

Quite often it is necessary to adjust an account for various reasons; the adjustment may take the form of posting a journal entry debit or credit amount to the file. Each record should include a JE date and source number.

DELETIONS FROM THE FILE

The great majority of journal entries are introduced into the processing run to find and delete records from the file for a variety of reasons:

- Bad debt charge-off: individual items or an entire account.
- Clearing offsetting debit and credit items: this is known as clearing "equals."
- When a check is sent to a customer covering open

credits, a cash disbursement journal entry is created to find and remove the open credit records from the file.

- Charging off uncollectible unadjusted deductions, remittance shortages, late interest billings, and other types of items.

CHANGES IN OPEN RECORDS

Changes effected in open records must be carefully controlled. The usual rule is that no change is permitted in dollar amounts—only in numeric data that serve to identify the record. For example, the system may permit changing the invoice number, store number, or the transaction code, but not the amount.

A very important type of change transaction is the *change of terms*. When a customer requests extra time for the payment of an invoice coming due, and his request is approved, then it is necessary to change the invoice terms which, in turn, changes the two vital due dates stored in the open record.

This requires identifying the customer and the specific open invoice. The input record for a change of terms brings in the new terms to be applied to the invoice. The updating program must include instructions that will write the new terms in the open invoice—and that will calculate and store the new due dates resulting from the change of terms; namely, the discount and final due dates.

An alternative method of handling a change of terms is to keypunch and post a new invoice record including the new terms; this requires the deletion of the original invoice through a journal entry. Merely changing the terms without deleting the original invoice seems to be the better approach, since it offers positive control and eliminates the possibility of introducing new errors when keypunching the replacement invoice.

OUT-TRANSACTION CODE

Journal entry transactions that search out and delete an open item from the customer file include their own identifying transaction code and a JE date and JE number. When the transaction "finder" record—created during a preliminary edit run—matches to an open record for the purpose of deleting it from the file, the program should move the JE date and number —and the *input transaction code—into the record being deleted.*

The purpose of this data move is to store in the deleted record itself the *authority or reason for deletion.* The "out-transaction code" (the JE code) itself provides the reason or authority code.

THE GENERAL JOURNAL

The printed General Journal provides details of every transaction that affected the customer file through journal entries. It should also develop all necessary proof and control totals for tie-back to batch totals initially developed for each group of input transactions.

The General Journal should provide separate columns for amounts posted as compared to amounts deleted for any reason. A further breakdown may be to show transferred records—those deleted by a transfer instruction—in a special column—because of the control situation represented by transfers "from and to."

SPECIAL INPUT REQUIREMENTS

Data input for journal entries may include the item *amount* as a key component of the input information. This would be in addition to the *finder number* which is the basic identifier for any record on the file that is to be changed or deleted. The inclusion of the amount provides the computer with two tests of the open item before deleting it—the finder number and the amount. If both do not match, the finder record should be ignored; unmatched finders should be printed on a proof sheet or register to inform the receivables supervisor of JE entries that were not acted on during the updating run.

HANDLING "EQUALS"

A well-designed receivables system will include methods and procedures for the routine removal of offsetting debit and credit records. Leaving offsetting records on the account file indefinitely is an example of very poor receivables administration and should not be tolerated.

USE SPECIAL INPUT REGISTER

For proper handling of "equals," design a special paper document or register for the adjusters or bookkeepers to use as the basis for cleaning off equal entries. Such a form includes columns for customer number, item finder number and amount—for each deduction or credit to be deleted from the open-item file.

Utilize the register page number as the voucher or JE number. This is a convenient device which solves the requirement that each JE input transaction include a voucher number (see Figure 18.1).

Differences. Quite often a credit memo that is issued to cover an unadjusted deduction is for an amount different than the deduction amount. The difference may be a small amount—or, in some instances, it may be a large amount. Bookkeepers or adjusters processing credits against the open deduction debits must be able to dispose of the difference in one of two ways:

- Charge the small difference amount to discount or an internal expense account.
- Set up a major difference amount to be posted to the account; usually identified on a Table of Transactions as a Partial Unadjusted Deduction or a Partial Credit.

To explain this further, consider the example below.

Customer Number	*TR Number*	*DR Amount*	*Credit Amount*	*Finder Number*
12-345-6	30	88.20		1-0022
12-345-6	50		70.20	1-0035

If the credit shown above applies against the debit amount of $88.20, there is an $18 difference remaining. The bookkeeper, therefore, may decide to offset the credit against the deduction debit—but set up the difference of $18 as a *Partial* Deduction debit. The procedures should provide for this routinely.

On the General Journal the above situation would be revealed by three entries on the computer-printed journal.

In the "Deleted Records" column, there would appear the $88.20 amount as a plus, and the 70.20 amount as a credit. In the "Records Posted" column the difference amount of $18 would appear and be identified by the transaction code as a partial deduction posted back to the account.

ACCOUNTING CONTROLS

Since each JE input transaction includes an item amount, the accounts receivable bookkeepers or supervisor preparing JE input entries can establish batches—and set up a dollar total for each batch. By restricting transactions in a batch to one type, accounting controls are easily established that tie in with subsequent totals developed by the computer.

Entries for deleting "equals" should be batched separately from other types of journal entry transactions. During the edit run when input transactions are being checked and tested by the computer, the computer should be programmed to accumulate individual counter totals for each type of journal entires:

- Equals
- Cash disbursements
- Bad debt chargeoff entries
- Other chargeoff entries
- Transfers
- JE items to be posted
- NG check entries to be posted

During the posting and delete runs, the programs should be constructed so as to accumulate comparable control totals in accordance with the breakdown listed above. This makes it possible to compare the preliminary totals with the final totals developed during the delete/post runs.

TRANSFERS

The necessity for transferring single records from one account to another arises for several reasons. Any miscoded invoice will be routinely posted to the wrong account. When the dunning process brings this to light, it is necessary to move the record from its present position in the file to the account where it properly belongs.

Cash application bookkeepers sometimes put unapplied cash on the wrong ledger account. This requires a subsequent transfer of cash from one account to another.

If a new account is opened up under the wrong name, or subsequent events reveal that it is not a new ledger account but is a subsidiary of an existing customer, it then becomes necessary to move all the items to a different position in the file. This situation may be handled two ways:

- Move each item individually to the new account.

Journal Entry Register

Date ____________

"EQUALS" Records to be Deleted

Page No. ____________

Trans. No.	Customer No.		Delete Amounts		Discount Adjustment +/−	Item FINDER NO.	
			MINUS Amounts	PLUS Amounts			
		Totals					
			DR A/Rec.	CR A/Rec.	Total Disc. Adjustment +/−		

SET UP PARTIAL DEDUCTIONS OR CREDITS

Trans. No.	Customer No.	JE REF.		New Entry Amount			Page Proof		
		Date	No.	Debits	Credits		Debit	Credit	
		Totals							
				DR A/Rec.	CR A/Rec.		Total Debits should equal Total Credits		

Figure 18.1 Journal entry register for input.

- Design a transfer instruction which moves the entire account intact to a new position in the receivables file.

It is obvious that the input transaction for a transfer must provide *two* customer numbers: the number that identifies the present account and the *new* account number. As the records are deleted from the file under the old number, move the *new account number* into the record in the regular customer number position for subsequent handling and posting.

Caution. When transferring a record do not change any indicative information found in the record, except the computer-assigned Finder Number. It is a mistake to change the item date or transaction number because of a transfer; always retain the original date and identifying transaction code.

REINSTATED RECORDS

A fundamental fact sometimes overlooked is that any system or procedure that provides for removing records from a file should include a well-planned procedure for putting certain records *back on the file.* In other words, your system should include provision for reinstating records that have been deleted for any reason at a prior time.

Reinstated records logically fall into two categories: those that represent sales-type transactions and all other. The ''all other'' is a broad category, since this includes remittance shortage records, unadjusted deductions, received on account records, journal entry adjustments, overpayment credits, and the like.

THE SPLIT APPROACH

Usually an invoice or credit invoice record is completely unlike all other types of records in data contents and record format. For this reason, you may want to handle reinstated sales through the regular sales edit runs. All other types of records to be brought back and put on the open file may be handled through the cash transactions input and edit run.

This eliminates the necessity of writing special edit runs merely to handle a few reinstated records from time to time.

MUST BE IDENTIFIED

Since reinstated sales or other records will be, by choice, merged in with regular input from time to time, it is essential for the program to recognize these entires and develop and print *separate control totals.*

A typical source register for keypunching invoices, credits and other types of records is shown in Figure 18.2.

JOURNAL ENTRIES: SINGLE OR DOUBLE ENTRY?

All journal entries in a double-entry bookkeeping system affect a minimum of two General Ledger accounts. At least one of the two or more entries found in a journal entry must have some effect on the receivables detail accounts, or the computerized receivables system should not receive the entry. If one part of the entry must be processed to the receivables file, what should be done with the entries affecting other General Ledger accounts?

TWO ALTERNATIVE APPROACHES

In a computerized system there are two different methods for handling the accounting aspects of journal entries:

1. Keypunch and process only part of the accounting entries—the ones that have some effect on customer accounts. Ignore the General Ledger accounting entries completely.
2. Keypunch all debit and credit amounts and code numbers that represent the entire journal entry, even though many multiple entries may be involved.

"SINGLE-LEGGED" METHOD

Option 1 is known as the ''single-legged'' method since, by choice, only the entry affecting receivables is keypunched and entered into the computer system. It is the simplest approach and works well in practice.

Let's examine an actual journal entry to see how this works:

DR Bad Debts Expense	$1234.67	
CR Accounts Receivable		1234.67

''To charge off the Robert Ayers account to bad debts as uncollectible.''

Under the single-legged approach only the second half of the entry is coded and keypunched for entry into the system—to delete the open-item records from the customer file. The only reference to the other side of the accounting entry is provided by the JE transaction code which indicates that the *reason* for removing the records is ''bad debts.''

Register for REINSTATED Items

Date _______________

Reinstated Invoices and Credits

Page No. _____________

Trans. No.	Division No.	Customer No.	Invoice Date	Invoice No.	Invoice Amount		Coded Invoice Terms			
							As of Date	Terms Code	Extra Days	
			Total							

Reinstated Unadjusted Deductions and all other item types

Trans. No.	Division No.	Customer No.	Check Date	Check No.	Amount	
				Total		

Reinstatement–Offset DELETIONS

Trans. No.		Customer No.	Check Date	Check No.	Amount	Serial No.	
				Total			

Prepared by __________________ Approved by __________________

Figure 18.2 Reinstated items entry register.

GENERAL LEDGER RECONCILIATION REGISTER

To back up the single-legged approach, the computer should develop a work file of all records removed from the customer file by journal entries during the month for any reason. At monthend, follow these procedures:

- *Use the computer to sort the work file on:*
  JE Transaction code (the out-transaction code number)
  Transaction date
- Then print a detailed Reconciliation Register that shows the details of every record deleted—and the grand total deleted for each different JE transaction number. This provides a recap of all entries for the General Ledger bookkeeper's use in reconciling his accounts with actions taken by the computer during the month.

The effect of cash disbursements on receivables provides an example of the need for reconciliation. During a given month the credit manager may have put through scores of requests for checks to be issued to customers to cover open credits on the respective accounts. At the same time he prepared input documents that resulted in clearing the credits from the receivables open-item file. Now suppose that the Cash Disbursements bookkeeper shows a total of cash charged to receivables for the month that *does not agree* with the total of items deleted because of cash. This situation requires checking details of checks drawn against credit amounts and totals actually deleted from the computer file because of the cash disbursements code. The recap list mentioned above makes a reconciliation effort easy and practical.

CHAPTER 19

How to Insure a Successful Receivables Conversion

The planning and proper control of the conversion of all customer open items from the existing customer records to the new computer system are of paramount importance. The vice-president of a large industrial firm, in a written memo to all personnel in the credit and receivables departments, expressed the situation as follows: ''I cannot stress enough the critical importance of the forthcoming receivables conversion. If this procedure is accomplished smoothly—the initial success of the new system will be assured. On the other hand, the conversion procedure *itself* can create problems of sufficient magnitude to sabotage the new system before it has had a fair chance. Errors made during this phase can result in a loss of customer goodwill and may require many weeks of clerical overtime work to correct them.''

TWO BASIC CONVERSION METHODS

There are two basic methods of approaching the conversion problem; each approach has its advantages and disadvantages:

1. The dual receivables system method
2. The inventory buildup method

OPERATE DUAL RECEIVABLES SYSTEMS

Under this approach you start the new computer system on a designated date by posting coded, edited sales transactions to the customer receivables file. Do not transfer any open items from the old records to the new computer system. Continue to operate the old receivables system until all open items have been closed by the application of cash or journal entries.

Apply cash to the open items on the old customer ledgers until the checks begin to pay items found on the new receivables file. At this point, the problem of ''split'' checks begins. That is, after a few weeks of operating the new computer system concurrently with the existing old system, checks will begin to cover items open on both sets of records. This requires allocating part of the cash to cover open items on the old records—and introducing the remaining amount of cash into the computer system for application to invoices found on the new customer file.

The theory behind the dual receivables method is very attractive, since the conversion problem is avoided. And, in theory, the old ledgers will be closed out in a reasonably short time, depending on the company's average number of sales days outstanding, which provides an indication as to the length of time that will elapse before most of the open items will be paid off.

DISADVANTAGES OF DUAL METHOD

Many ''feasible fallacies'' are encountered in data processing and in systems work. The dual method, although very attractive in concept, has many serious disadvantages that must be fully considered:

1. It requires operating two complete, separate receivables systems for a period of time.
2. It requires two separate groups of bookkeepers each with a supervisor; each handling a system totally unlike the companion system.
3. Two sets of controls must be carefully maintained.
4. After a short period of dual operations, it becomes increasingly necessary to "split" remittances between the two sets of records.
5. As customers use open credits as part payment of invoices, the problem of transferring or splitting credits arises.
6. Credit and collection control becomes difficult, because the customer account status is reflected on two different sets of records.
7. The preparation of past due statements is awkward; dunning procedures are relatively inefficient because of the spread over two different systems.
8. The dual system tends to remain in existence longer than anticipated. A large firm in New York City that adopted this approach to avoid the problem of converting open items to the new computer system found the old ledgers still open *one year* after beginning the computerized system!

INVENTORY BUILDUP METHOD

The alternative approach recognizes the necessity for making a clean break from the old receivables system by transferring all open items, under full control, to the new computer system on a designated date. The inventory buildup conversion plan *spreads out the work over a period of months,* and it assures positive accuracy of all invoice details contained in all sales records that eventually are selected from the inventory of open item records.

The theory behind the inventory plan is that, at the time of final conversion, we will have available and ready for selection *machine-readable sales transactions* in "inventory" to match most of the open items still remaining on the old customer ledgers or other types of receivables records. The data included in these records are apt to be accurate because this approach requires setting up the customer coding function and all sales edit runs several months before the final conversion date. Sales and credit transactions found in the inventory have been routinely processed with no undue pressure during this time period. (If no inventory is built up, the tremendous pressure of coding, keypunching, and verifying scores of thousands of open items during a short conversion period creates hundreds of errors that may cause the new system to fail).

TWO TYPES OF INVENTORY RECORDS

The sales items included in the inventory may be in the form of punched cards or records stored on magnetic tape or disks. If records are stored on a magnetic tape customer file for conversion purposes, we recommend using the ledger printout method at the time of conversion.

If the punched-card approach is utilized, then the cards must be interpreted and sorted on customer account number and transaction date before being handed over to the conversion teams for use in the conversion process (see Figure 19.1).

REQUIREMENTS OF INVENTORY METHOD

Building the inventory of open items requires careful planning and timing of certain basic work phases that are involved in designing and implementing the new receivables system:

1. The new customer numbering system must be selected and installed. Numbers must be assigned to all existing customer accounts.
2. Invoices and credit invoices must be properly coded, keypunched, and processed through sales edit runs for some months before the conversion date. This obviously requires that these new programs receive priority and are completed ahead of those not required until after conversion.

   To accomplish the above requires a dual staff for several months preceding the conversion date.
3. The input department must be ready to handle sales transactions.
4. The new open-item and customer master files are constructed, programmed, and tested ahead of other programs.

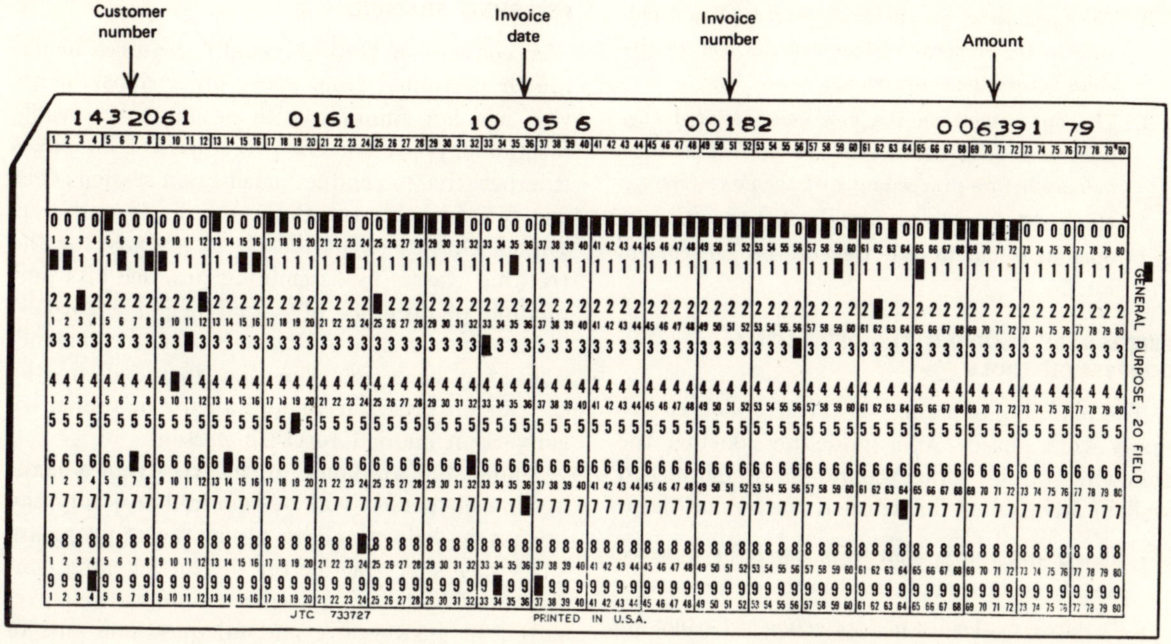

Figure 19.1 Sample interpreted invoice card.

NOT NECESSARY TO PURGE INVENTORY FILE

It is not necessary to apply cash to the inventory file. It is recognized that, at conversion time, the inventory will include thousands of records that have been paid or cleared and are not needed for conversion. The excess of records over the ones actually needed presents no particular problem. For example, if the printout of open items from magnetic tape is the selected method, the ledger review clerks merely *circle the* "finder number" for items that are to be *retained*—to match open items still remaining on the old customer ledger. (This requires a special computer program that subsequently *discards all open items* on the customer file except the circled items which are keypunched and fed into the computer as those to be retained on the new customer file).

MAJOR BENEFITS OF INVENTORY METHOD

The most significant benefit of the buildup method or approach to the conversion problem is that up to 85% of all-open item transactions —prepunched, coded, and edited under routine processing conditions—are available in machine-readable format without any clerical work other than the indicating of the open items to be retained.

Another hidden benefit is that a massive number of actual, live sales transactions is available for extensive testing of all file updating programs and for testing cash application and related runs. In effect, the inventory method captures the benefits of a full parallel operation without the costs of paralleling.

Organizing the Conversion Project

Planning the final conversion project is a vital function of the systems team, assisted by an advisory committee that should include one or two members of top management. Thorough planning and preparation are of vital importance. Before detailing what is involved in the preparatory stages, consider the prerequisites of a sound conversion plan.

PREREQUISITES OF A SOUND CONVERSION PLAN

1. Programs for the new system must be functionally tested and debugged extensively using "live data" over a period of time.
2. The approach and time table for conversion must assure that a minimum of time will elapse between opening the new system and closing out the old system. THE APPLICATION OF CASH MUST NOT BE UNDULY DELAYED.

3. The open items on customer ledgers should balance to the General Ledger control over receivables before the conversion.
4. The open items on the new computerized customer file must balance to the *present account balance* before proceeding with the new system.
5. Every effort must be made to balance the new open-item file to the General Ledger control total.

PRELIMINARY PLANNING AND DEVELOPING CONVERSION TOOLS

The planning of a successful conversion covers many work phases. As a guideline, consider the following things which should be accomplished well in advance of the selected conversion date:

- Design and test special work sheets or punched card forms that will be used in the conversion.
- Prepare a master list of *transaction codes* that are acceptable to the new computer system for coding open items manually transcribed from the old records during the conversion process.
- Photograph one or more typical customer ledger records and illustrate how each type of open transaction can be properly identified:

  Invoice
  Credit Memo
  Unadjusted deduction debit item
  Received on Account credit
  Overpayment credit
  JE debit or credit, etc.
- Fill out one or more work sheets with sample entries for the various types of open items that will be encountered during the conversion process and place them in the conversion manual for training and reference.
- Prepare a master list of all sales terms that will be found in connection with open invoice items—and describe how the applicable terms are to be handled by the conversion personnel.
- Prepare a floor plan showing the physical location of each team participating in the conversion project.
- Determine desk and equipment requirements and make the necessary arrangements (desks, chairs, tables, adding machines, adding machine paper, pencils, etc).
- As a final step, prepare complete, illustrated written procedures and assemble all of the material described above into *conversion manuals*.

PERSONNEL TRAINING

A conversion project usually requires bringing in personnel from many other departments who are not familiar with accounts receivable terminology, systems, or procedures. This makes it imperative to conduct orientation sessions that are followed by training periods for all personnel. One excellent idea is to prepare for the training classes by assembling practice kits that include photocopies of actual ledger records—the new conversion work sheets—written instructions for each job function included in the conversion procedures—and a copy of the entire conversion manual for each person.

Under the guidance of the receivables manager, each person will be required to study the open-item ledger and to fill in the appropriate work sheets as practice for the forthcoming conversion. The training leader should be well prepared to answer any and all questions and to evaluate the progress of the people present in understanding what has to be accomplished, how and why. Remember that training is the key to a smooth, efficient conversion.

ORGANIZE CONVERSION PERSONNEL INTO TEAMS

Let us assume that the inventory method has been selected for your conversion—and that sales and credits transactions covering a period of several months will be stored on a customer open-item file kept on magnetic tape, instead of stored in the form of punched cards. (All subsequent discussions will be based on these two assumptions.)

3-MAN WORK TEAM

As the result of considerable trial and error with many large-volume receivables conversions, I recommend the use of work teams consisting of three persons:

- Two customer ledger analysts
- One auditor

For purposes of explaining typical conversion steps and procedures in detail, let us assume that the old receivables system consists of machine-posted customer ledgers and that open items are detected by the absence of any "key-off" code or date. Furthermore, the ledger sheets are kept in trays in alphabetic sequence. (Account numbers have been written on ledgers in advance of conversion.)

PHYSICAL ARRANGEMENTS AND WORKING TOOLS

Seat the team at a table or desk with the team auditor seated across from and facing the two ledger analysts. Provide the team with red-and-black lead pencils for handling debits and credit items. Equip the team auditor with an adding machine.

The conversion director places one or two ledger trays containing the accounts assigned to the team on the desk, ready for the conversion work to begin.

The team also requires a supply of work sheets or work cards for recording open items of any type found on the customer ledgers and that are *not* included in the computer inventory. (Items that fit this category are past due invoices, old deduction debits, received-on-account credits, overpayment credits, and journal entries, etc.)

The primary documents that represent the greatest bulk are the *computer-printed list of open items* posted to the customer's computer file during the past several months. For convenience and speed of identification, the computer has assigned a 4-digit, consecutive serial number to each open item on the file. This number is printed along with indicative data such as the invoice date, invoice number, store number, and invoice or credit amount.

CONVERSION PROCEDURES USING PRINTED OPEN ITEM LISTS

Each of the ledger analysts pulls a customer ledger sheet and scans it for open items. When a current invoice or credit amount is found, the analyst refers to the computer-printed list, finds the comparable item—and merely circles the consecutive, 4-digit identifier or ''finder'' number.

When the analyst sees an old invoice amount not included in the inventory, or an open item of any type not in inventory, she records the indicative data in pencil on the *work sheet* provided for this purpose.

After completing the review of a ledger sheet, the analyst paper clips the work sheet and the computer-printed list to the old ledger sheet—and hands them across the desk to the auditor (see Figure 19.2).

DUTIES OF TEAM AUDITOR

The team auditor is basically responsible for turning in open items that balance to the old customer ledger balance. To accomplish this, he performs as follows:

- Adds all amounts found on the printed list—identified by the circled identifier number.
- Adds amounts found on the attached work sheet.
- Totals the adding machine and compares the total with the ledger balance. Or, the auditor may enter the account balance from the ledger as a minus amount—to print .00* on the adding machine tape if the account is in balance.

If the computer is required to print an out-of-balance account list later, as part of conversion control, the auditor may be required to write the account balance—taken from the ledger—on the work sheet as his final step before releasing the conversion papers for input.

ACCOUNT REVIEW

In those instances where the open-item total does not agree with the ledger balance, give the auditor no more than five minutes to review the ledger items, prior cash application, pencil entries of any type, and the like, in an attempt to find the reason for the discrepancy. Quite often this time period is sufficient simply because the analysts overlooked an open item during their review of the ledger.

CONVERSION DIFFERENCES

If the auditor is unable to reconcile the difference between the total of the items brought forward and the ledger balance, he introduces a manual entry on the work sheet that ''plugs'' the account balance. That is, he writes up a special transaction with a code that identifies the amount as a *conversion difference amount* (plus or minus). This forces the total open items brought forward to the new system to agree with the customer ledger balance.

GROUP SUPERVISOR

Assign a group supervisor to control and guide the functions of about five conversion teams. He assembles all of the completed documentation routed to him from team auditors for review and checking. He scans the work sheets for completeness, and he reviews the transaction codes used looking for invalid codes. If in doubt, he returns the work sheets and computer print-

Team No.	Customer No.

WORK SHEET—ITEMS NOT ON PRINTED INVENTORY LIST

Rev. 7/15/69

Trans. Code	Item		Date		Invoice No. or Check No.	Terms Codes	Store No. or Location Letters	OPEN — ITEM AMOUNT		Div. No.	
	Mon Name	Mon No.	Day	Yr				DEBIT	CREDIT		

Auditor's Conversion Difference Amount						
TR. No.	Date	Ref. No.		Debit	Credit	

Ledger Balance					
TR. No.	Date		Debit	Credit	Copy balance from old ledger

Figure 19.2 Sample work sheet used in a conversion.

outs to the conversion team for checking before routing the material into keypunching.

COMPUTER RUNS

The keypunch section converts all open items appearing as pencil entries on work sheets into punched transaction cards. They also punch cards intended to find and "retain" open items in inventory that are to be held as part of the new customer file.

After the computer has created a new customer file by dropping all unwanted sales and credits—and by adding the old items that appeared on the work sheets—then the computer should print a special list of out-of-balance accounts; one or more pages per customer.

After the conversion teams have an opportunity to review the out-of-balance accounts and submit additional cleanup input, the computer corrects the accounts that were out of balance. Then, a complete account list can be printed.

PRINT NEW CUSTOMER LEDGERS

A final step is to print a complete package of new customer ledgers, showing all open items effectively part of the new account file. Print an account balance for each account.

Balance the new trial balance with the old receivables total; if a discrepancy remains, the conversion and audit teams must remain on the job until the discrepancy between each new ledger and the old ledger is resolved.

Post-Conversion Procedures

Several suggestions are in order for the post-conversion period:

1. Retain the old customer ledgers in alphabetic sequence for approximately six months for reference when required.
2. Retain the printout indefinitely representing the new customer ledgers showing all open items *at the time of conversion.* This is very important because of reference problems that will arise in the future because of transfers, record changes, for account reference and reconstructions, and the like.
3. Begin to apply cash on hand (which has probably accumulated during the conversion process) as soon as possible.
4. *Begin the cleanup of "conversion differences" as soon as possible.*

An essential element of conversion planning is to set up a special review and audit team, which goes into action the day after the actual file conversion has taken place. This team has a list of all accounts that required the introduction of a conversion difference. Team members take one account at a time, analyze it, trace prior cash applications back in time and do everything possible to reconcile the open items to the ledger balance. If this is not possible within a reasonable length of time, they are empowered to charge off the difference amount to an adjustment account.

This audit project should move forward as rapidly as possible, since it is recognized that future cash application to an account that includes an unknown difference will be difficult and may lead to troublesome errors.

Summary

The conversion aspect of computerizing receivables deserves to be set up on your master schedule of projects and events as a separate and distinct project. Planning should begin several months in advance of the projected date selected for the actual conversion.

As the deadline approaches, constantly review the status and condition of every computer program, and the readiness of the computer hardware. If one or more programs continues to display problems when running actual, "live" data, postpone the massive conversion project until you are completely confident that all programs and the computer configuration of equipment are ready, dependable, and will support a full-blown receivables operation without faltering.